THE MICROECONOMICS
OF CAPITALISM

THE MICROECONOMICS OF CAPITALISM

John Broome
Department of Economics,
University of Bristol

 ACADEMIC PRESS, INC.

(Harcourt Brace Jovanovich, Publishers)

London   Orlando   San Diego   New York

Toronto   Montreal   Sydney   Tokyo

ACADEMIC PRESS INC. (LONDON) LTD.
24/28 Oval Road
London NW1

United States Edition published by
ACADEMIC PRESS, INC.
Orlando, Florida 32887

British Library Cataloguing in Publication Data
Broome, John
    The microeconomics of capitalism.
    1. Macroeconomics
    I. Title
    339   HB172.5

ISBN 0–12–135780–5
ISBN 0–12–135782–1 Pbk

PRINTED IN THE UNITED STATES OF AMERICA

85 86 87 88   9 8 7 6 5 4 3 2

PREFACE

In order to analyse such a complicated system as an economy we need an approach that is simple enough to begin with but eventually leads to an understanding of the whole system with all its complications. Most textbooks on microeconomics start by breaking the economy down into parts small enough to be easily analysed individually. They analyse the behaviour of individual consumers and producers, and only when that is done do they put these parts together to present a picture of the economy as a whole. This approach has advantages and also disadvantages. The chief disadvantage is, I think, that it is not a good way of investigating the inter-connections within the economy, what influences what and how. Consumers and producers one learns about in detail, but when it comes to the general equilibrium of the whole system one learns only a few broad facts about such things as marginal rates of substitution, and not much about what actually determines people's incomes, the quantities produced of different goods, their prices, and so on.

This book has another way of making the analysis simple enough to begin with. From the start it deals with the economic system as a whole, but models it in a very simple way. As the book progresses the model is brought nearer to reality. Throughout I have tried to keep a firm grip on the relationships between different parts of the economy. Of course this approach too has its disadvantages. One is that taking account of each new complicating feature of reality can be a lengthy business, because its effects have to be traced through the whole system; the approach that concentrates primarily on the system's individual parts does not have to be so thorough. Consequently I have had to limit the scope of this book to the analysis of long-run equilibrium in competitive economies. But then, when they come to talking about the economy as a whole, most textbooks are equally limited. My method's advantages, on the other hand, seem to me to outweigh the disadvantages. It keeps a proper perspective on what is important and what is not. It naturally turns the emphasis away from consumers' behaviour and even the behaviour of individual producers towards the productive system as a whole and the interrelationships within it, and to the distribution of its product amongst the classes of society.

An incidental benefit of my approach is that it gives special attention to capital and its working, something that the marginalist methods of other textbooks seem less suited to. In analysing a capitalist economy it is surely a good idea to pay close attention to capital.

Capital and Wages

Some features of this book will, I dare say, seem controversial. Most of those that do arise from my assumption that workers are paid their wages before their product is completed and sold, so that wages have to be financed out of capital. I doubt that many people will object to this assumption in itself; in practice wages are generally "advanced" in this way. But some of its consequences may seem objectionable.

Many of the differences between this assumption and the alternative one that wages are paid in arrears are simply matters of form. Any input to a production process may be paid for in advance or in arrears, and the input's price will behave differently in the two cases, but that is easy to account for. If the price is paid in arrears we can say that it contains an element of interest, and we can say the same for wages. For instance, the two assumptions lead to a different relationship between the wage and the marginal productivity of labour: if wages are paid in arrears labour will be employed up to the point where the value of its marginal productivity is equal to the wage; if they are paid in advance the value of labour's marginal productivity will have to be greater than the wage in order to afford profit on the wages advanced. But the conclusions are easily reconciled by saying that the wage in the former case includes an element of interest. The difference is really no more than a matter of what we choose to call the "wage". I prefer to use the term for something close to what it is in practice: a payment for labour alone without any significant interest (in practice at most a month's).

But one consequence of my assumption may appear to be more than a matter of form. Since wages are, according to the assumption, paid out of capital, capital in the aggregate includes a component that may be called a "wages fund". If the economy's stock of capital grows faster than the labour force, two things can happen to it. It can supply workers with more machines and materials to work with, or it can pay them higher wages. Most economists will agree that accumulating capital can have the effect of increasing wages, but many will doubt that an increase in wages can actually absorb capital. So let us ask whether this is an acceptable idea.

It is natural to suppose that this question is to be answered by looking at an economy's stocks of consumer goods. Do they need to be increased if wages are increased? The answer may be yes or no. For various reasons, including the seasonal nature of some production, any economy has to hold stocks of wage goods, which will certainly have to be built up if wages rise. On the other hand there are also stocks of goods for capitalists' consumption. A rise in wages means a fall in profits, so while one stock is built up the other will be run down. The final result may be a greater or a smaller total. But in any case this is not what concerns us. It is merely a matter of the technology of stockholding. It depends on how the stock of wage goods is related to the flow, and the stock of capitalists' goods to their flow. Stockholding we can think of as an industry. Stockholding of wage goods may be more or less capital intensive—require a greater or a smaller stock per unit flow of consumption—than stockholding of capitalists' goods. If it happens to be more capital intensive then an increase in the wage will increase the economy's need for capital invested in stockholding. In the same way, if the manufacture of wage goods is more capital intensive than the manufacture of capitalists' goods, an increase in the wage will increase the need for capital invested in manufacturing. But neither of these things depends on whether wages are paid in advance or in arrears, and neither is what is at issue in deciding whether or not capital contains a wages fund.

To see what really is at issue let us resort to a model. Imagine an economy where corn is grown in the following way. Workers working for one day sow some corn as seed. One year later, with no further labour, a crop of corn appears. Assume that workers are paid for their labour on the day they do it, and that they are paid in corn. A capitalist invests in corn growing by employing workers to sow seed. The seed corn and the wages paid together constitute the capital invested. Here capital is thought of as goods "advanced" to set production in motion. A stock of goods is needed before production can occur, and this stock includes both materials and wage goods. An increase in wages obviously requires an increase in capital conceived this way.

The stock advanced, however, may only exist instantaneously, and it needs to be renewed each year. Consequently there is room for an alternative conception of capital. In our model let us make production continuous. Suppose that seed can be sown on any day of the year and that it always comes to fruition a year later. The economy's capitalists each employ a constant labour force. Each day a capitalist's employees sow new seed. Each day a crop appears that was sown a year earlier. The crop is divided between wages paid to workers for the present day's work, profit for the capitalist, and seed corn. Workers and the capitalist consume their shares at once, and the seed is sown at once. So this economy has no standing stocks of either materials or goods for consumption. That need not prevent us from thinking of capital as a stock of corn advanced, including wages; each day corn needs to be advanced to renew production—capital needs to be replenished. A census of the economy's standing stocks, though, would reveal no corn. Instead it would reveal stocks of part-grown corn of different ages, which would stay constant from day to day. An alternative way to think of capital is to identify it with these standing stocks. A change in the wage will leave them unaltered, so wages form no part of capital conceived this way. To be sure, an increase in the wage will cause an increase in the *value* of capital (measured in ripe corn), because an increase in the wage (with a corresponding fall in the rate of profit) will increase the value of part-grown corn relative to ripe corn. But this way of thinking will make a sharp distinction between the value of capital and the quantity of capital, and say that the quantity of capital—the standing stocks—has stayed the same.

In this book I have adopted the notion of capital as stock advanced. It seems to me that the alternative can be misleading. It suggests that if the wage increases we should treat the consequent increase in the value of capital as a mere upvaluing of an unchanged quantity. But an increased wage will actually be the result of real saving on the part of capitalists, a deliberate diversion of goods away from consumption to add to capital. To see why, we shall have to examine saving in our model.

An individual capitalist saves, and invests, by refraining from consuming all of his or her profit and instead using it to employ more workers and supply them with seed to sow. The result will be a greater output in a year's time. But now suppose there are many capitalists and an inelastic supply of labour. If capitalists save simultaneously they will increase the competition for labour and pull up the wage. In saving they intend to employ more workers but they will not succeed in doing so. Unless some substitution is possible of seed corn for labour—and let us assume it is not—they will not succeed in expanding production either. So their saving will be entirely absorbed by the increase in the wage. But it is no less saving for that. If we think of capital as corn advanced we shall say that capital has been increased and been absorbed by the wage too. Each day the stocks of corn advanced need to be replenished; but capitalists have more than replenished them, they have added to them out of their income.

Capital treated this way is the total of past saving. The amount of capital the economy has, or the amount per worker, is a measure of its state of development. That is how I have used it throughout this book. Capital treated the other way, however, is not so well linked to saving. Saving will sometimes add to capital (when it brings a new technique into use), and sometimes not. Since the saving is equally real in either case that seems to me unsatisfactory.

The point of this primitive model is to show that the notion of capital as stock advanced, including wages, represents a real quantity of goods invested by capitalists in production, and that increasing wages requires a real investment. But when it comes to a world of many products I have allowed this notion to develop naturally into a treatment of capital as a *fund*, the value of the goods advanced. The alternative is to identify capital strictly with capital *goods.* (There is no reason why wage goods should not be included.) My reason for preferring the former is that it makes capital a unitary quantity and it makes the rate of profit the rate of return to capital, which is the most natural way to think of it. The alternative conception takes capital to be a collection of disparate goods. To aggregate them one needs an index, and even then the rate of profit is not the rate of return to aggregated capital but the rate of return to the *value* of capital. To calculate that one also needs a price index for capital. In the process of forming these indexes difficulties occur that are by now well-known (see Section 4.5 of this book). All these complications seem to me unnecessary. Identifying capital with capital goods is no more than a habit that has sprung up amongst economists of the twentieth century.

That, rather than aggregation, is the real source of the problems in capital theory. Treating capital as a fund that can be used to buy capital goods or labour is, I think, altogether more natural and more straightforward. One problem remains, a much simpler sort of index-number problem: the choice of a numeraire. This is discussed in Section 3.5. The criterion I have used is simply that the link between saving and capital should be preserved; the numeraire should be chosen in such a way that saving leads to an accumulation of capital.

Readers' Guide

In principle this book can be read without any prior knowledge of economics, though a reader who has not come across the notion of a competitive market will have to look at Appendix A before coming to Section 2.3. But I do not recommend it as an introduction to economics; it is too theoretical for that. It is intended for students in their second or third year of studying economics.

Some parts of the book are more difficult than others, and some parts can safely be skipped. Chapters 1 and 2 are both indispensible, and neither is difficult. Chapter 3 is harder in that it contains some mathematics, but most of it must be read because it presents the core of the theory. Section 3.5, however, can be skipped. Most of Chapter 4 is also essential, but not Section 4.5 or the Appendix. The most difficult parts of Chapter 5 are Sections 5.3 and 5.5, and both can be skipped. Section 5.5 in particular contains the hardest mathematics in the book. Chapter 6 contains little difficult analysis; it only outlines further ways of developing the theory, and all of it ought to be read.

Readers of this book will need to know some simple matrix algebra: what vectors and matrices are, how to add and multiply them, and what the inverse of a matrix is. Appendix B explains all the matrix algebra that is needed outside Section 5.5, but many readers will want a fuller explanation and will have to consult a textbook on mathematics for economists. Appendix C describes some extra notation that is used in Section 5.5. In Sections 4.5 and

5.5, and also in some other parts of Chapter 4, there is some differential calculus including partial differentiation. But neither Section 4.5 nor 5.5 is essential to the book's argument, and a reader who skipped the calculus in the rest of Chapter 4 would not miss anything essential either. So calculus is a help to reading the book, but not indispensible.

Acknowledgements

This book has been very much improved during the long course of its writing by the advice I have received from many people. I should like to mention particularly John Beath, Vivienne Brown, Michio Morishima, John Muellbauer, Ian Steedman and John Whitaker, but many others have helped me a great deal, including especially the students on whom I tried out versions of several chapters. Mary Harthan and Elizabeth Church did most of the typing, which is no doubt a more tedious job even than the author's.

My debts to the literature will be obvious. This is a textbook and does not pretend to be original.

CONTENTS

1.

SUBJECT MATTER AND METHODS

This book investigates some aspects of the workings of capitalist economies. It is about capitalist economies only, and only about their "microeconomic" aspects. That is to say, it deals with such things as the prices of individual goods, the quantities of them that are produced and where they are used, the methods that are chosen for producing them, and so on. It also concentrates on the relationships between these things and the distribution of income amongst the classes of people that make up society.

Models

The book's method is to examine the workings of simple imaginary economies defined by clearly specified assumptions. Imaginary economies like this are called **models**. Because the models leave out many of the complexities of real economies it is comparatively easy to analyse their behaviour. And because their assumptions are chosen to reflect some of the most important features of real economies, the models' behaviour casts light on the behaviour of real economies. The book starts in Chapter 2 with a model that is very simple indeed, and proceeds by adding complicating features step by step, chapter by chapter.Each successive model is a little closer to reality. Even so, by the end of the book the model of Chapter 5 will still be a long way from an adequate representation of a modern capitalist economy. For instance, it will still assume that the economy is fully competitive, whereas modern capitalist economies are in many respects not competitive at all. In principle it is possible to go on adding to the model more and more realistic features, such as monopolies, though of course the analysis becomes more difficult at each step. This book brings the process of elaboration to an end at an arbitrary and rather early stage, where the analysis is already quite hard enough for a textbook of this sort. Chapter 6 describes in outline how the process might be continued, to accommodate monopoly and other complications. But even from the very simplest model in Chapter 2 there are some lessons to be learnt.

One of the model's unrealistic assumptions is that the economy's capital is owned by a class of "capitalists" who manage their own productive enterprises using their own capital. A better picture of modern capitalism would include managers and entrepreneurs who organize production and obtain the capital to finance it through a capital market. However, it turns out to be inconvenient to introduce these other classes until Section 6.3, near the end of the book. But it will emerge in that Section that their existence makes very little difference to the conclusions reached earlier, so nothing is lost by sticking to the simpler model of society until then.

Another unrealistic feature of the models is that, by means of various assumptions I shall not go into now, they ignore the possibility of inflation and unemployment. These are "macroeconomic" problems that are simply beyond the scope of the book. Of course this is a serious limitation. The models could be extended to take account of them but I shall not have the space, even in Chapter 6, to discuss how.

Equilibrium

We shall be looking only at the **equilibrium** states of the models. An economy, or any other system, is in equilibrium if it would continue indefinitely in its present state without changing unless some outside influence disturbed it. If there are some inherent forces that will cause change then the economy is not in equilibrium. Suppose, for example, that capital invested in some industries receives a greater rate of return than it does in others, without any compensating disadvantages such as greater risks. Then, unless something prevents them, capitalists will transfer their capital from the less profitable to the more profitable industries. There is an inherent force for change; the economy is not in equilibrium. It can only be in equilibrium if all rates of profit are equal or balanced by some other advantages and disadvantages the industries may have, or else if there are some barriers to the movement of capital (such as a law protecting a monopoly).

Stability

It is generally much easier to identify the equilibrium states of an economic model than to work out how it will behave when it is not in equilibrium. That is the great advantage of equilibrium analysis. Its disadvantage is that we often need to know what will happen out of equilibrium, and it gives us no help over that. It does not even tell us, for one thing, whether or not a particular equilibrium is **stable**. An equilibrium is defined as stable if, when the economy is near the equilibrium, it will move nearer of its own accord. A ball resting at the bottom of a hollow is in a stable equilibrium, whereas one balanced at the top of a hill is in an equilibrium that is not stable. Obviously, to know whether an equilibrium is stable we need to know how the economy will move when it is not in the equilibrium, and that is beyond the scope of this book's analysis. This is a serious deficiency. In practice no economy is ever going to be exactly in equilibrium; there will always be outside disturbances. The only justification for concentrating on equilibrium analysis is the idea that even though an economy is not exactly in equilibrium it will generally not be far away. Then many of the conditions that apply in equilibrium, such as the equations that determine the prices of products, will apply quite accurately most of the time. But that idea is not even plausible if the equilibrium is not a stable one, since then the economy will have no tendency to move towards it. There is no reason to expect an economy to be anywhere near an equilibrium that is not stable. So only stable equilibriums have any real interest. Yet the techniques of this book do not allow us to distinguish stable equilibriums from others. This severely limits the value of our equilibrium analysis. We shall simply have to assume that the equilibriums we investigate are stable ones. It is true that there will often be informal considerations to support that assumption. For example, I mentioned just now that, given certain conditions, the rates of profit in different industries will have to be the same if the economy is to be in equilibrium. But if the rates of profit are not equal there is reason to think they will move towards equality. Capital will flow into the more profitable industries, increasing competition within them and, we should normally expect, reducing their profitability. Similarly the less profitable industries should be made more profitable by an outflow of capital. It seems likely, then, that the forces of change will move the economy towards its equilibrium. But this is only an informal argument that needs thorough analysis before it can be relied on. It *suggests* that the equilibrium is stable, and within the methods of this book that is the best we can hope for.

Comparative Statics

One of our main concerns will be with how the different variables that interest us are related together. We shall want to know how the prices of products are related to the wage, how they are related to the amount of labour used in making them, how the techniques selected for use in different industries are related to the rate of profit, and so on. The method I shall use for investigating these relationships is known as **comparative statics**. It compares equilibrium states of the economy under different given conditions. For instance, I may work out what the equilibrium is like when the wage is given at one level and then when the wage is given at a higher level. In each case I might calculate the prices of the products. Suppose the price of spoons turns out to be higher in the equilibrium that has the higher wage. I shall often express a discovery like this by such remarks as "A higher wage brings about a higher price for spoons" or "Increasing the wage increases the price of spoons". Remarks of this sort when they occur in this book need to be interpreted carefully. They mean only that the *equilibrium* price of spoons is higher than it was before. Suppose the economy is initially in equilibrium and then the wage goes up. If the new equilibrium is stable and if there are no large external disturbances the price of spoons should eventually approach its new equilibrium level. So under these conditions increasing the wage will indeed cause the price of spoons to rise in the end. But we do not know what the initial effect will be, nor what will happen even in the long run if the equilibrium is not stable. That depends on how the economy behaves out of equilibrium, which is beyond the reach of our methods. So the results of comparative statics must be treated with caution.

2

A CORN ECONOMY

Section 2.1 Technology

Assumptions

Let us imagine a primitive economy where people work the land. If somebody works for a year, cultivating one acre of ground, he or she can grow one ton of corn from a quarter of a ton sown as seed. In an obvious notation, the process is:

$$1/4 \text{ corn } \& \text{ 1 land } \& \text{ 1 labour} \longrightarrow 1 \text{ corn.} \qquad (2.1.1)$$

I call this a **technique** for producing corn. The units are tons for corn, acres for land and person-years for labour.

Although the meaning of (2.1.1) is obvious enough, the formula hides some assumptions that must be brought into the open.

(1) Production is assumed to occupy a definite length of time: one year. This includes all the time spent preparing the ground and, if necessary, waiting idly for the seasons to come round. The essential thing is that the period from one harvest to the next cannot be shortened.

(2) This is absolutely the only way to grow corn; there are no alternative techniques. If, for instance, any less than a quarter of a ton of seed were sown, no amount of extra labour and no commitment of extra land could coax from it a whole ton of output. Nor can a deficiency of labour or land be made up for by applying more of the other inputs.

(3) The technique can be employed, separately, by as many people as choose to. One person can produce a one-ton crop on one acre from a quarter of a ton of seed; two people, working independently, can produce two tons on two acres from half a ton of seed; and so on.

(4) There are no benefits to be had from cooperation; workers can do no better working together than separately. In whatever way they go about their work, a million workers will always need a million acres and a quarter of a million tons of seed, and their crop will always be a million tons, no more and no less. Assumptions (3) and (4) together amount to the assumption of **constant returns to scale**.

Inputs

Land, corn and labour, the three inputs to the production process, have some crucial differences between them.

(1) Land is a **scarce resource**; it cannot be created. As an economy expands, its scarce resources will eventually run out, and this limits its capacity to produce. In our example, if the country contains only a million acres then it can never grow more than a million tons of corn in a year. We shall see in Chapter 5 that scarce resources need not constrain an economy quite so inflexibly, but all the same it is essential to treat them in a category of their own, apart from inputs that can be produced. Besides land, some other examples of scarce resources are: fish stocks, minerals, clean water and heads of water capable of generating electric power.

(2) Corn is an input to production but it is also itself a produced good. At any particular time an economy's production may be restricted by the corn it has available for seed, but the restriction will only be temporary. In principle, given enough time, any desired amount of seed can be made available by growing it, provided a shortage of scarce resources does not intervene. Produced inputs such as corn I shall call the **materials** of production. One characteristic of materials is that they are completely used up during production.

(3) **Labour** fits neither of these two categories. It is not properly a scarce resource since, given time, the labour force can grow. But neither is it produced by some technical process that can augment the labour force at will. We should therefore keep it in a category of its own. There are, besides, some further reasons for doing so. For one thing, labour has a special position in the productive process since it is what actually does the producing; the other inputs are used or worked on *by* labour. Another reason has to do with the social system surrounding the productive process. In this book, we are going to be concerned with economies where some of the people receive an income simply because they own some of the inputs to production. Workers are

differently situated from the *owners* of inputs, because they gain their income by actually working.

(4)   There is another category of inputs worth mentioning now but which is not represented in the primitive technology of our example. I shall call it the **instruments** of production. It includes tools, machinery, buildings, improvements to land, and other things. They are distinguished from scarce resources in that they can be produced and from materials in that they are not used up in the course of a single year's production but can be re-used several times. We shall have to ignore instruments of production until Chapter 6, and suppose until then that workers labour with their bare hands.

Net Production and the Stock of Materials

Suppose that one year our economy's harvest is 40 million tons of corn. Ten million tons will have been used up as input. The excess of output over input, 30 million tons, is called the economy's **net production** for the year. The whole 40 million tons is its **gross production**. Net production is defined as gross production less materials used up.

Net production is, in a sense, what is available to the people for their own consumption. This statement, however, needs to be carefully qualified. Part of any year's gross production is consumed and the rest is used as input, but as input for the next year's production, not its own. So consumption is the difference between a year's gross production and the next year's input, whereas net production is the difference between a year's gross production and the same year's input. Since production may change from one year to the next, these need not be the same. Imagine, for example, that this year our economy grows 40 million tons of corn but next year's crop is to be 44 million. Eleven million tons will be needed for seed, which leaves 29 million for consumption. Net production, however, is 30 million, as we have seen. We can say this: net production is what can be consumed *if* the economy's production is neither to increase nor decrease. It is, however, always possible for some of net production not to be consumed and instead set aside as input for increasing production in the future. Alternatively, consumption can be greater than net production,but then production will decline.

In effect, the economy possesses a stock of corn for use as seed. Any economy needs such a **stock of materials** because the output from the production process comes into existence only after the inputs have already been used up; inputs cannot be supplied out of the production they engender. Each year the stock is apparently destroyed by being used, and each year it has to be recreated. But though it seems to come and go the quantity of stock persists from year to year as a population of butterflies persists: it survives from the sowing to the harvest in larval form. In fact, as I shall be emphasizing later, it is wrong to identify the *stock* of corn with the actual corn that composes it. The actual corn gets used up each year, but the stock survives. From year to year it may grow or shrink or stay the same. A part of the crop is always needed to restore the stock, or otherwise there can be no production in the next year. After the stock has been restored to exactly what it was at the beginning of the year, what is left out of the crop is just the net production. If all of this is consumed the size of the stock will stay the same. However, instead some of it may be added to the stock, or else the stock may be reduced by consuming part of it.

Distribution

What happens to an economy's net production is one of this book's principal subjects. Normally it will be shared out among the people in some way. In a capitalist economy, even the part of net production that is not consumed, if there is one, will pass into people's ownership and add to their wealth. And of course the part that is consumed must be consumed by somebody. So we can say that net production is **distributed** to the people. We shall investigate some of the causes and effects of different patterns of distribution.

The business of distributing net production is rather easily understood in our present model, because there is only one good. On the other hand it is easy to see that some difficulties of analysis will occur when there are several goods to be distributed. Imagine we found, in a more complicated economy, that the working class received as their share of net production various things including 500 million loaves of bread and 100 million bars of soap. Then suppose that the next year they get the same amounts as before of all other goods but 400 million loaves of bread and 200 million bars of soap. Has their share gone up or down? As it stands, the question has no clear meaning, since they are getting more of one thing but less of something else. However, we could say whether the *value* of their share has gone up or down if we knew about the prices of bread and soap. If a bar of soap costs more than a loaf of bread, the value of the workers' share has gone up; if the soap costs less than the bread it has gone down. Thus, in order to speak without ambiguity about the distribution of the economy's net production we should first of all need to know something about prices. And this is awkward because one of the things that can easily affect prices is the distribution itself (as we shall discover, if it is not obvious at once). So already the subject has gathered difficulties. If, on the other hand, there is only a single type of product to be divided amongst the people, that sort of problem cannot come up. As a matter of fact, this is the very reason why I chose to start this book with a one-product economy: we shall see clearly some of the essential features of distribution before being faced with complications.

The various quantities we shall need to deal with, such as wages, profits, costs and capital, will all be quantities of corn.

The Productivity of Labour, and Fertility

In our single-product economy we can identify the net production of a single worker, something that will not be possible in more complicated cases. It is three-quarters of a ton of corn, obviously. A worker's gross production is one ton. The net production is what is available to be distributed to the worker and anybody else who is to share in his or her production. A worker's net production is an indication of the productivity of the technology. It may be called the **productivity of labour**.

Another measure of productivity is the technology's **fertility**, which is defined simply as the proportion by which the gross output of corn exceeds the input. To put it another way, it is net output as a proportion of input. In our example it is three. The fertility is the fastest rate at which the economy could theoretically expand its output, if all of each year's output was used as the next year's input. Of course, expansion at this pace is not a practical possibility, since it leaves nothing for the workers to live off. All the same we shall find that our theory has some use for the notion of fertility.

It is important to realize that the process of production in any economy, not just our simple model, is to some extent *circular*. It is tempting to conceive of production as a conveyor belt travelling in a straight line, collecting things from nature and delivering them to consumers, with some manufacturing on the way. But a much better image is a merry-go-round. Goods are produced, and then they go round again, back into the production process as inputs. On each round there can be some expansion; more goods can be produced than on the round before. Fertility measures this capacity for growth. But in practice on each circuit some or all of the extra production is diverted off the merry-go-round to be consumed. Net production is just what can be taken off whilst leaving the process the same size as before.

Do not think a high fertility is a sign of advanced technology. We shall see in Chapter 4 that as an economy's capital accumulates the techniques it adopts are likely to have a greater and greater productivity of labour but to be less and less fertile. Productivity of labour is gained at the expense of more circular production.

The Integrated Requirement of Labour

According to our assumptions, to produce a ton of corn at the end of a year requires one person-year of labour performed during the year. This amount may be called the **direct requirement** of labour for the ton of corn. But in a sense it takes more labour than that to produce the corn, because the input of materials, the seed corn, has itself to be produced by labour. The labour needed to produce the materials is the **indirect requirement** of labour. The sum of the direct and indirect requirements I shall call the **integrated requirement**.

We can work out the integrated requirement of labour for a ton of corn as follows. Let it be l^* years. The materials needed for producing a ton of corn are 1/4 ton of corn, whose integrated requirement is obviously $l^*/4$. This amount of labour is, by definition, the indirect requirement for a ton of corn, being the labour necessary for producing its materials. If we add to it the direct requirement of 1 year, we must get the integrated requirement. And this we originally defined to be l^*. So

$$l^* = 1 + l^*/4.$$

The solution of this equation is $l^* = 4/3$. That is to say, the integrated requirement of labour for a ton of corn is 4/3 years. Of this 1 year is the direct labour and 1/3 year the indirect.

An instructive way to confirm this calculation is to imagine an economy where the labour performed each year is just 4/3 person-years. (Perhaps there are two people each working 2/3 of the time.) Its annual gross production would evidently be 4/3 tons of corn. Its net production would be one ton since each year 1/3 ton would be used up as seed. So the net effect of the 4/3 year of labour is to produce just one ton of corn; all the labour is devoted ultimately to this production and nothing else. Clearly, then, this is the total amount of labour required, directly and indirectly, for producing a ton of corn.

A different light can be shed on the integrated requirement of labour by calculating it in another way. To grow a ton of corn, one year of labour is required directly, and also required is 1/4 ton of seed corn. This 1/4 ton must be grown by 1/4 year's labour, working with 1/16 ton of seed. That in turn requires 1/16 year's labour and 1/64 ton of seed, and so on. The production of a ton of corn, then can be looked at as the final result of a long drawn-out process divided into a series of stages. At each stage the materials are produced that are needed for the next. Each requires some labour, and we may add up the amounts to get the integrated requirement:

$$1 + 1/4 + 1/16 + 1/64 + \ldots$$

This is a geometric series whose sum is 4/3.

A product's integrated requirement of labour is often called the **labour embodied** in it.

In exactly the same way as we worked out the integrated requirement of labour for corn we could work out the integrated requirement of land. The latter is a notion we shall not be needing until Chapter 5.

Section 2.2   Capitalism

Capitalists and Workers

Section 2.1 was almost entirely to do with technological matters. Once we knew the economy's technology we could work out such things as the indirect requirement of labour and a worker's net production, without needing to make any reference to the nature of the society. I am not suggesting that the technology itself is likely to be independent of society; obviously it is not. After all, technologists and inventors are members of society and may well be influenced by it. But, once the technology is given, wherever it comes from, the subjects discussed in Section 2.1 follow from it alone.

On the other hand, for most questions in economics the nature of society is extremely relevant. Even in our elementary model questions arise which cannot be answered just from a knowledge of the technology: how is net production going to be divided up among the people?, what fraction of the population will form the agricultural work-force?, and so on. To answer questions like these we should have to know, for instance, whether the economy's stock of materials is privately owned and if so by whom, what are the traditions about the sharing of labour between men and women, whether there is some obstruction in the system that causes unemployment, and so on.

Of course, many quite different types of society could employ the technology described in Section 2.1. One possibility is that farming is administered by a government that owns both the land and the stock of seed corn. Such a government might simply direct a number of people to do the work, and distribute their net production in some way it thinks suitable. Another possibility is that the population consists of free peasant families that grow their own food from seed they own themselves. Perhaps each year there is a public meeting at which land is distributed to families according to their needs. Each family would consume its own net production, unless it chose to expand or contract its stock of seed in order to be able to alter the size of its farm.

One feature of a society that goes a long way towards determining the character of its economy is its pattern of ownership. Some societies may not recognize private property at all. At another extreme, some may even permit one person to be owned by another. In this book we are going to be concerned with one particular sort of economic system, whose defining characteristic is that the stock of materials and (when we come to them) the instruments of production are owned by a class of people who do not themselves work with them. These people are called **capitalists** and the system is known as **capitalism**.

I shall be assuming, actually, that the capitalists own rather more than the stock of materials. In our simple model, each year a part of the crop must be set aside as seed corn, the materials for future production. Another part will be needed for the consumption of workers and their families during the next agricultural year. This latter I shall call the **subsistence stock** for workers (though I do not mean to suggest that workers' consumption is necessarily only just enough to subsist on). I assume that the capitalists in the economy own both the stock of seed and the subsistence stock. These two together constitute what is called their **capital**. Naturally, after the harvest they will also have to lay up a stock of corn for their own consumption and their families', but this is not a part of their capital. The difference is that capital is engaged in farming, as I shall explain, in order to gain a return, whereas what is consumed by capitalists and their families is, simply, used up.

The capitalist economy works as follows. Workers are not able to farm on their own account because, when the harvest is done, they own neither the seed needed for the next year's production nor the wherewithal for living through the year. To get their subsistence they have to become employed by capitalists, who pay it to them as wages during the course of the year. Wages are paid in the form of corn. The capitalists, having hired their workers, set them to sow and cultivate the seed, which they, the capitalists, also own. When the crop is brought in it will of course belong to the capitalists. They will expect it to be enough to replace their capital and give them something more besides.

For example, think about some capitalist—call him Charles—who owns a capital of 3/2 tons of corn. Suppose the wage rate he pays is 1/2 ton a year. He would use his capital to employ two workers, paying out 1 ton in wages during the course of the farming year and using 1/2 ton for seed. From this amount of seed the two employees will grow 2 tons of corn, which is left in Charles's possession at the end of the year. This restores his capital of 3/2 tons, ready to repeat the process, and leaves him a gain of 1/2 ton. The gain is called **profit**. Charles obtained it, not by working, but by being in possession of capital and setting others to work with it. It is therefore to be thought of as a "return" to his capital. And we can speak of the rate of return, or **rate of profit**, as the amount of profit divided by the capital needed to obtain it. In Charles's case it is 1/2 divided by 3/2, or 1/3 (i.e. $33\frac{1}{3}\%$).

Profit obtained like this forms the capitalists' income. They may consume it if they choose, or else they may add it to their capital in order to make more profit in the future.

Classes

In all this I have implicitly assumed that there is no difficulty over getting land for farming, and at no cost. This assumption will be maintained until Chapter

5. We shall assume that there is so much land in the country that there is always some available for anyone who wants to farm it. Furthermore, we shall assume that the land is not owned by anybody, so there is nothing to stop anyone using it, and no question of rent.

If, contrary to these assumptions, there were any landowners and they managed to extract a rent, then they would form a third class in the society. As it is, there are only capitalists and workers. Notice that the distinction between the classes is not some matter of degree like the size of their income. They participate in the productive process in entirely different ways. The workers do the actual work in the fields. Since they own neither what they need for farming nor what they need to live off while farming, they have to gain their livelihood by selling their labour for wages. Capitalists, on the other hand, being in possession of capital, can use it to obtain an income without working. They put themselves in control of the productive process and take possession of its product. It yields them a profit because the product is more than what they give up to obtain it.

It is natural to imagine that, in a capitalist economy like the one I have described there might be families that own a stock of seed corn and also cultivate it themselves. Free peasant families they might be called. Now, of course there might indeed be free peasants besides capitalists and workers, but I shall flatly assume that there are not. At least, if there are any they keep themselves to themselves and have no influence on the rest of the economy. I want to concentrate on a *pure* capitalist economy in which workers and capitalists are sharply divided. There is one class that owns the stock, another that does the work, and that is all.

The Rate of Profit

Now, let us go back and think about the rate of profit in more detail. Remember Charles with his 3/2 tons of capital and two workers employed at a wage of 1/2 ton each. His annual profit is 1/2 ton, which is calculated as the annual gross production, 2 tons, less the **cost** of producing it, 3/2 tons. The cost is made up of wages, 1 ton, and seed corn, 1/2 ton. It happens that cost in this case is the same quantity as capital, but it is important to distinguish between the two concepts all the same. They will not be equal in quantity if some of the costs arise at the end of the farming year, after the harvest is in. Suppose, for instance, that there is a tax of 1/8 ton of corn per ton produced, collected at harvest time. Then to produce 2 tons of corn the cost including tax will be 7/4 tons (3/2 tons as before plus the tax of 1/4 ton). But still only the capital of 3/2 tons is required.

The rate of profit is the gross production less the cost of producing it, reckoned as a fraction of the capital required in the operation: (gross production–cost)/capital. The rate of profit, note, is not a quantity of corn but a plain number, the ratio of one quantity of corn to another.

The rate of profit obtained by any capitalist is not affected by the scale of his or her enterprise. This is a direct consequence of the assumption of constant returns to scale. Charles's farm has a gross production of 2 tons of corn a year and yields a profit rate of 1/3, given that the wage he pays is 1/2 ton. Now, Julia's farm, say, produces 1 ton per year. She employs, therefore, one worker. Her costs of production are 3/4 ton, consisting of 1/2 ton for the worker's wage and 1/4 ton for seed. Her profit is 1/4 ton. The capital she requires to finance her enterprise is 3/4 ton, which covers the costs each year. Her rate of profit is 1/4 ton divided by 3/4 ton, i.e. 1/3, the same as Charles's. The different scales of production yield just the same rate of profit.

In view of this, when we want to know the rate of profit we need only calculate it for an enterprise of some convenient size. The same answer will apply to all. Generally we shall work with an enterprise whose gross production is just one unit.

The Wage–Profit Equation

Something that does make an important difference to the rate of profit is the wage. To see why, consider a capitalist who pays a wage w, and whose farm has a gross production of 1 ton. The cost of producing this output is $(1/4 + w)$, the seed plus the wages of one worker. The capital needed to finance the operation is $(1/4 + w)$. So the rate of profit, r, is:

$$r = \frac{1 - (1/4 + w)}{(1/4 + w)} . \qquad (2.2.1)$$

Once w is given, (2.2.1) tells us r. I shall call this **the wage–profit equation**.

Clearly, the bigger is w the smaller will be r. There are two reasons. First, a bigger wage increases costs and hence decreases profit. Second, a bigger wage demands more capital to finance it. Thus a smaller profit is returned on a bigger capital.

A graph of equation (2.2.1) is shown as the solid curve in Fig. 2.2.1. (Note that by convention r is on the horizontal axis and w on the vertical one.) The graph is called **the wage–profit curve**. Marked in the diagram are the wage of 1/2 ton and profit rate of 1/3 that were mentioned in the examples above.

The wage–profit curve shows two things, which are both important. First, there is a definite relationship between the wage and the rate of profit; once one is known so is the other. Second, the curve slopes downwards, which means that an increase in the wage must be accompanied by a decrease in the rate of profit, and vice versa. We have discovered these rules for the case of a

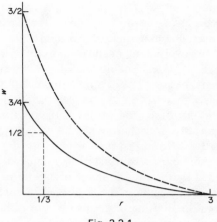

Fig. 2.2.1

very simple single-product economy, but we shall see that they apply in more complicated cases, too. It is essential to keep them in mind. It would be futile, for instance, to think about the effects of an increase in the wage without taking account of the effects of the simultaneous decrease in the rate of profit.

The Division of Net Production

The negative connection between the wage and rate of profit is absolutely fundamental, so it is important to have some intuitive understanding of why it happens. Remember that in Section 2.1 we defined a worker's net production with our technology to be 3/4 ton of corn. This is what is available to be distributed between the worker and his or her employer. Should it happen that the worker gets all of it, then the capitalist will get none. The wage will be 3/4 ton and the rate of profit nought. One end of the wage–profit curve stands for this possibility. At the other end the worker's wage is nought and all of net production goes to the capitalist. The capitalist's profit is in this case 3/4 ton. Since there are no wages to pay the capital needed to get it is only the 1/4 ton of seed. Hence the rate of profit is 3/4 ton divided by 1/4 ton, i.e. 3. Generally, for a wage of w the capitalist's share is $(3/4 - w)$ and the capital needed $(1/4 + w)$. So the rate of profit is $(3/4 - w)/(1/4 + w)$, which is just what equation (2.2.1) says. From this point of view, then, the wage–profit curve simply represents the division of net production between worker and employer. If one gets a bigger share the other gets a smaller one, and therefore the curve slopes downwards.

All this applies to one capitalist farm on its own. If we make the extra assumption that all capitalists pay their employees the same wage, we shall also be able to interpret the wage–profit equation in terms of the net production of the economy as a whole. Equality of wages might result from a competitive labour market, but it might also result from collective bargaining, convention, an edict of government, or something else. Whatever the cause the consequence will be the same: each capitalist will get the same rate of return on capital as all the others, because (2.2.1) applies to each of them. In that case it is obvious that the economy's aggregate net production will be divided between the classes in the same proportions as the net production of a single farm. If one class gets a bigger share it gets it at the expense of the other. Clearly, also, the rate of profit, just as it is equal to the income of a single capitalist divided by his or her capital, is also equal to the income of the capitalist class divided by the total amount of capital in the economy.

Although the connection between the wage and the rate of profit can fairly be said to result from the division of net production, I have one warning to issue about it. Think of the wages and profits that arise from a particular year's farming. The profits come out of that year's crop, but the wages are paid before the crop is available; they come out of the previous year's harvest. So it is a little odd to treat wages and profits as sharing a particular year's production. Everything works out, however, because in calculating the profit of any year we deduct costs, including wages, from that year's total production even though they were actually paid from the previous crop.

Technology and the Wage–Profit Curve

The wage–profit curve does, of course, depend on the economy's technology. The maximum wage, i.e. the wage that corresponds to a profit rate of nought and appears as the vertical intercept in the diagram, is the net production per worker. It is what I called in Section 2.1 the productivity of labour. On the other hand, the maximum rate of profit, the horizontal intercept, is the same as the technology's fertility, because when there are no wages to be paid capital consists of materials alone and profit consists of the whole amount by which the technology is capable of increasing those materials in a year. Thus the two intercepts of the wage–profit curve represent the two indicators of productivity mentioned on p. 9.

The wage–profit curves of different one-product technologies will all have the same bowed-in shape but they will intersect the axes at different points. For example, suppose that in our economy some discovery reduces the amount of labour required in farming. Suppose the technology becomes

1/4 corn & 1 land & 1/2 labour →1 corn.

Then the productivity of labour doubles but fertility stays the same. The new wage–profit curve is the dotted curve in Fig. 2.2.1.

The Determination of the Wage and the Rate of Profit

I have not yet said anything about what actually determines the wage and the rate of profit. We have only found a connection between the two: once one is determined, so is the other. We know the wage–profit curve but not the economy's position on it. The assumption I shall make to settle the question is that the wage is determined in a competitive labour market. Section 2.3 describes the labour market and the wage that emerges from it.

A competitive labour market is, of course, only one of many possible mechanisms for setting the wage and the rate of profit. Tradition and collective bargaining are others. An important possibility is that the labour market may be obstructed in its working by a failure of aggregate demand. (See p. 24 in Section 2.3 for some further explanation.) Unemployment may result. But whatever happens — however the wage and rate of profit may be determined and whether or not there is unemployment — the wage–profit equation always applies.

The Integrated Requirement of Capital

Before we come to the labour market there is one other concept to be developed, which will be needed in Chapter 3. Suppose the wage is w. To finance the production of one ton of corn, a capital of $(1/4 + w)$ is required, as we have seen. This I shall call the direct requirement of capital for a ton of .corn. There is also an indirect requirement because capital is also needed to finance the production of the 1/4 ton of seed used as input. The **integrated requirement of capital** for a ton of corn is the sum of the direct and indirect requirements. It may be calculated just as we calculated the integrated requirement of labour. Let the integrated requirement of capital for a ton of corn be k^*. Then the indirect requirement, which is the integrated requirement of 1/4 ton, is $k^*/4$. Add to this the direct requirement $(1/4 + w)$ and we must get the integrated requirement. So:

$$k^* = k^*/4 + (1/4 + w).$$

The solution for k^* is $(4/3)(1/4 + w)$.

This calculation displays some symmetry between the treatment of labour and capital. But do not be deceived into thinking they are more alike than they are. Labour is an input into production, as defined in Section 2.1. The labour requirement is given simply by technology. Capital is not an input like that; it exists at all only because the economy has a particular type of society, namely a capitalist one. And the quantity of capital required depends on the wage, which is not given technologically but results from the working of society.

Trying to treat capital like labour as an input to production has led to important mistakes in economics. From Chapter 3 onwards we shall see some of the reasons why.

Section 2.3   Competition: Capital and Labour

The Labour Market

Imagine that in our model bargaining over wages takes place each year just after the harvest. At that time workers are hired for the next year and their wages are agreed. I shall make the major assumption that this labour market is competitive. Furthermore, I shall assume that each year the bargaining achieves an equilibrium where demand is equal to supply. There will, consequently, be a uniform wage w throughout the economy.

To get any further we need to set up **supply and demand functions** for labour. Now, the labour force may be growing or shrinking, but let us pick a year when it happens to be just one million workers. And let us suppose that the supply of labour in that year is perfectly inelastic — unaffected by w — at one million. The supply curve, a vertical line, is shown in Fig. 2.3.1. The supply function is

$$S(w) = 1\ 000\ 000.$$

To find the demand function we have to remember where the demand for labour comes from in the first place: it comes from capitalists. They have a certain amount of capital, which they use to employ workers. As with the

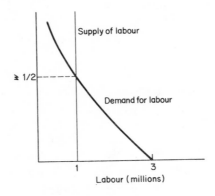

Fig. 2.3.1

labour force, the economy's total capital (the sum of the capitals of all the individual capitalists) may be growing or shrinking, but let us suppose for the moment that in the year we are considering it is three-quarters of a million tons of corn. Suppose, too, that this amount is inelastic — unaffected by the wage or the rate of profit. Now, to employ a worker requires a definite quantity of capital. First, his or her wage needs to be paid from capital and, second, there is not much point in employing somebody without providing him or her with the materials to work on. To be exact, to employ a single worker requires $(1/4 + w)$ tons of corn as capital, w to pay the wage and $1/4$ as seed. The capitalist class as a whole possesses 750 000 tons of capital. Therefore they can employ with it $750\,000/(1/4 + w)$ workers. For any wage w, this is the amount of labour capitalists will want to buy. It is nothing else but $D(w)$, the demand for labour.

$$D(w) = \frac{750\,000}{(1/4 + w)}.$$

The graph of this function is shown in Fig. 2.3.1 together with the supply curve.

Clearly, from Fig. 2.3.1, the equilibrium wage where $S(w)$ is equal to $D(w)$ is $1/2$. At this wage it takes $3/4$ ton of capital to hire one worker, because of the need to supply him or her with $1/4$ ton of seed. Hence the economy's $3/4$ million tons of capital will be just what is needed to employ the whole labour force. At any higher wage, capitalists would simply not have the resources to employ every worker; unemployment would be inevitable. A lower wage, on the other hand, would mean that capitalists with unoccupied capital would be going around looking, unsuccessfully, for somebody to hire with it.

All this is easily made more general. Suppose now that the labour force is L, not necessarily a million. And suppose the capital in the economy is K, not necessarily three-quarters of a million. Then the supply and demand functions for labour are:

$$S(w) = L$$

and
$$D(w) = K/(1/4 + w),$$

by the same reasoning as before. Since we assume the labour market to be in equilibrium, the wage is given by the requirement that $S(w) = D(w)$, or:

$$L = K/(1/4 + w). \tag{2.3.1}$$

Solving this equation for w yields

$$w = K/L - 1/4. \tag{2.3.2}$$

The ratio K/L is the economy's **aggregate capital/labour ratio**. It is the amount of capital per worker in the economy as a whole. Equation (2.3.2) is easy to interpret. The capital available for employing each worker is K/L tons of corn. Of this 1/4 ton has to be kept as seed. The rest is available for the wage, and that is what (2.3.2) says. Notice also that from (2.3.2) and (2.2.1) on p. 14 we can find that

$$r = \frac{1}{K/L} - 1. \qquad (2.3.3)$$

The Distribution of Net Production

Assuming that there is a competitive labour market, we have discovered that the aggregate capital/labour ratio fixes the wage and rate of profit. So it takes us to a particular point on the wage–profit curve. Thus it completes the determination of the distribution of the economy's net production. Let us look at this distribution more closely. The income of the working class is wL, the number of workers times the wage earned by each. The income of capitalists is rK, the total capital times its rate of return. From (2.3.2)

$$wL = (K/L - 1/4)L. \qquad (2.3.4)$$

From (2.3.3) $$rK = \{\frac{1}{K/L} - 1\}K,$$

or $$rK = (1 - K/L)L. \qquad (2.3.5)$$

Equations (2.3.4) and (2.3.5) tell us the size of the shares of the two classes. Added up, they obviously ought to come to the total net production of the economy, since that is what there is to be shared. Let us check that they do.

$$\begin{aligned} wL + rK &= (K/L - 1/4)L + (1 - K/L)L \\ &= (1 - 1/4)L \\ &= (3/4)L. \end{aligned}$$

And $(3/4)L$ is indeed the economy's net production, since there are L workers and each has a net production of 3/4.

Figure 2.3.2 illustrates the distribution of net production, and how it depends on the aggregate capital/labour ratio. It is what I shall call a **distribution diagram**. The vertical axis shows production *per worker* and its division. The horizontal axis shows different values of K/L. Changes in K/L cannot make any difference to total production, gross or net, because a worker always produces the same amount. The only thing that changes is his or her wage. The graphs start when K/L is 1/4 because unless the capital/labour ratio is at least this there is just not enough capital to employ all the workers, even for no wage. They could not all be provided with seed corn to cultivate. For greater values of K/L, the workers' share is given by $(K/L - 1/4)$ and the capitalists' by $(1 - K/L)$, according to (2.3.4) and (2.3.5). When K/L is 1, the

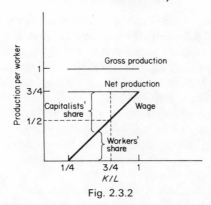

Fig. 2.3.2

capitalists get nothing, and there is not much point in continuing the graphs beyond here.

The sloping line in the distribution diagram is nothing more than a graph of the wage w against the capital/labour ratio K/L. It is obvious from (2.3.2) that its slope is one.

Economic Growth

We now know what the economy will be like in any particular year, depending on its aggregate capital/labour ratio. But we have not yet finished our job, because this ratio is unlikely to be entirely accidental. Over the years, the wage and the rate of profit will doubtless influence the progress of the economy's supplies of labour and capital. In a single year the wage and the rate of profit are determined by the capital/labour ratio, but in time the capital/labour ratio may itself respond to the wage and the rate of profit. In fact, the ratio may respond a little even in a single year. I have assumed that the supplies of labour and capital in a single year are inelastic, but they need not be. Workers may be influenced by the wage in deciding how much to work during a year, and capitalists may be influenced by the rate of profit in deciding how much of their income to add to capital in a year. But the influences there can be in a single year are small compared with those that can work during the course of many years, and for simplicity I shall continue to ignore them.

To simplify things, let us suppose that the growth of the labour force proceeds at a steady rate, say 1/10 (i.e. 10%), per year, and is not at all affected by the wage. But we must certainly take account of the influence of the rate of profit on the accumulation of capital. Capital accumulates because capitalists save a part of their profit and add it to their capital. Therefore, the higher the rate of profit the faster capital is likely to grow. Let us assume, for instance, that capitalists regularly save a constant fraction, say 3/10, of their profit.

Now, suppose that in some year the economy's aggregate capital/labour ratio is, say, 2/3. By (2.3.3) the rate of profit is 1/2. That year, then, capitalists receive as income an amount equal to half the stock of capital. Of this they save 3/10, which means they add to capital an amount equal to 3/20 (i.e. 3/10 of 1/2) of the stock already in existence. Capital is accumulating, then, at a rate of 3/20 (i.e. 15%) per year. Obviously, since this is faster than the labour force is growing, the aggregate capital/labour ratio must be rising. In Fig. 2.3.2 the economy is moving towards the right. The distribution of income is altering in favour of the working class. The rate of profit is falling. As a result of this, saving is becoming progressively smaller in relation to capital, and the rate of accumulation must be decreasing.

As the rate of accumulation of capital decreases, there will eventually come a point where it is just the same as the rate of growth of the labour force. Actually, in our example, this point will be reached when the rate of profit has fallen to 1/3. For then capital will be growing at a rate given by 3/10 of 1/3, which is 1/10, the same as labour's rate of growth. The wage that corresponds to this critical rate of profit is 1/2, by the wage–profit equation (2.2.1) on p. 14. I have marked this wage on Fig. 2.3.2, which shows that it will be attained by the time the capital/labour ratio has got up to 3/4 ((2.3.2) confirms this). From then on the capital/labour ratio will no longer change. Capital and labour will grow in step. Each year the economy will be just as it was in the year before, but on a 10% larger scale. The wage and the rate of profit will stay constant, and net production will be divided between workers and capitalists in a constant proportion (actually two to one).

I have just described a state known as **proportional growth**, because everything in the economy stays in the same proportions. Setting aside the particular numbers I assumed, there must always be *some* rate of profit that will cause capital and labour to expand proportionally. If capitalists save a fraction s of their profit, capital will grow at the rate rs. So, to achieve proportional growth rs must be equal to the rate of growth of the labour force, which I shall call g. That is to say, r must be g/s. Put this into (2.3.3.):

$$g/s = \frac{1}{K/L} - 1.$$

Hence $\qquad\qquad K/L = s/(g+s).$

We have here a neat formula to determine what aggregate capital/labour ratio will bring about proportional growth. An economy that does not have this particular ratio will move towards it. For if its ratio is higher the profit rate will be too low to allow capital to grow as quickly as the labour force, and the ratio will fall. The opposite will happen if the ratio is initially lower.

States of proportional growth in an economy are convenient to analyse (as we shall see in later chapters), but other patterns of growth also have some interest. Even though an economy will move towards proportional growth it may have a long and varied career in getting there. If, for example, the labour force is entirely static then proportional "growth" means no growth at all, but if also the stock of capital is initially quite small it will have to increase a lot before accumulation finally stops. The course of accumulation will move the economy towards the right in Fig. 2.3.2. As time goes on, income will be diverted more and more from capitalists towards workers. Only when the aggregate capital/labour ratio reaches one, bringing the rate of profit down to nought, will accumulation finish.

This last example brings out two points worth mentioning. One is that the accumulation of capital against a constant labour force does absolutely nothing to help production. It only alters distribution. This is a consequence of our fundamental assumption that there is only one way to grow corn. Given that, production is rigidly determined by the labour force. It seems more plausible to assume that increasing amounts of capital will make it possible to employ techniques that are more productive in the sense of yielding greater net production per worker. I shall consider in Chapter 4 economics that can alter their techniques in this way.

The second point is that accumulating capital is plainly a bad thing for the capitalists who are doing it. But they can be expected to do it all the same. There is a disjunction between the interests of the class as a whole and the interests of the individuals within it. Any individual's income depends on the size of his or her capital; whatever the rate of profit, more income means more capital. To get more income any individual capitalist has to accumulate. Indeed, given that other capitalists are accumulating, the rate of profit will be falling, and any individual will have to accumulate too even to stand a chance of keeping the *same* income. Each capitalist will have to pile up capital to try and stay afloat, yet the end result is to sink the class as a whole.

To summarize our conclusions we may say that in a single year the economy's rate of profit is determined by its aggregate capital/labour ratio, but in the long run it is rather the other way round. There is only one rate of profit that can keep capital growing in step with labour, and eventually the economy will have to move towards it. The capital/labour ratio will adjust itself accordingly.

Aggregate Demand

The account I have given of the workings of the labour market is, in one way, too facile. It makes the achievement of equilibrium seem straightforward, just as in any other market. It suggests that we might normally expect anyone who wants a job to be able to get one. But it would be a serious gap in our theory if we took no account of the possibility of unemployment. Sometimes people cannot find a job even though they are keen to work for the going wage.

There are, to be sure, some ways that unemployment could occur in our model. One is that there might not be enough capital in the economy to provide all the labour force with materials to work on, let alone with wages. Another is that the labour market might not be entirely competitive. The wage might be held up, by trades unions for instance, at a level too high to permit everyone to be employed by the existing stock of capital. But a phenomenon typical of modern economies is that capital and labour are unemployed at the same time, and our model is too primitive to accommodate that possibility. I shall try to explain why not.

In any ordinary economy people receive their income in the form of money. Consequently they have the option of not spending all of it on goods, and occasionally they may spend more than their income. In the first case they will be saving up some of their money; in the second they must be spending some money they already have. So the value of the products people choose to buy need not be the same as their income. It may be more or less. Taking everybody together, the value of the **aggregate demand** for products in the economy as a whole can be different from the total income of the people.

Crucial to this possibility is the existence of money. For our purposes, the important characteristics of money are two. It is, first of all, valuable, so it can be worth storing up rather than spending immediately on products. Second, it is not a product itself; no labour or capital is employed in the production of money (or, at least, the cost of its production is an insignificant part of its value). Thus the storing up of money does not constitute a demand on the economy's production.

In our model economy without money, on the other hand, there is no distinction to be made between total income and aggregate demand. People get their income as corn and have to use it as corn. They may consume it or add it to their capital. Either way it constitutes a demand for corn. Even if people were to throw away a part of their income, they would be throwing away corn, which would have to be produced. Even wasted corn is a demand on the economy's production.

The significance of this is as follows. The economy's net production of corn is, by definition, the same as the total of people's income. Since, in our model, all income is automatically aggregate demand, demand will exactly match net production. All the corn produced, that is to say, will be demanded by the people. There will be no difficulty about getting rid of it. Of course, this never even appeared to us as an issue before, because the net production is actually handed out to people, as it were, in the very same process as paying them their incomes. But in a monetary economy it really is an issue. Income is paid out as money and people then have to come and buy up the net production on their own initiative. There is no guarantee that all of it can automatically be sold. It may be that only a limited quantity of goods can be disposed of, so that the economy's production may actually be restricted by the demand for it. There might not be enough demand to give work to everybody who would like to be employed, in which case there is bound to be unemployment. The details of such a failure of aggregate demand do not concern us now, but we can see the contrast with our own model. There demand imposes no limits on production. However much corn the economy may choose to grow, all of it will be taken up by demand. In particular, if the labour market reaches its equilibrium, all that is then produced can be sold. No shortage of aggregate demand will prevent capitalists from employing everyone who wants to work.

In summary, it is a very special feature of our model, caused most immediately by the absence of money, that aggregate demand is automatically the same as aggregate income. Only this permits the untroubled working of the labour market.

Section 2.4   Single-product Economies in General

Technology

So far in this chapter I have adopted a particular numerical example for the technology. Nevertheless, all the points I have made apply to any single-product capitalist economy. In this section I shall express the model in general terms. Most of the equations will be echoed on another level (containing vectors and matrices) in Chapter 3. When reading that chapter, it may occasionally be helpful to refer back to here.

Let the technology be:

$$a \text{ corn } \& \ m \text{ land } \& \ l \text{ labour} \rightarrow 1 \text{ corn.} \qquad (2.4.1)$$

Evidently, for this to be an intelligible economy a, m and l must be non-negative, and actually I shall assume that a and l are both positive. Also, if a were one or greater the technology would be **unproductive**; the output of corn would be no greater than the input. Evidently we must assume a to be less than one, as a minimal condition for the model to make sense.

If the economy's gross production is x, its net production, y, is

$$y = (1-a)x. \qquad (2.4.2)$$

An individual worker's net production is $(1-a)/l$, since l workers produce, net, $(1-a)$. The technology's fertility is $(1-a)/a$. We can calculate the integrated requirement of labour for a ton of corn as we did on p. 10. Let it be l^*. Then

$$l^* = l^*a + l.$$

The solution gives

$$l^* = \frac{l}{1-a}. \tag{2.4.3}$$

Equilibrium under Capitalism

Now, take the economy to be a capitalist one with a wage of w. Let the integrated requirement of capital for a ton of corn be k^*. Then, by the same argument as on p. 17.

$$k^* = k^*a + (a + wl).$$

Therefore

$$k^* = \frac{a + wl}{1-a}. \tag{2.4.4}$$

Let the profit rate be r. By an argument like the one on p. 14.

$$r = \frac{1 - (a + wl)}{(a + wl)}.$$

The wage–profit curve is shown in Fig. 2.4.1. A more convenient way of writing the equation is:

$$1 = (1 + r)(a + wl). \tag{2.4.5}$$

Now let us assume a competitive labour market and consider its equilibrium. Let the total quantities of labour and capital be L and K respectively. When the wage is w the capital required to finance the production of one ton of corn is $(a + wl)$. This employs l workers, so the amount of capital needed to employ one worker is $(a + wl)/l$. Divide this into the aggregate of capital in the economy and we get the demand for labour to be $Kl/(a + wl)$. In equilibrium this must be equal to the supply of labour. So:

$$L = Kl/(a + wl).$$

Hence $$w = K/L - a/l. \tag{2.4.6}$$

This is the more general form of (2.3.2) on p. 19.

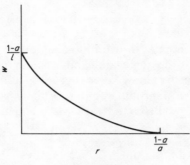

Fig. 2.4.1

Employment of Capital and Labour

For the sake of future comparisons, it is worth relating the economy's gross and net production to its labour supply and stock of capital. In producing x tons of corn, gross, the economy must evidently employ lx workers. In equilibrium, therefore

$$L = lx. \tag{2.4.7}$$

The capital needed to finance the growing of one ton of corn is $(a + wl)$. To grow x tons, then, requires $(a + wl)x$. In equilibrium

$$K = (a + wl)x. \tag{2.4.8}$$

Since x is $y/(1 - a)$ by (2.4.2), these equations may be written

$$L = \frac{l}{1 - a}y$$

and

$$K = \frac{a + wl}{1 - a}y.$$

That is to say (bearing in mind (2.4.3) and (2.4.4))

$$L = l^*y \tag{2.4.9}$$

and

$$K = k^*y. \tag{2.4.10}$$

Growth

Figure 2.4.2 is the economy's distribution diagram showing production and distribution related to the aggregate capital/labour ratio (it is constructed from (2.4.6)). Suppose the labour force is growing at a rate g and capitalists save a fraction s of their profit. For proportional growth (see p. 22) the rate of profit must be g/s. From the wage–profit equation (2.4.5), the corresponding wage is

$$\frac{1}{l}\left\{\frac{s}{g+s}-a\right\}.$$

Entering this in Fig. 2.4.2 shows the long-run capital/labour ratio. Actually it is (from (2.4.6))

$$\frac{s}{l(g+s)}.$$

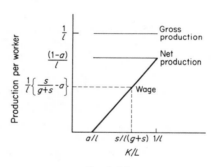

Fig. 2.4.2

Income and Net Production

From (2.4.5) we can derive

$$(1-a)=wl+r(a+wl).$$

Multiply by the gross production x:

$$(1-a)x=wlx+r(a+wl)x.$$

Substitute from (2.4.2)

$$y=wlx+r(a+wl)x. \tag{2.4.11}$$

Now, y is the economy's net production and lx is the number of workers employed, so wlx is the total income of the working class. Also, $(a+wl)x$ is the amount of capital engaged in the production, so $r(a+wl)x$ is the income of the capitalist class. Equation (2.4.11), then, tells us that the income of workers and capitalists together amounts to exactly the same as net production. Of course, we knew already that this has to be true, since net production is precisely what is distributed as income; now we have an algebraic demonstration.

When the labour market is in equilibrium, (2.4.7) and (2.4.8) allow us to write (2.4.11) as

$$y = wL + rK.$$

Questions on Chapter 2

1. If you were trying to make a fairly complete model of a modern capitalist economy, what classes would you include? Define each one with care.
2. Suppose that for the same input of corn and labour some farmers were able to get a bigger output than others. Would competition equalize the wage or the rate of profit?
3. Suppose land is in limited supply and owned by landlords who charge rent for its use. Suppose the level of rent is determined by a competitive market in land. Describe as thoroughly as you can the workings of this new model.
4. What would be the shape of the wage–profit curve if wages were paid in arrears out of the harvest instead of in advance out of capital? What difference would it make to the analysis in Section 2.3 of the demand for labour?
5. Suppose these two alternative techniques are available:

    1/2 corn & 1 labour → 1 corn
    1/4 corn & 2 labour → 1 corn.

    What determines which one will be adopted? What will the economy's wage–profit curve be like? What will the demand curve for labour be like?
6. Let the economy's technology be (2.1.1). Let the supply of capital be a constant K. Write down the demand function for labour and work out the elasticity of demand for labour. Do the same assuming now that the supply of capital is this function of r:

$$K(r) = \frac{c}{1 - (1/4)(1+r)},$$

    where c is a constant. How will the total income of the working class be affected by changes in the supply of labour?
7. Suppose that farming is more productive if done on a large scale than on a small. When workers are employed in multiples of ten they can apply this technique:

    5/2 corn & 10 labour → 11 corn,

whereas when employed in smaller numbers they must use this one

$$1/4 \text{ corn \& } 1 \text{ labour} \rightarrow 1 \text{ corn.}$$

How will the model work now? Is there any reason to expect a market in capital to develop?

8. Assume that the growth rate of the labour force depends on the wage. There is some wage, called the "subsistence" wage, at which the labour force neither grows nor shrinks. The higher the wage is above this level the faster the labour force grows. The lower the wage is below this level the faster the labour force shrinks. Analyse the growth of the economy, first assuming that capital grows at some steady rate, and then assuming that capitalists save some constant fraction of their income. What will happen when land becomes scarce?

9. Let the technology be (2.1.1). Suppose farmers, to avoid the trouble of paying wages in kind, find it convenient to set up a corn-exchange. Farmers take corn to the exchange, which issues them with corn-tokens in return. Wages are paid in the form of tokens, which the workers then use to buy their food at the exchange. Now suppose that if the wage ever goes above a half ton per year workers save for a rainy day all the tokens they receive above this amount. Suppose the wage slowly rises as capital accumulates. What will happen when it reaches a half?

3.

ECONOMIES WITH SEVERAL PRODUCTS

Section 3.1 Technology

The Technology Defined

Let us now give our model a number of industries, each having a product of its own. I shall frequently use this technology as an example:

$$\left.\begin{array}{l} \text{1/6 corn \& 1/6 fertilizer \& 1 labour} \rightarrow \text{1 corn} \\ \quad\text{1 corn} \qquad\qquad\quad \text{\& 1 labour} \rightarrow \text{1 fertilizer} \\ \quad\text{1 corn} \qquad\qquad\quad \text{\& 2 labour} \rightarrow \text{1 bread.} \end{array}\right\} \quad (3.1.1)$$

Corn, fertilizer and bread are all measured in tons. I assume that each industry takes the same length of time over its production process, say a year. None of the industries has any alternative technique available to it. Each has constant returns to scale. Each employs exactly the same type of labour; any worker can work in any industry.

I have not mentioned land in (3.1.1) because I assume it is free and plentiful. Consequently, as we found in Chapter 2, it does not come into our analysis at all, and may as well be ignored.

In this chapter we shall be doing our work in quite general terms, so it will be useful to express the technology in a general way. The formula for a general technology with n products is:

a_{11} product 1 & a_{21} product 2 & . . . & a_{n1} product n & l_1 labour $\rightarrow$ 1 product 1⎫
a_{12} product 1 & a_{22} product 2 & . . . & a_{n2} product n & l_2 labour $\rightarrow$ 1 product 2⎬ (3.1.2)
. . . .
a_{1n} product 1 & a_{2n} product 2 & . . . & a_{nn} product n & l_n labour $\rightarrow$ 1 product n. ⎭

This is to be interpreted in exactly the same way as numerical examples like
(3.1.1). It says that a unit of the first product (product 1) is made by l_1 units of
labour out of a_{11} units of product 1, a_{21} of product 2 and so on up to a_{n1} units
of product n. Similarly for the other products. The previous assumptions still
apply: there are constant returns to scale, no alternative techniques, and each
process of production takes one year to complete.

For convenience I shall often use matrix notation as a way of writing the
technology. Arrange the coefficients a_{11}, a_{12}, a_{21}, etc., in a matrix like this

$$\begin{pmatrix} a_{11} & a_{12} \ldots a_{1n} \\ a_{21} & a_{22} \ldots a_{2n} \\ \cdot & \cdot & \cdot \\ \cdot & \cdot & \cdot \\ \cdot & \cdot & \cdot \\ a_{n1} & a_{n2} & a_{nn} \end{pmatrix}$$

and call it A. A is often known as an **input–output matrix** or a **matrix of
technical coefficients**. Remember that the input requirements of any
particular industry appear as a *column* in A; they are listed vertically in
contrast to formulas like (3.1.2) which list them horizontally. Of course, this is
simply a matter of convention. The labour inputs into the various industries
write as a row vector

$$(l_1, l_2, \ldots l_n)$$

and call it l.

The matrix A and the vector l together specify the technology completely.
To help make it clear how they work, here is Technology (3.1.1) expressed in
that form:

$$A = \begin{pmatrix} 1/6 & 1 & 1 \\ 1/6 & 0 & 0 \\ 0 & 0 & 0 \end{pmatrix}$$
$$l = \quad (1 \quad 1 \quad 2).$$

Of course for this notation to work we have to agree in advance to count corn,
fertilizer and bread as products 1, 2 and 3 in that order.

Basic and Non-basic Industries

Now we need to make a fundamental distinction. In Technology (3.1.1) the
farming and fertilizer industries are both indispensible. Without either of

them there could be no economy at all. On the other hand, the bread industry is not essential in the same way. Since bread is not used as an input for production it is evidently simply a consumer good. The bread industry's function, from the technological point of view, is to convert corn into a form acceptable to consumers.

Industries that are needed to keep the economy going, like corn and fertilizer, are called **basic**, the others **non-basic**. The distinction is, more or less, between industries whose products serve somewhere as inputs, and those whose products do not. Strictly that definition needs qualifying. Suppose, in our example, that an industry were to spring up that transforms bread into toast, where toast is another consumer good. Evidently bread would now have acquired a role as an input, but that is not enough to make it basic. It is no more essential to the economy than before. A non-basic good, then, may serve as an input, but only in non-basic industries. However, this point is a minor refinement of the definition and for simplicity I shall always assume that, whatever non-basic goods there may be, they are never used as inputs. And I shall make all numerical examples conform to that rule. A side-effect of this assumption is to simplify the mathematics of the model in certain obscure ways I need not spell out. From time to time I shall have to make assertions without proving them, and one or two of these would not actually be true without the assumption.

For our purposes, then, basic industries are those whose products are used as inputs. The others are non-basic.

There is something else to point out. Non-basic industries are not indispensible in the way that basic ones are, but they may not be dispensible either. The economy needs a labour force, which needs some consumer goods to sustain it. If bread happens to be an essential food, then the economy cannot run without a bread industry, even though it is classed as non-basic. This is, in one way, a rather unsatisfactory state of affairs. The whole idea of dividing industries into basic and non-basic is to separate the essential core of the economy from its inessential periphery. **Subsistence industries** are essential and therefore ought really to count as basic. And actually we only need to reformulate things a bit to make them so. Suppose, for instance, that in (3.1.1) each worker needs, as an essential minimum, 1/4 ton of bread annually. Workers' needs could be treated simply as extra input requirements for production. The technology would become:

$$1/6 \text{ corn} \quad \& \; 1/6 \text{ fertilizer} \; \& \; 1/4 \text{ bread} \; \& \; 1 \text{ labour} \rightarrow 1 \text{ corn}$$
$$1 \text{ corn} \qquad\qquad\qquad\qquad\quad \& \; 1/4 \text{ bread} \; \& \; 1 \text{ labour} \rightarrow 1 \text{ fertilizer}$$
$$1 \text{ corn} \qquad\qquad\qquad\qquad\quad \& \; 1/2 \text{ bread} \; \& \; 2 \text{ labour} \rightarrow 1 \text{ bread}.$$

Now bread has become basic by our original definition because it is listed as an input. There is no reason why we should not always interpret our formulae for technologies in this way and suppose that subsistence needs have been included among the inputs. It will make no difference to the argument. I shall not normally adopt this interpretation, though, because it is a little inconvenient; it means that the wage has to be thought of as a payment to workers over and above what they need for a minimum level of life, because that has already been accounted for.

Gross and Net Production

Look at the example (3.1.1). Suppose that in a year the economy produces altogether x_1 tons of corn, x_2 of fertilizer and x_3 of bread. These amounts are its **gross production**. But some is used as inputs. We can see directly from (3.1.1) that the input of corn needed for all this production is $(1/6)x_1 + x_2 + x_3$, made up of $(1/6)x_1$ used in farming, x_2 in the fertilizer industry and x_3 in baking. Similarly the input of fertilizer is $(1/6)x_1$, all applied in farming. Bread is not used as an input at all. The **net production** of the three goods is defined as their gross production less the amounts absorbed as inputs in the course of production. It is, in the sense described on p. 7, what is available for consumption. Alternatively, some of it may be added to the economy's stock of materials so as to allow increased production in the future. If we write the net production of the three goods as y_1, y_2 and y_3, then

$$\left. \begin{array}{l} y_1 = x_1 - ((1/6)x_1 + x_2 + x_3) \\ y_2 = x_2 - (1/6)x_1 \\ y_3 = x_3. \end{array} \right\} \quad (3.1.3)$$

These equations can be used to tell us what gross production is needed to deliver any given net production, and that will be useful later in the chapter. If, say, 25 tons of corn and 15 of bread are needed, net, then $y_1 = 25$, $y_2 = 0$ and $y_3 = 15$. We may insert these values in the equations and solve for x_1, x_2 and x_3. The answer is $x_1 = 60$, $x_2 = 10$ and $x_3 = 15$; the gross production of corn, fertilizer and bread must be 60, 10 and 15 tons. Clearly this economy has to produce a lot more altogether than it can deliver as net production.

All this can be generalized for the technology shown in (3.1.2). Let the first industry produce, gross, x_1, the second x_2 and so on up to the nth, which produces x_n. Write these quantities together as a column vector called x:

$$x = \begin{pmatrix} x_1 \\ x_2 \\ \cdot \\ \cdot \\ \cdot \\ x_n \end{pmatrix}.$$

To find the net productions we have to subtract from the gross productions what is used as input. So how much of the first product is used as input?

Some is used in the first industry—actually $a_{11}x_1$. And $a_{12}x_2$ is used in the second, $a_{13}x_3$ in the third and so on. Altogether:

$$a_{11}x_1 + a_{12}x_2 + \ldots + a_{1n}x_n.$$

In the same way an amount

$$a_{21}x_1 + a_{22}x_2 + \ldots + a_{2n}x_n$$

of the second product is used as input. We can write all the inputs together as a column vector

$$\begin{pmatrix} a_{11}x_1 + a_{12}x_2 + \ldots + a_{1n}x_n \\ a_{21}x_1 + a_{22}x_2 + \ldots + a_{2n}x_n \\ \cdots\cdots\cdots\cdots\cdots\cdots\cdots \\ a_{n1}x_1 + a_{n2}x_2 + \ldots + a_{nn}x_n \end{pmatrix},$$

which conveniently happens to be the vector Ax. Having found the vector of inputs we only have to subtract it from the vector of gross production to get net production. If the (column) vector of net production is y, then

$$y = x - Ax.$$

The right hand side $(x - Ax)$ may be written $(Ix - Ax)$ where I is the identity matrix. And this may be factorized to $(I - A)x$. So

$$y = (I - A)x. \tag{3.1.4}$$

Equations (3.1.3) are simply (3.1.4) applied to the numerical example and written out component by component.

We were able to solve (3.1.3) for gross production given net production. The counterpart in the general case involves inverting the matrix $(I - A)$. From (3.1.4)

$$(I - A)^{-1}y = (I - A)^{-1}(I - A)x$$

where $(I - A)^{-1}$ is the inverse of $(I - A)$. Of course $(I - A)^{-1}(I - A)$ is just I, by the definition of matrix inversion. So

$$(I - A)^{-1}y = Ix.$$

Since Ix is just the same as x

$$x = (I - A)^{-1}y. \tag{3.1.5}$$

Of course, for this to work $(I - A)$ has to have an inverse. In other words, it must be non-singular. I shall soon explain the significance of this restriction (p. 39).

Fertility

In Chapter 2 I defined something called "fertility" for a single-product technology. It was the proportion by which gross production exceeds the input (see p. 9). Something similar can be done for our new complicated technology, but not straight away. Normally in the new situation production will not be directly comparable with the inputs. Output and input both consist of collections of goods, probably rather differently composed. For one thing, output is bound to contain some consumption goods, and these will not appear amongst the inputs. Take technology 3.1.1, for example. Gross production might be 30 tons of corn, 5 of fertilizer and 10 of bread. Then it is easy to work out that the inputs used in making it are 20 tons of corn (5 used in farming, 5 in the fertilizer industry and 10 in baking) and 5 tons of fertilizer (all used in farming). In vectors, gross production is

$$x = \begin{pmatrix} 30 \\ 5 \\ 10 \end{pmatrix}$$

and inputs are

$$Ax = \begin{pmatrix} 20 \\ 5 \\ 0 \end{pmatrix}$$

Obviously there is no definite proportion between inputs and outputs; it depends which product you look at.

However, there is nothing to stop us *imagining* the technology's being applied to producing a combination of outputs that is directly comparable with the inputs, even if that is not actually likely to happen. Imagine that, still with technology 3.1.1, gross production was 30 tons of corn and 10 of fertilizer. The inputs would be 15 tons of corn and 5 of fertilizer. In vectors:

$$x = \begin{pmatrix} 30 \\ 10 \\ 0 \end{pmatrix} \quad ; \quad Ax = \begin{pmatrix} 15 \\ 5 \\ 0 \end{pmatrix}.$$

Now for *each* product gross production is double the amount used as input. Without ambiguity, we may say that gross production is twice the input. The proportion by which gross production exceeds the input is one (i.e. 100%). And this is what is meant by the technology's **fertility**. As in the single-product case it is defined as the proportion by which gross production exceeds input, but only when gross production and input are proportional to one another. Only then does the comparison make clear sense.

To generalize, what we are looking for is a vector, x, of gross outputs that is proportional to the inputs, Ax, it uses. If we can find some x to work this trick, then each component of x will exceed the corresponding component of Ax by the same fraction. That fraction will be the fertility. Algebraically:

$$x = (1 + R)Ax$$

where R is the fertility.

It can be proved (though I shall not prove it) that there always will be an x that works the trick. Furthermore, there is only one, which means that the fertility is uniquely defined. To be more exact, it is not strictly true that there is only one x that works the trick. For if

$$x = (1 + R)Ax$$

then obviously

$$\lambda x = (1 + R)A(\lambda x)$$

for any positive number λ. That is to say, λx works the trick of proportionality just as well as x. There is, then, a whole range of vectors that do it, each a scalar multiple of x. Of course, each gives the same fertility R. What can be proved is that there is only one such range.

Self-reproducing Combinations of Products

The vectors from this range stand for combinations of products that, as it were, reproduce themselves. If one of the combinations is used as input for the technology the output will be just the same in composition but on a larger scale. Look back to the numerical example. The input vector $\begin{pmatrix} 15 \\ 5 \\ 0 \end{pmatrix}$ reproduces itself on twice the scale, emerging as an output $\begin{pmatrix} 30 \\ 10 \\ 0 \end{pmatrix}$, and if this latter vector were fed back as input the output would be double again: $\begin{pmatrix} 60 \\ 20 \\ 0 \end{pmatrix}$. Each of these vectors belongs to the range of self-reproducing combinations for technology 3.1.1. If there was no consumption the economy could in principle grow like this from year to year along the range of self-reproducing vectors. One year's output would serve as the next year's input. The industries would grow proportionally, all at a rate equal to the technology's fertility. As a matter of fact, this is the fastest the economy could possibly grow; I shall leave you to work out why.

Notice that a non-basic product cannot be included in the self-reproducing combination, simply because non-basics, we assumed, are never used as inputs.

The self-reproducing combinations of products are economically interesting for several reasons, so it is worth giving them a special symbol, e. If e is a self-reproducing vector, then

$$e = (1 + R)Ae. \qquad (3.1.6)$$

Equation (3.1.6) defines both e and R.

For a historical reason, a self-reproducing vector is often called a **standard commodity**. Mathematically, the vectors e are known as "eigen vectors" or "characteristic vectors" of the matrix A, and $1/(1 + R)$ is one of its "eigen values" or "characteristic roots".

Productive and Unproductive Technologies

For some matrices A fertility is negative. No economy could exist for long with a technology like that. It would not be able to produce each year even as much as it used as input. This sort of technology is called **unproductive**.

To get an idea of what an unproductive technology is like, look at (3.1.1) and imagine that agriculture suddenly needs a lot more fertilizer than before. Let its technique become

1/6 corn & 1/2 fertilizer & 1 labour $\longrightarrow$ 1 corn.

The matrix A is then

$$\begin{pmatrix} 1/6 & 1 & 1 \\ 1/2 & 0 & 0 \\ 0 & 0 & 0 \end{pmatrix}.$$

This technology is not unproductive, but production is, one might say, harder than before. To achieve any given net production we can find out what gross production is needed by solving these equations, which correspond to (3.1.3):

$$y_1 = x_1 - ((1/6)x_1 + x_2 + x_3)$$
$$y_2 = x_2 - (1/2)x_1$$
$$y_3 = x_3.$$

Take, as we did before (p. 34), $y_1 = 25$, $y_2 = 0$, $y_3 = 15$. Then the solution is $x_1 = 120$, $x_2 = 60$ and $x_3 = 15$. Compare these with the results we got on p. 34. Clearly with the new less productive technology a lot more gross production of corn and fertilizer is needed to deliver the same net production as before.

Now suppose agriculture's need for fertilizer goes up even more, and A becomes

$$\begin{pmatrix} 1/6 & 1 & 1 \\ 1 & 0 & 0 \\ 0 & 0 & 0 \end{pmatrix}.$$

This *is* an unproductive technology. It cannot produce any net output at all. Attempting to solve the equations for gross output will, it is easy to check, give negative answers, and that is nonsense of course. It is easy to see what is happening. To produce a ton of corn requires as input 1/6 ton of corn directly, and on top of that another whole ton to make the fertilizer it needs. More corn must go in than comes out. Mathematically, a technology's unproductiveness shows itself by the inverse matrix $(I-A)^{-1}$ having negative components.

There is a borderline state between productiveness and unproductiveness. In our example it occurs when the matrix is

$$\begin{pmatrix} 1/6 & 1 & 1 \\ 5/6 & 0 & 0 \\ 0 & 0 & 0 \end{pmatrix}.$$

Each ton of corn produced uses as input precisely one ton of corn when we take account of the amount used indirectly through the fertilizer industry. In these borderline cases the matrix $(I-A)$ is singular.

We shall always deal only with productive technologies. Consequently, they will always have positive fertilities, and we may always assume that $(I-A)$ has an inverse and that its inverse has no negative components.

The Integrated Requirements of Labour

If the gross output of the first industry is x_1 the labour employed in it is $l_1 x_1$. If the output of the second industry is x_2 the labour employed in it is $l_2 x_2$, and so on. Total employment is therefore $l_1 x_1 + l_2 x_2 + \ldots + l_n x_n$, or in vector form lx. But x is equal to $(I-A)^{-1}y$ by (3.1.5). Employment, then, is

$$l(I-A)^{-1}y.$$

Now suppose we artificially make y $\begin{pmatrix} 1 \\ 0 \\ 0 \\ . \\ . \\ . \\ 0 \end{pmatrix}$. That is to say, we imagine the

economy's producing, net, nothing but a unit of the first product. Then the labour employed is evidently the first component of the vector $l(I-A)^{-1}$. This labour is doing nothing, in the end, but producing that one unit of the first product. It must, therefore, be the total, direct and indirect, requirement of labour for that product, its **integrated requirement** in fact (see p. 10). Similarly the second component of $l(I-A)^{-1}$ is the integrated requirement for the second product, and so on. If I write the row vector of integrated requirements of labour as l^*, then

$$l^*=l(I-A)^{-1}. \tag{3.1.7}$$

The labour that goes into making a good is employed, not just in its own industry, but all over the economy in the making of the good's inputs and the inputs into those inputs and so on. By means of a mathematical device we can go in more detail into the pattern of labour inputs needed in making a product. Take this infinite series of matrices:

$$I+A+AA+AAA+\ldots\; .$$

Now multiply it by $(I-A)$:

$$(I+A+AA+AAA+\ldots)(I-A)$$
$$= (I+A+AA+AAA+\ldots)I-(I+A+AA+AAA+\ldots)A$$
$$= I+A+AA+AAA+\ldots-A-AA-AAA-AAAA-\ldots$$
$$= I.$$

Multiplying the series by $(I-A)$, then, turns out to produce the identity matrix I. So the series must be the inverse of $(I-A)$:

$$(I-A)^{-1}=I+A+AA+AAA+\ldots\; .$$

Hence, since l^* is $l(I-A)^{-1}$ by (3.1.7),

$$l^*=l(I+A+AA+AAA+\ldots).$$
$$\therefore l^*=l+lA+lAA+lAAA+\ldots\; . \tag{3.1.8}$$

The right hand side of this equation has an intelligible interpretation. It is, of course, a row vector. Let us attend, for the sake of discussion, to its second component, which is the sum of the second components of each of the terms l, lA, lAA, $lAAA$ and so on. The second component of l is just l_2, the labour used *directly* in producing a unit of the second product. The second component of lA is

$$l_1a_{12}+l_2a_{22}+\ldots+l_na_{n2}.$$

Now, a_{12} is the first input into a unit of the second product, and l_1a_{12} is the labour that (directly) produced it. And a_{22} is the second input and l_2a_{22} the labour that (directly) produced that, and so on. So this sum is all the labour needed (directly) to produce the inputs used in making a unit of the second product. It is, we might say, the first level of indirect labour. The second component of lAA is the next level of indirect labour, the labour needed (directly) to make the inputs into the inputs. (I leave you to spell out the details.) The second component of $lAAA$ is the labour needed (directly) to make the inputs into the inputs into the inputs, and so on. Adding up all these quantities will give us the total, direct and indirect, labour required to produce a unit of the second product: l_2^* in fact. This is what (3.1.8) tells us when we look at its second component. Of course, the same analysis applies for each component. The point of the equation is that it splits up the vector of integrated requirements of labour into a series of direct and indirect requirements of increasing remoteness.

We can think of it as a remoteness of time. The vector l specifies for each product the labour that must be employed on its production during the actual year when it is delivered as a finished product. The vector lA is the labour employed in the previous year, and so on. The making of each product is a process drawn out through time, and each has a pattern of labour inputs distributed across the years. Table 3.1.1 represents the time distribution of labour inputs for the three products of technology 3.1.1. Provided the technology is productive, the very remote indirect requirements of labour will become infinitely small, as the table suggests.

Table 3.1.1   Years before final production

Corn	1	1/3	2/9	5/54	17/474	. . . . .
Fertilizer	1	1	1/3	2/9	5/54	. . . . .
Bread	2	1	1/3	2/9	5/54	. . . . .

Section 3.2   Competitive Capitalism

The Markets for Products

It is time to go beyond technology and introduce some assumptions about the society. Let us assume it to be capitalist. Besides farming capitalists there are now, in the example we have been following, fertilizer capitalists and bread capitalists. They all employ workers, whose job is to process materials owned by the capitalists. Capitalists have to possess enough capital to cover both wages and materials. The product belongs to them.

Think about the farming capitalists' position just after harvest. They own a quantity of corn that has just been brought in from the fields. But they need other things besides corn. Next year's farming demands fertilizer, and perhaps next year's employees want to be paid in bread. Perhaps the farmers want to consume some bread themselves. How do they get these things? Well, I assume that they trade in **competitive markets**. (Of course, this is not the only possibility; there might be a centrally regulated system of allocation, or markets that are not competitive, or some other mechanism.) They have to sell their corn to people who want it and can offer bread or fertilizer in exchange, namely the capitalists in other industries where corn is needed as an input. In this way competitive exchange serves the purpose of circulating goods between industries — getting them to where they are required as inputs. Of course, goods for consumption can be traded in the same markets, and workers who are paid in one commodity may exchange it for something different if they want.

Prices and the Numeraire

I assume once more that there is a competitive market for labour.

Competitive trading between the various goods will establish a **price** for each. Leaving the example aside for the moment, let p_1 be the price of the first product, p_2 of the second and so on. Put these together as a row vector

$$p = (p_1, p_2, \ldots p_n).$$

There will also be a **wage**, w, which we may think of as the price of labour. Now, since we are talking about a barter economy where goods exchange for other goods rather than money, there are really only **relative prices**: the price of bread in terms of corn or the wage in terms of bread, for example. We need to pick a **numeraire**, one good in which to measure the price of the others. Only then will prices be properly defined. The operation of picking a numeraire amounts simply to defining its price as one. We might decide, say, to make

$$p_1 = 1$$

and thereafter all other prices would automatically be expressed in terms of the first product. Sometimes in this chapter I shall have to talk about the significance of various alternative choices of numeraire, so I do not want to commit myself to any particular one at the moment. The important thing now is not to settle on a numeraire but to recognize that there has to be one. Until one is selected we cannot expect our theory to tell us prices as opposed to ratios of prices. No system of equations that purports to determine prices can be complete without some definitional equation specifying the numeraire.

I shall sometimes want to use a whole collection of goods as the numeraire rather than just one. That is to say, I shall want to fix the price of the collection at one. Suppose the collection consists of z_1 of product 1, z_2 of product 2 and so on; in fact the collection is the vector

$$z = \begin{pmatrix} z_1 \\ z_2 \\ . \\ . \\ z_n \end{pmatrix}$$

Then the price of the collection — what it would cost to buy — is $p_1 z_1 + p_2 z_2 + \ldots + p_n z_n$ or in vector notation pz. If z is to be numeraire we want to make

$$pz = 1. \tag{3.2.1}$$

This is a useful general way of writing the numeraire equation. It accommodates any choice of numeraire we are likely to want. For instance, if product 1 is to be numeraire by itself we make

$$z = \begin{pmatrix} 1 \\ 0 \\ . \\ . \\ 0 \end{pmatrix}$$

and (3.2.1) is still the correct numeraire equation.

Requirements of Capital

Capitalists will finance and control the operation of the various industries. Think about the first. For it to produce, gross, one unit of its product, the inputs needed are $a_{11}, a_{21}, \ldots a_{n1}$ of the various products and l_1 of labour. These will cost altogether

$$p_1 a_{11} + p_2 a_{21} + \ldots p_n a_{n1} + w l_1.$$

All of this will have to be paid out of capital. This sum, then, is actually the capital required in the first industry, per unit of output. Let us write the per unit requirements of capital in all the industries as a row vector:

$$(p_1 a_{11} + p_2 a_{21} + \ldots + p_n a_{n1} + w l_1, \ p_1 a_{12} + p_2 a_{22} + \ldots p_n a_{n2} + w l_2, \ \ldots \ldots,$$

$$p_1 a_{1n} + p_2 a_{2n} + \ldots + p_n a_{nn} + w l_n).$$

It is easy to check that this is simply $(pA + wl)$.

Now, to produce a unit of the first product actually needs more capital altogether than is required in the first industry alone. There must be inputs from other industries, whose production must be financed by capital. So must the production of the inputs to these inputs, and so on. There is, then, an indirect requirement of capital as well as a direct one. To find the total—the **integrated requirement of capital**—we may go through an exercise like the one we went through to find the integrated requirement of labour. If the economy's gross production is x, the capital employed in it must be altogether

$$(pA + wl)x,$$

which equals

$$(pA + wl)(I - A)^{-1}y,$$

where y is net production. The same reasoning as in the case of labour (pp. 39–40) leads to the conclusion that $(pA + wl)(I - A)^{-1}$ must be the vector of integrated requirements of capital. If we write these requirements as a row vector k^* then

$$k^* = (pA + wl)(I - A)^{-1}. \tag{3.2.2}$$

I must repeat the warning issued on p. 17 against being too impressed by the symmetry of capital and labour. In Section 3.3 it will become obvious why.

Free Entry and Exit

I now make a quite new assumption: a capitalist with an amount of capital may invest it in any industry he or she chooses. This is generally called the assumption of **free entry and exit** for every industry. A farmer, for instance, is free to make an exit from farming and enter baking instead. I shall also make two associated assumptions. First, a capitalist moving into or out of an industry never accounts for more than a very small part of its production. Second, capitalists always choose to invest their capital in the industry where the rate of return is greatest. These assumptions are meant as an extension of the notion of competition: capitalists compete with one another for the greatest profit.

In a competitive economy free entry and exit ensures that the rate of profit in every industry must, in equilibrium, be the same. If some industry happened to be less profitable than another, capital would migrate from the first to the second. Therefore, if there are any differences in the rate of profit the economy cannot be in equilibrium.

The **equality of the rate of profit** is the main prop of the analysis in this chapter and those that follow.

The Long Run and the Short Run

Arriving at equilibrium in our more complicated economy will be a much more long drawn-out affair than in the simple world of Chapter 2. If the economy is not in equilibrium then, for one thing, there will be more produced of some goods than is demanded, and less of others. Their prices will have to adjust to sort this out. For a good in excess supply its price will presumably have to fall in order to encourage demand and bring it into line with the quantity being made. The opposite must happen for goods in excess demand. But matching demand to existing supply is only the beginning of the movement to equilibrium. The prices that do that job may be called short-run prices. Inevitably they will make some industries more profitable than others. So the migration of capital will begin. Capital will leave the less profitable industries and in the process reduce their output. It will move into the more profitable ones and increase theirs. Where output is reduced we would expect prices to rise because the market is less well supplied. The drain of capital from less profitable industries, then, should improve their rates of profit as their products' prices increase. The opposite should happen in industries where profit was originally high. Eventually rates of profit will become equal everywhere; the equilibrium will be achieved. Obviously this will not happen quickly. It is what people often call a **long-run equilibrium**, to contrast it with a short-run equilibrium where only markets clear and the rate of profit is not necessarily equalized. Of course, what happens in the short-run is not really an equilibrium at all, and since this book is about equilibrium only, the long-run is what concerns us. We do have to take account, though, of the length of time it takes to get there. It makes a difference to how we analyse economic growth.

In the single-product economy of Chapter 2 I assumed in Section 2.3 that equilibrium was established from year to year. Each year conditions might be different — perhaps the supply of capital was always altering — but each year the economy started afresh and found an equilibrium for that year. But in our more elaborate model we must allow several years for an equilibrium to be reached. Consequently, if there is some sort of continuous change going on — if for example capital is growing — the economy may never be in equilibrium at all. This is a serious problem, since our methods of analysis can only deal with equilibrium states. How we can get around it is discussed in Section 3.5. In the meantime we shall simply study the characteristics of equilibrium and investigate its comparative statics.

Section 3.3   Prices, the Wage and the Rate of Profit

The Equations of Equilibrium

Assume that the economy is in equilibrium. One consequence is that prices do not change from year to year. Another is that the rate of profit is the same in every industry. Call it r.

Consider a capitalist in the first industry. We shall work out the rate of profit she obtains on her capital. For simplicity we may as well suppose her output to be one unit a year, since the scale of production makes no difference to the rate of profit. The value of this output is p_1. We have already worked out (p. 43) that the cost of producing it is

$$p_1 a_{11} + p_2 a_{21} + \ldots + p_n a_{n1} + w l_1.$$

The profit, then, is

$$p_1 - (p_1 a_{11} + p_2 a_{21} + \ldots + p_n a_{n1} + w l_1).$$

We already know, too, that the capital employed in this operation must exactly cover the costs. The rate of profit (profit divided by capital) is therefore

$$r = \frac{p_1 - (p_1 a_{11} + p_2 a_{21} + \ldots + p_n a_{n1} + w l_1)}{(p_1 a_{11} + p_2 a_{21} + \ldots + p_n a_{n1} + w l_1)}.$$

Rearranging leads to

$$p_1 = (1+r)(p_1 a_{11} + p_2 a_{21} + \ldots + p_n a_{n1} + w l_1). \tag{3.3.1}$$

Similarly, from the second industry

$$p_2 = (1+r)(p_1 a_{12} + p_2 a_{22} + \ldots + p_n a_{n2} + w l_2).$$

There is a corresponding equation for every product, including this for the last:

$$p_n = (1+r)(p_1 a_{1n} + p_2 a_{2n} + \ldots + p_n a_{nn} + w l_n).$$

These equations say that the price of each product is its cost of production raised by the rate of profit. This is a fundamental rule about prices that will remain true for more and more complicated models throughout this book. In a competitive economy, so long as costs have to be financed out of capital, no capitalist will stay in an industry unless its product sells for enough to cover the costs and add the going rate of profit.

The rule does not mean that capitalists will *set* their prices by adding a mark-up to the costs. Under competition capitalists cannot set their prices at all. The market fixes prices, and capitalists as individuals can do nothing about it. They are price-takers. What our rule says is that under competition prices will, in equilibrium, *turn out* like that.

All the price equations can be put together in a single vector equation:

$$p = (1+r)(pA + wl). \tag{3.3.2}$$

This is the chapter's most *fundamental equation*. It is really n equations in compressed form. We have to remember that there is also a numeraire equation, such as (3.2.1) on p. 43, to be taken into account before prices and the wage can be completely determined. Our system so far, then, has effectively $(n+1)$ equations. Its unknowns are r, w and p. (A and l represent the technology, which we are taking as given.) Since p is a vector of n components this makes $(n+2)$ unknowns altogether—one more than the number of equations. Consequently, if one unknown is given from somewhere else, the equations will determine all the rest. The equations leave us, we may say, one degree of freedom. It is not surprising that we cannot yet fix the variables completely. In Chapter 2 we could not find the economy's equilibrium until we had looked into the demand and supply of labour. The same is true now; we shall have to wait until Section 3.4 for that. Meanwhile, though, (3.3.2) does at least settle a definite *relationship* between the unknowns. In this section we are going to study this relationship. We shall start by looking at the connection between the wage and the rate of profit. Then we shall look at prices and how they are linked to these two distributional variables.

The equations, remember, apply in equilibrium only, and the relationships among the variables apply in equilibrium only, too. We shall, in fact, be doing comparative statics. Do not be confused by the expressions I shall sometimes use, such as "a rise in the wage leads to ...". They are not describing immediate dynamic effects, but changes in the equilibrium.

An Example

It will be helpful to have an example in front of us. For technology (3.1.1) the equations of equilibrium are

$$\left.\begin{array}{l} p_1 = (1+r)((1/6)p_1 + (1/6)p_2 + w) \\ p_2 = (1+r)(p_1 + w) \\ p_3 = (1+r)(p_1 + 2w). \end{array}\right\} \quad (3.3.3)$$

These are just (3.3.2) spelled out for the particular example. If we now appoint corn to be the numeraire by setting p_1 equal to one, they become:

$$\left.\begin{array}{l} 1 = (1+r)(1/6 + (1/6)p_2 + w) \\ p_2 = (1+r)(1+w) \\ p_3 = (1+r)(1+2w). \end{array}\right\} \quad (3.3.4)$$

We have here three equations linking the four unknowns r, w, p_2 and p_3.

The Wage and the Rate of Profit

Once the wage is given, then, our equations fix the rate of profit, and vice versa.

The two are rigidly connected. In the example we can find the connection as follows. Substitute for p_2 in the first equation of (3.3.4) from the second:

$$1 = (1+r)(1/6 + 1/6(1+r)(1+w) + w). \qquad (3.3.5)$$

This, in a rather complicated implicit form, is the relationship between r and w. It is the economy's wage–profit equation. Its graph, the wage–profit curve, is the solid curve in Fig. 3.3.1.

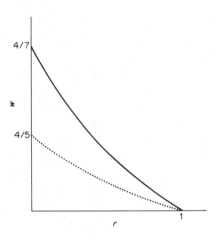

Fig. 3.3.1

Notice that to find the wage–profit equation we took no account of the third equation in (3.3.4), representing the bread industry. The bread industry is this economy's only non-basic one, and this is an instance of an important general rule: in any economy the relationship between the wage and the rate of profit is fixed by the basic industries alone, subject to a qualification I shall be coming to. The reason is that non-basic industries can adjust passively to whatever rate of profit is established elsewhere. Competition will raise or lower their products' prices until they match the given rate of profit, and this adjustment will not itself affect that rate. It is different with basic industries. Certainly, competition will adjust their prices to make all the rates of profit equal, but the adjustment will be a process of mutual interaction. An increase in the price of a basic product increases profit in its own industry but simultaneously decreases it in any other where it happens to be an input. Basic industries, therefore, all have a hand in fixing the general rate of profit.

But there is the qualification I mentioned. In the numerical example we happen to be using a basic product, corn, as numeraire. Suppose we were to change the numeraire to bread. Then in (3.3.3) we should make p_3, not p_1, equal to one. The equations would become

$$\left.\begin{array}{l} p_1 = (1+r)((1/6)p_1 + (1/6)p_2 + w) \\ p_2 = (1+r)(p_1 + w) \\ 1 = (1+r)(p_1 + 2w). \end{array}\right\} \quad (3.3.6)$$

Finding the wage–profit equation, which means eliminating p_1 and p_2, is now bound to involve all three equations. All three industries, then, affect the relationship between the wage and the rate of profit. It is scarcely surprising that the numeraire industry has to be taken into account. When the wage is expressed in terms of some numeraire, the level of the wage for any given rate of profit must depend partly on the cost of producing the numeraire.

From (3.3.6) the following wage–profit equation can be obtained by some algebra I shall not write out:

$$w = \frac{(r+4)(r-1)}{(r+1)(r-5)(r+3)}.$$

Its graph is the dotted curve in Fig. 3.3.1. Naturally the two wage–profit curves in the diagram, being constructed with different numeraires, are not the same. The behaviour of the wage depends partly on the behaviour of the price of the good it is measured by, and the prices of corn and bread will behave differently. By contrast, the rate of profit is conceptually independent of the numeraire. Consequently, both the curves intersect the horizontal axis at the same maximum rate of profit (which, as we shall see on p. 52, is actually the technology's fertility).

That the numeraire industry helps determine the relationship between the wage and the rate of profit is not, of course, an interesting fact about the economy. It is just the result of our happening, arbitrarily, to have chosen that numeraire. Something that *is* an interesting fact about the economy is the relationship between the *real* wage and the rate of profit. The **real wage** is the wage measured in terms of wage goods — the sort of goods that workers buy — as numeraire. Clearly enough, then, its relationship to the rate of profit is given by the basic industries and wage-goods industries together.

The Downward Slope of the Wage–Profit Curve

Both the wage–profit curves in Fig. 3.3.1 slope downwards. The same is true of any wage–profit curve. It is a quite general rule that, whatever product serves as numeraire, *an increase in the wage always goes along with a decrease in the rate of profit, and vice versa.* I shall explain why. The explanation is much harder than in the case of the single-product economy (see pp. 15–16).

Suppose the economy starts in equilibrium and then the wage goes up.

Think what happens initially before any prices change. Every industry finds its costs increased. (I assume that every industry employs some labour.) Initially, then, the rate of profit in every industry must fall, though not to the same extent in each; industries where labour accounts for a large fraction of costs will be worst affected. Prices will next have to adjust to make the rates of profit equal once again. Now the question is: in the course of this adjustment could it happen that the prices of products increase enough to restore the industries' profits to their original rate, or perhaps higher?

At this point I want to prove a general proposition which I shall use again in Chapter 4. Consider an economy that is not necessarily in equilibrium. Certain prices prevail but the rates of profit in the industries are not necessarily all the same. Then suppose the prices of products alter (in any arbitrary way) while the wage stays constant in terms of some numeraire. Then the rates of profit in the various industries will change. The proposition I shall prove is that there is at least one industry where the rate of profit either rises or stays constant, and at least one where it either falls or stays constant. To prove it pick out from all the products the one whose price rises by the greatest percentage; if all prices fall in terms of the numeraire then pick out the numeraire. This product's price evidently rises by at least as much as any of its inputs including labour. The rate of profit in its industry must therefore rise, or at least stay constant. Similarly, if we pick out the product whose price falls by the greatest percentage, the rate of profit in its industry must either fall or stay constant.

It follows that if ever a situation arises where different industries have different rates of profit and then prices alter to equalize the rates, then the final equalized rate must lie somewhere between the previous highest and lowest rates, or it may be equal to one or the other. And that answers the question I asked just now. Once the wage has risen, reducing the rate of profit in every industry, there is no way prices can move so as to restore the original rate of profit. A higher wage inevitably leads to a lower rate of profit.

Because we shall need it in Chapter 4 I shall mention in passing a refinement that can be applied to these propositions. If prices change (in any arbitrary way) while the wage stays constant, and if furthermore the change involves some change in the relative prices of basic goods, then in at least one industry the rate of profit definitely rises and in at least one it definitely falls. It follows that if prices change to equalize rates of profit, and if initially not all basic industries have the same rate, then the final equalized rate lies between the previous highest and lowest rates and is equal to neither. The proof I leave to you; it is a more complicated version of the one I gave above.

It makes no difference to the argument I have just recounted which product is the numeraire. An increased wage is associated with a reduced rate of profit however the wage is measured (provided it is measured in terms of some product or other). Whatever the numeraire, the wage–profit curve slopes downwards. One consequence is that when the wage goes up or down in terms of one product it goes up or down in terms of them all, because the rate of profit must have gone down or up. A rise or fall in the wage in terms of *any* numeraire means a rise or fall in its purchasing power over *every* product — a rise or fall, then, in the *real* wage. The numeraire may be arbitrary, but we can be sure that the wage measured against it does always correctly indicate the direction of movements in the real wage.

Intuitively it seems obvious enough why the wage and the rate of profit have to move in opposite directions. The economy has a limited productive capacity, and its output has to be divided between workers and capitalists. If one class gets more the other has to get less. That was the account I gave on p. 16 of Chapter 2 for the single-product model. But the proof I have given in this chapter does not have much connection with that intuition. It worked by looking at the prices of individual products. It said nothing about distributing total net production. The reason is that now we have a more complicated model total net production is an unreliable concept. Net production consists of several different goods. To put them together in a single total they have to be valued at their respective prices and added up. Now, we know from (3.3.2) on p. 46 that their prices are affected by the wage and the rate of profit. A change in these distributional variables is therefore likely to change the value of total net production. Furthermore, a change in distribution may change the actual quantities of the various goods produced, because workers and capitalists may have different demands (this is something I shall be discussing later). But if net production is no longer a fixed quantity we cannot rely any more on the intuition that one class can get more of it only if the other gets less. The distribution of income may, in a sense, be the dividing up of the national cake, but the size of the cake now alters when we alter the size of the slices. Therefore I had to fall back on other arguments.

All the same it is hard to reject the idea that the ultimate reason why the wage–profit curve slopes downwards must be to do with competition between the classes for the products of a limited productive capacity. I am sorry to say, however, that I cannot make this intuition into a precise argument.

The Mathematics of the Wage–Profit Equation

Equation (3.3.2) on p. 46 can be reorganized as follows:

$$p = (1+r)(pA + wl).$$
$$\therefore\ pI = (1+r)pA + (1+r)wl.$$
$$\therefore\ pI - p(1+r)A = (1+r)wl.$$
$$\therefore\ p(I - (1+r)A) = (1+r)wl. \tag{3.3.7}$$
$$\therefore\ p = (1+r)wl(I - (1+r)A)^{-1}. \tag{3.3.8}$$

(The last step assumes that $(I-(1+r)A)$ is not singular, a point I shall come back to later.) Let the numeraire be the vector z (see p. 43), so that pz is one by definition. Postmultiply (3.3.8) by z:

$$pz = (1+r)wl(I-(1+r)A)^{-1}z.$$
$$\therefore \ 1 = (1+r)wl(I-(1+r)A)^{-1}z.$$
$$\therefore \ w = \frac{1}{(1+r)l(I-(1+r)A)^{-1}z}. \qquad (3.3.9)$$

This is the economy's wage–profit equation relating w and r.

By differentiating (3.3.9) it is possible to obtain a mathematical proof that the wage–profit curve slopes downwards. But since we have a proof already I shall not bother with that. However, we ought to look at the question of whether or not $(I-(1+r)A)$ is singular, because it affects the validity of (3.3.9). When r is nought this matrix is simply $(I-A)$, and we have already assumed that to be non-singular as a consequence of A's being productive (see p. 39). When r is nought we are, in a diagram such as Fig. 3.3.1 on p. 48, at the extreme left hand end of the wage–profit curve. Increasing r takes us down the curve. To begin with, while r is small, $(I-(1+r)A)$ will be sufficiently like $(I-A)$ to be non-singular too. It will stay non-singular as long as w stays positive. (This is a fact, but I shall not prove it.) At the right hand end of the wage–profit curve w drops to nought and simultaneously $(I-(1+r)A)$ becomes singular. (Equation (3.3.7) shows it has to be singular when w is nought.) Before r reaches that point—and this of course covers all the economically significant rates of profit—(3.3.9) is valid.

The Maximum Rate of Profit

The rate of profit, then, reaches its economic maximum when $(I-(1+r)A)$ first becomes singular in the course of increasing r from nought. (Other, higher, values of r may also make this matrix singular, but they have no relevance to economics.) Look back to (3.1.6) on p. 38, which defines the technology's fertility R. It may be written (e, remember, is the self-reproducing vector):

$$e-(1+R)Ae = 0.$$
$$\therefore (I-(1+R)A)e = 0.$$

Hence $(I-(1+R)A)$ is singular. Of the values of r that make $(I-(1+r)A)$ singular, one is R. Furthermore, it can be proved that R is actually the lowest of these values of r, the one we have already decided is the economy's maximum rate of profit in that it corresponds to a wage of nothing.

The maximum rate of profit, then, is the technology's fertility. We found the same thing on p. 16 of Chapter 2. The intuitive explanation in our more complicated economy is more complicated. Imagine, first, the economy's producing the self-reproducing combination of goods. The net production of each product is a fraction R of the input of that product. If, also, profits are at their maximum and workers are paid nothing, all this net production will go to the capitalists, and it will be a fraction R of their capital. In that case, R is certainly their rate of profit. In a self-reproducing economy, then, the maximum rate of profit is definitely the fertility. But now, the composition of production has not been mentioned at all in this section of the chapter; it makes no difference to the wage–profit equation. Therefore, what is true of this equation in a self-reproducing economy is true in any.

Prices and Demand

Now let us turn to prices. With changes in the wage and rate of profit prices change too. It is essential to understand that this has absolutely nothing to do with the demand for the products from consumers. Consumers' demand does have some role in determining the economy's equilibrium; we shall see in Section 3.4 that it helps fix where on its wage–profit curve the economy will be. But once the wage and rate of profit are given, demand cannot affect prices. They are determined solely by the requirement that every industry should return the same rate of profit.

Let me put it another way. In the market for each product the supply curve is horizontal. There is one price for bread, say, that makes baking exactly as profitable as farming or making fertilizer. At that price capitalists will supply as much or as little bread as will satisfy demand. Bread cannot, in equilibrium, sell at a lower price for then no capitalist would make it. It cannot, in equilibrium, sell at a higher price for then every capitalist would make it and nothing else. The supply of bread is perfectly elastic; therefore demand cannot influence its price.

Prices and the Requirements of Labour and Capital

Equation (3.3.2) tells us, as I have already pointed out, that each product's price is its cost raised by the rate of profit. By manipulating (3.3.2) we can arrive at another rule about prices:

$$p = (1 + r)(pA + wl).$$
$$\therefore \ p = pA + wl + r(pA + wl).$$
$$\therefore \ p - pA = wl + r(pA + wl).$$
$$\therefore \ p(I - A) = wl + r(pA + wl).$$
$$\therefore \ p = wl(I - A)^{-1} + r(pA + wl)(I - A)^{-1}.$$

Now $l(I-A)^{-1}$ and $(pA+wl)(I-A)^{-1}$ are respectively l^* and k^*, the vectors of integrated requirements of labour and capital (see p. 40 and p. 44). We can conclude, then, that

$$p=wl^*+rk^*. \qquad (3.3.10)$$

This is a vector equation having n components. For example, the first is

$$p_1=wl_1^*+rk_1^*.$$

The term wl_1^* is the wages paid to all the workers employed, directly and indirectly, in producing a unit of the first product. And rk_1^* is the profit paid to all the capitalists. Equation (3.3.10), then, says simply that each product's price is made up of the payments for the labour and capital employed in producing it. This is scarcely a surprise.

Let us examine the equation some more. When w is high we know that r is low, and vice versa. At the extreme where r is nought, the vector of prices is just the wage times the vector of integrated requirements of labour. In other words: prices are in proportion to labour embodied. At the other extreme they are in proportion to the integrated requirements of capital. In between, the pattern of prices is a sort of weighted average of the two. If the distribution of income swings towards wages, prices become more like the requirements of labour; if it swings towards profits they become more like the requirements of capital.

The Effect on Prices of Changes in Distribution

One question of interest is how prices will alter when there is an alteration in the wage and the rate of profit. (Remember, I am always speaking of "alterations" in the sense of comparative statics.) At first sight it looks as though our formula (3.3.10) provides an easy answer. A rise in the rate of profit, with its accompanying decline in the wage, brings relative prices closer to proportionality with the requirements of capital. So products that use a lot of capital ought to go up in price relatively. Let me be more precise. Compare any two products and suppose that of the two the second requires in its production the higher ratio of capital to labour. Then an increase in the rate of profit ought to increase its price relative to the first. Quite apart from (3.3.10) that is what one would naturally expect. When the wage goes down and the rate of profit up, the products that will benefit least from the saving in wage costs are the ones that use a lot of capital in proportion to labour, and these are also the products that will suffer most from having to pay greater profits. These, then, are the products that should become relatively more expensive.

That describes what we should *expect* of the behaviour of prices. Unfortunately, though, they need not always conform. We shall have to work it out more carefully. The price of the second product relative to the first is, from (3.3.10),

$$\frac{p_2}{p_1} = \frac{wl_2^* + rk_2^*}{wl_1^* + rk_1^*} = \frac{l_2^*(1 + (r/w)(k_2^*/l_2^*))}{l_1^*(1 + (r/w)(k_1^*/l_1^*))}.$$

Now l_1^* and l_2^* are constants, given by the technology. Imagine for a moment that the same applied to k_1^* and k_2^*. Then an increase in r/w—a shift of distribution from wages towards profits—would increase the top line of the above fraction proportionally more than the bottom line if and only if k_2^*/l_2^* is bigger than k_1^*/l_1^*. This, therefore, would be the condition for a rise in the rate of profit to increase p_2/p_1, and it would precisely confirm our expectations. It can, however, go wrong because k_1^* and k_2^* are *not* constants of the technology. Nor are any of the components of k^*. The vector k^*, remember, is

$$(pA + wl)(I - A)^{-1}.$$

Besides the technological coefficients contained in A and l, this also depends on p and w. When r changes, so do p and w. So, therefore, do k_1^* and k_2^*. Capital requirements are, in fact, subject to **revaluation** when the wage and prices alter. A further misfortune is that there is no straightforward rule for predicting the size and direction of the change. We cannot tell, then, whether the above fraction will rise or fall. The relative price p_1/p_2 may go up or down.

Our putative rule that seemed so natural has failed us, because capital requirements are liable to revaluation. It turns out, too, that there is no other rule to put in its place. There is no straightforward rule at all to tell us which way prices will move when distribution changes. However, it is still tempting to think our natural-seeming rule describes the normal case, even though it has exceptions. Instances where an increase in the rate of profit cause a fall in the relative price of a product that uses relatively more capital it is tempting to think of as "perversities" and probably uncommon. I am inclined in that direction myself. Nevertheless, I do not see how one can validly make judgements like this about what is common or exceptional on the sort of theoretical grounds we have available. So I prefer to say what can and cannot happen and not commit myself on likelihoods.

I can give an example of a technology where prices move in the unexpected direction, but I shall not go through all the calculations involved. The technology is:

$$\left.\begin{array}{l} \text{1/5 manure \& 10 labour} \rightarrow \text{1 turnips} \\ \text{3/5 turnips \& 10 labour} \rightarrow \text{1 cattle} \\ \text{3/5 cattle \& 1 labour} \rightarrow \text{1 manure.} \end{array}\right\} \quad (3.3.11)$$

Let cattle be the numeraire. The price of turnips (relative to cattle) is the interesting one. When the rate of profit is $1\cdot0$ it is $0\cdot67616$ but if the rate of profit rises to $1\cdot12551$ it rises to $0\cdot68025$. (These figures may be calculated from

(3.3.8) on p. 51.) Yet the ratio of the integrated requirement of capital to the integrated requirement of labour is actually lower for turnips than for cattle. Details are shown in Tables 3.4.3 and 3.4.4 on pp. 65, 66. They can be checked by using the various formulae in this chapter.

Wicksell Effects

Changes in k^* and changes in capital requirements generally, when they result from a revaluation following a change in the rate of profit, are commonly known as **Wicksell effects**. I have mentioned before the dangers of assimilating capital too much to labour, and Wicksell effects are the reason why. Labour is a technical requirement of production; a particular amount of production demands a particular amount of labour. Labour is an input that appears in the specification of the technology. Capital is not. For one thing it is not a technical necessity that the economy is capitalist in the first place. And even given that it is, the *amount* of capital needed in production depends not just on the technology, but also on the wage and prices, and these emerge from the workings of social processes. When the wage changes, and prices with it, the requirements of capital change, even if technology is unaltered. Of course, the actual materials and labour used in production stay the same, but these are not the capital. They are what the capital is spent on. It is unwise to identify capital with the goods — "capital goods" — that capital is used to buy.

Wicksell effects are a nuisance in economics. The trouble is that they are unpredictable. A change of distribution will change the capital requirements of different products, but there is no simple rule that tells us in which direction or by how much. These effects can upset all sorts of expectations one might naturally have about the economy; we have just seen one example. Of course, if capital *were* a technical input to production it would not be troubled by annoying changes in valuation. There would be no Wicksell effects, and the behaviour of prices and other things would be more predictable. But the world is more complicated than that.

Prices and the Compounded Costs of Labour

Though illuminating in one way, Equation (3.3.10) is unsatisfactory in another. Since the vector k^* contains prices in its definition, prices occur on both sides of the equation. To give a proper account of prices it would be best to express them in terms of something independent of themselves. We ought really to *solve* (3.3.2) on p. 46 for prices, rather than converting it in the way that leads to (3.3.10). Actually, I have already done that in (3.3.8) on p. 51:

$$p = (1+r)wl(I-(1+r)A)^{-1}$$

Here we have prices given in terms of the wage, the rate of profit and the constants of the technology. Let us look at the equation more closely.

It is rather unprepossessing as it stands. But it can be made more informative by expanding the matrix $(I-(1+r)A)^{-1}$ by the same trick as I applied to $(I-A)^{-1}$ on p. 40.

$$(I-(1+r)A)^{-1}=I+(1+r)A+(1+r)^2AA+(1+r)^3AAA+\ldots \quad .$$

Hence

$$p=(1+r)wl\{I+(1+r)A+(1+r)^2AA+(1+r)^3AAA+\ldots\}$$
$$=(1+r)wl+(1+r)^2wlA+(1+r)^3wlAA+(1+r)^4wlAAA+\ldots \quad .$$

On pp. 40–41 I interpreted the vectors l, lA, lAA, etc. They tell us the products' requirements for labour to be applied at various intervals before the final appearance of the output. First, l is the direct requirement — the labour needed in the year of production itself. Its cost is wl. This will have to be financed by capital, and the owner of the capital will demand a profit. The term $(1+r)wl$ represents the cost of direct labour plus the profit on it. Second, lA is the labour required in the penultimate year of production. The capital that finances *its* cost, wlA, will not receive a return for two years. Profit at the rate r must therefore be added twice. The term $(1+r)^2wlA$ expresses this cost plus profit. Third, $(1+r)^3wlAA$ is the cost of labour in the previous year, plus three years' profit. And so on.

We have here, then, the prices of products broken down into labour costs at different dates, **compounded** at the rate of profit forward to the date of final production. It is a formulation that makes good intuitive sense.

Equal Compositions of Capital

If it were to happen that two products had the same distribution of labour requirements through time, their relative price would never alter. It would be fixed by the technology alone, and independent of the distribution of income. It is not necessary for the products to have the *same* requirements of labour from year to year, but they should always be in the same proportion. The following technology provides an example.

$$\left.\begin{array}{l}\text{1/6 corn \& 1/6 fertilizer \& 1 labour} \rightarrow 1 \text{ corn}\\ \text{1 corn} \qquad\qquad\qquad \text{\& 2 labour} \rightarrow 1 \text{ fertilizer.}\end{array}\right\} \quad (3.3.12)$$

The pattern of labour inputs, distributed through time, is shown in Table 3.3.1. Since in every year fertilizer needs twice as much labour as corn does it will sell for twice the price. This is obvious even before we take account of the wage and the rate of profit.

In an economy where every product had the same distribution of labour inputs, relative prices could never change at all. It is obvious, too, from the above example, that they would be in proportion to the total labour embodied in the products. In this case, then, prices are directly related to the technology in a neat and simple way.

Because it is theoretically convenient if prices do not change, model economies of this sort have had an important place in the history of economics. Fortunately, to tell whether all products have the same pattern of labour inputs it is not necessary to work out the entire pattern for each of them. It is good enough to check that all products absorb direct and indirect labour in the same proportions. If they do, then the whole distribution through time of labour inputs must be the same for each; I leave you to think out why.

Table 3.3.1   Years before final production

Corn	1	1/2	1/4	1/8	1/16	. . . . .
Fertilizer	2	1	1/2	1/4	1/8	. . . . .

In economies of this type, and only in these, the ratio of capital to labour will be the same in every industry. (Again, I leave you to think out the reason.) Therefore, each industry divides its capital in the same proportions between the part spent on wages and the part spent on materials. The **composition of capital**, as it is called, is the same in every industry. By tradition, this is most often taken as the defining characteristic of these special economies: every industry has the same composition of capital.

Section 3.4   Capital, Labour and Final Demand

The Distribution of Capital and the Demand for Labour

We have done what can be done to sort out the links between the wage, the rate of profit and prices. Once the numeraire was chosen, the equations contained in (3.3.2) on p. 46 left one unknown to be settled. In our earlier investigation of the single-product model we had come to an equivalent stage by the end of Section 2.2. By then we had discovered a connection between the wage and the rate of profit, and had only to find the value of one to settle them both. Then in Section 2.3 we finished determining the model by taking the wage to be fixed in a competitive market for labour. We found that it was given simply by the economy's aggregate ratio of capital to labour. Our present model will be completed in the same way, by settling the wage in a **competitive labour market**. But the working of the market is more complicated.

The supply of labour is no special problem; it is whatever the economy's labour force happens to be. The difficulty is with demand. In the earlier model, for each wage there was a definite number of workers the economy's capital was able to employ. We could therefore draw the demand curve for labour straight away. The difficulty in our present case is that a given quantity of capital will employ different numbers of workers in different industries. The cost of the materials supplied to workers is not the same in every industry. Different industries, therefore, require different amounts of capital for financing the employment of a worker. For an example take the economy whose technology is (3.1.1) (see p. 31). When the wage is 1/5 in terms of corn the rate of profit is 1/2 (see (3.3.5) on p. 48), and the price of fertilizer in terms of corn is 9/5 (see (3.3.4) on p. 47). Then to employ a worker in farming requires, in terms of corn, 2/3 ton, of which 1/5 ton is for wages and the rest for materials. In the fertilizer industry employing one worker requires 6/5 ton of corn as capital; in baking 7/10 ton. Thus, some given amount of capital, say 100 tons, will employ 150 workers in farming, about 143 in baking and only about 83 in the fertilizer industry.

Capital's demand for labour, then, depends on the industry where it is applied. To find the total demand we shall have to take account of how capital is divided up between industries. As a matter of fact, it is more convenient to look at its division, not between industries, but between the net production of the various goods. The capital that is ultimately engaged in the net production of, say, cauliflowers, is not all directly applied in the cauliflower industry. A good part of it will be financing the making of whatever inputs cauliflower cultivation needs, and *their* inputs, and so on. I want to lump all this capital together and call it the cauliflower-growing **segment** of total capital. It is easy to segment capital in this way. On p. 44 we found that the economy's total capital is k^*y, where k^* is the vector of integrated requirements of capital and y the vector of net outputs. Of course

$$k^*y = k_1^*y_1 + k_2^*y_2 + \ldots + k_n^*y_n.$$

The first term on the right is the segment of capital devoted to the net production of the first product. Similarly for the other terms. An increase in y_2 and a decrease in y_1 will mean a transfer of capital from the first segment to the second. This implies, not just a transfer from the first industry to the second, but a complicated movement of capital out of all the industries that contribute in one way and another to the making of the first product and into those that contribute to the making of the second.

The labour force can be segmented similarly. Its total size we found on pp. 39–40 to be l^*y, l^* being the vector of integrated requirements of labour. And

$$l^*y = l_1^*y_1 + l_2^*y_2 + \ldots l_n^*y_n.$$

The terms on the right represent the segments of labour employed, directly and indirectly, in producing the various goods.

The ratio of capital to labour in the first segment is k_1^*/l_1^*. This is the number of units of capital required to employ a worker in that segment. The larger the fraction of capital employed in segments where the ratio is low, the larger will be the demand for labour and, normally, the higher will be the wage. Only if all segments have the same capital/labour ratio will capital's distribution among segments not affect the demand for labour.

Final Demand

The size of the economy's various segments, and hence the distribution of capital, depends on the pattern of net production. The next question is what determines the pattern of net production.

The answer is **demand**. Ultimately the movement of capital and labour among industries must be regulated by demand. We assumed that capital will wander from industry to industry looking for the highest rate of profit, until every industry offers the same. Now, given any particular wage, there is a definite price for each product that will make all industries' rates of profit equal. To these prices will correspond a definite quantity of demand for each product, and this must be exactly matched by the output of each industry. If, say, one industry were to produce too much it would be forced to sell its product at too low a price, one that would yield profit at less than the general rate. Capital would go elsewhere, causing output to fall. Similarly, an industry that produced too little would naturally expand. If demand should alter, capital will redistribute itself accordingly, enlarging industries where demand has grown and shrinking those where it has fallen. Labour, of course, will move in company with the capital that employs it.

Capital and labour will be distributed according to demand. More precisely, they will be distributed to make the economy's *net* production match what is called *final* demand. Final demand has two components. There is, first of all, the demand by workers and capitalists for consumption goods. Second, in a growing economy there is the demand from capitalists for goods to add to their stock of materials. Both have to be supplied out of net production. What is *not* counted in final demand is the demand from one industry for the products of another to serve as inputs (unless they represent an *increase* in the industry's stock of materials). Inputs come out of gross, not net, production.

Final demand controls net production. So final demand directly controls the size of the economy's segments. That is the point of dividing up capital and labour by segments instead of industries. The size of industries is one step removed from final demand.

Final demand, then, influences the distribution of capital, hence (unless all segments have the same capital/labour ratio) the demand for labour, hence (normally) the wage.

Aggregate Demand and the Composition of Demand

Something about what I have just said may be puzzling. I said that in equilibrium the economy's net production of the various products will be equal to the demand for them. But how do we know that is even possible? Might it not be that the stock of capital, for example, is simply not big enough to finance all that production? If so, then the argument I gave to show that capital would distribute itself so as to meet demand would not work. All industries might simultaneously find themselves unable to meet their demands, and unable to get capital for expansion just because every other industry is also short of capital. Alternatively, might not demand turn out to be less than the economy's productive capacity, so that every industry might have too much capital? Unemployment of capital and labour would then be a possibility.

As it happens, though, in our present model these difficulties cannot arise. Final demand issues from the economy's workers and capitalists. They decide what to buy with their income and their decisions determine the distribution of capital. It is essential to understand that the *total* of final demand is not one of the things they decide. People automatically spend their whole income on products — no more and no less. They have to because there is no money in our model. Everybody receives his or her income in the form of some product or other. It may be exchanged for other products of equal value, but whether exchanged or not it always constitutes demand. The aggregate value of demand cannot but be the same as aggregate income.

Now, aggregate income in the economy is, by definition, exactly equal to the value of its net production. To see why, remember that in each industry the capitalists' income is defined to be what is left out of the value of gross production, after deducting wages and the cost of materials. Wages are, of course, the workers' income. So, putting all industries together, capitalists' and workers' incomes in the whole economy add up to the value of its gross production less the cost of the materials it uses up. But, since gross production less materials is just net production, the value of gross production less the cost of materials is just the value of net production. We have arrived at our conclusion: capitalists' and workers' incomes together amount to the value of net production.

The consequence is that the aggregate value of final demand must always be the same as the value of net production. However much is produced there will always be enough demand in total to buy it all. If (before equilibrium is reached) one industry is producing too much to meet its demand, some other must be producing too little. Hence demand imposes no limitation on the *total* of the economy's production. (This is explained more fully in Chapter 2 on p. 24.) What it does require of the economy is that its total production be composed of the right sorts of goods, the goods people want to buy. To put it another way, all the capital capitalists supply will be able to find an occupation provided it is put into the right industries. Demand does not determine how much capital can be employed, but it does determine how it must be distributed. The important thing is not the total of demand, because that looks after itself, but the *composition* of demand — its division amongst the different products.

An Example

We must have an example of all this. Look at Tables 3.4.1 and 3.4.2. They describe two different states of an economy that employs technology 3.1.1 (on p. 31). To make things as simple as possible I have suppressed the baking industry by supposing there is no demand for bread. Corn is the numeraire.

In each table I have assumed that the economy's labour force is 1 000 000 workers, and that its capital, measured in corn, is 800 000 tons. The Tables show, for one thing, how the labour and capital is divided up, both by industries and by segments. Take Table 3.4.1, for instance. The labour force in the fertilizer *industry* is 142 857 people. However, none of them are employed in the fertilizer *segment* because it happens that in Table 3.4.1 there is no net production of fertilizer at all. All the producers of fertilizer are evidently simply producing input for the corn industry.

The Tables also show the net and gross productions arising from the segments and industries. And they give various other pieces of information, including the income received by workers and capitalists in the segments and industries (found by multiplying the labour force by the wage and the quantity of capital by the rate of profit) and the integrated labour and capital requirements of the different products.

All the quantities in the Tables can be worked out from the various formulae presented in this chapter, including particularly ones given later in this section.

Now, the basic difference between the two Tables is simply this: in Table 3.4.1 final demand is for corn only whereas in Table 3.4.2 there is some final demand for fertilizer too. Actually in Table 3.4.2 I set y_2/y_1 at 1/4. All the other differences flow from this. If we imagine a transition from Table 3.4.1 to 3.4.2, labour and capital move into the fertilizer segment, which means in

Table 3.4.1

Technology 3.1.1; $L = 1\,000\,000$; $K = 800\,000$; $y_2 = 0$.
$w = 0.26433$; $r = 0.38387$; $p_1 = 1$ (numeraire); $p_2 = 1.74967$.

| | Industries | | |
	Corn	Fertilizer	Total
Gross production	857 143	142 857	
Labour employed	857 143	142 857	1 000 000
Capital employed	619 381	180 619	800 000
Workers' income	226 571	37 762	264 332
Capitalists' income	237 762	69 334	307 096
Total income	464 332	107 096	571 429

| | Segments | | |
	Corn	Fertilizer	Total
Net production	571 429	0	
Value of net production	571 429	0	571 429
Labour employed	1 000 000	0	1 000 000
Capital employed	800 000	0	800 000
Workers' income	264 332	0	264 332
Capitalists' income	307 096	0	307 096
Total income	571 429	0	571 429
Integrated requirement of labour	1.75	2.75	
Integrated requirement of capital	1.4	2.66433	
Integrated capital/labour ratio	0.8	0.96885	
Integrated requirement of materials	0.93742	1.93742	
Integrated materials/labour ratio	0.53567	0.70452	

practice increasing the size of the fertilizer industry. Thus some net production of fertilizer is provided to meet the demand. Since the fertilizer segment has the higher capital/labour ratio the result is a reduction in the demand for labour. Consequently, to maintain equilibrium in the labour market the wage falls. Because of the wage–profit equation the rate of profit rises.

A point that emerges from the Tables is that a product's integrated capital/labour ratio is not an immutable quantity. It varies with the wage and prices, because the integrated requirement of capital does. It is possible for a product to have a lower ratio than another when the wage has one value and a higher ratio when it has another. Then at one level of the wage a shift of demand between products may raise the wage, whereas at another level a similar shift reduces it. But the same rule always applies: when demand is transferred from one product to another it raises the wage if and only if the former requires the higher ratio of capital to labour in its production. The ratios in question are, naturally, the ones existing when the demand is transferred.

Table 3.4.2

Technology 3.1.1; $L = 1\,000\,000$; $K = 800\,000$; $y_1/y_2 = 4$.
$w = 0.21146$; $r = 0.47806$; $p_1 = 1$ (numeraire); $p_2 = 1.79061$.

Industries	Corn	Fertilizer	Total
Gross production	769 231	230 769	
Labour employed	769 231	230 769	1 000 000
Capital employed	520 432	279 568	800 000
Workers' income	162 661	48 798	211 460
Capitalists' income	248 798	133 650	382 449
Total income	411 460	182 449	593 909

Segments	Corn	Fertilizer	Total
Net production	410 256	102 564	
Value of net production	410 256	183 652	593 909
Labour employed	717 949	282 051	1 000 000
Capital employed	540 598	259 402	800 000
Workers' income	151 817	59 643	211 460
Capitalists' income	258 439	124 010	382 449
Total income	410 256	183 652	593 909
Integrated requirement of labour	1.75	2.75	
Integrated requirement of capital	1.31771	2.52917	
Integrated capital/labour ratio	0.75298	0.91970	
Integrated requirement of materials	0.94765	1.94765	
Integrated materials/labour ratio	0.54152	0.70824	

Final Demand and Prices

One consequence of the rule is that we can say something, as it happens rather inconclusive, about the influence of final demand on the prices of products. The demand for a product does not affect its price directly, but the pattern of final demand in general affects the wage, which in turn affects prices. Any alteration in demand may alter any price. But it is most interesting to see what the demand for a particular product does to its own price.

More exactly, let us ask: when demand shifts from one product to another what happens to the relative price of these products? Suppose for the sake of argument that the second product has a higher integrated capital/labour ratio than the first. Then the demand for labour will fall as a result of the shift, the wage will fall too, and the rate of profit will rise. Now, the natural expectation is that the fall in the wage, with its accompanying rise in the rate of profit, will raise the relative price of products that use relatively more capital in their production. If this expectation were fulfilled, the second of our two products would rise in price relative to the first. And that is very plausible. It is, after all, the one whose demand has gone up. But I explained on p. 55 that our natural expectations about the movements of prices are not necessarily fulfilled. On occasions when they are not then our second product, the one whose demand has risen, will actually fall in price against the first.

A shift of demand from one product to another can, then, reduce the price of the second relative to the first. Tables 3.4.3 and 3.4.4 give an example. They use Technology 3.3.11 from p. 55. The Tables are to be compared in the way we compared Tables 3.4.1 and 3.4.2. Cattle are the numeraire. The labour

Table 3.4.3

Technology 3.3.11; $L = 1\,000\,000$; $K = 45\,611$; $y_2 = y_3 = 0$.
$w = 0.00943$; $r = 1.00000$; $p_1 = 0.067616$; $p_2 = 1$ (numeraire); $p_3 = 1.21886$.

	Industries Turnips	Cattle	Manure	Total
Gross production	87 719	10 526	17 544	
Labour employed	877 193	105 263	17 544	1 000 000
Capital employed	29 656	5 263	10 692	45 611

	Segments Turnips	Cattle	Manure	Total
Net production	81 404	0	0	
Value of net production	55 042	0	0	55 042
Labour employed	1 000 000	0	0	1 000 000
Capital employed	45 611	0	0	45 611
Integrated requirement of labour	12·28448	17·37069	11·42241	
Integrated requirement of capital	0·56031	0·83618	1·11114	
Integrated capital/labour ratio	0·04561	0·04814	0·09728	

force is 1 000 000 and constant. The supply of capital (in terms of cattle) is 45 611 and constant. Compare the turnip and cattle industries. Of the two the cattle industry has the higher capital/labour ratio. Accordingly when, in Table 3.4.3, final demand is for turnips only the wage is higher than in Table 3.4.4 where it is for cattle only. However, the price of turnips is lower (relative to cattle) in Table 3.4.3 than 3.4.4. The reason is that, because of Wicksell effects, the price does not respond to the wage in the way we might expect. This I explained on pp. 55–56.

I do not know how to judge whether this sort of "perverse" response of price to demand is likely to be common or rare.

Table 3.4.4

Technology 3.3.11; $L=1\,000\,000$; $K=45\,611$; $y_1=y_3=0$.
$w=0.00623$; $r=1.12551$; $p_1=0.68025$; $p_2=1$ (numeraire); $p_3=1.28855$.

	Industries Turnips	Cattle	Manure	Total
Gross production	37 221	62 035	7 444	
Labour employed	372 208	620 347	7 444	1 000 000
Capital employed	11 912	29 186	4 513	45 611

	Segments Turnips	Cattle	Manure	Total
Net production	0	57 568	0	
Value of net production	0	57 568	0	57 568
Labour employed	0	1 000 000	0	1 000 000
Capital employed	0	45 611	0	45 611
Integrated requirement of labour	12.28448	17.37069	11.42241	
Integrated requirement of capital	0.53636	0.79229	1.08161	
Integrated capital/labour ratio	0.04366	0.04561	0.09469	

The Equations of the Model

What I have said so far in this section is accurate but rather informal. I should spell out the model more exactly.

We have already investigated the basic system (3.3.2) of equations connecting the wage, the rate of profit and prices. I repeat the equations here:

$$p=(1+r)(pA+wl). \tag{3.4.1}$$

To complete their sense another equation is needed to define a numeraire, say,

$$pz=1. \tag{3.4.2}$$

We know that after (3.4.1) and (3.4.2) there is just one unknown left to be determined. The job of this section is to determine it by means of supply and demand in the labour market.

Suppose the economy has a labour force L. It must, in equilibrium, be the same as lx, the labour actually employed (x is gross production). Similarly, if K is the economy's stock of capital, it must be equal to $(pA+wl)x$, the capital employed.

$$L=lx$$
$$K=(pA+wl)x.$$

Now, x is the same as $(I-A)^{-1}y$, where y is net production. So

$$L=l(I-A)^{-1}y \tag{3.4.3}$$

and

$$K=(pA+wl)(I-A)^{-1}y. \tag{3.4.4}$$

By substituting the definitions of l^* and k^* ((3.1.7) on p. 40 and (3.2.2) on p. 44) we can if we choose write these equations in the simpler form

$$L=l^*y$$

and

$$K=k^*y.$$

It is worth comparing the various equations above with the equivalent ones in Section 2.4 of Chapter 2.

I shall treat L and K as given constants. (There is some difficulty in treating K as something given, but I shall postpone worrying about that till Section 3.5.) We have, therefore, in (3.4.3) and (3.4.4) added n unknowns to our system: the n components of y. On the other hand we have only added two equations. Previously there was one unknown still to be determined. Now there are evidently $(n-1)$.

Now, y is net production, which is determined by final demand. Final demand comes from capitalists and workers, and they may intend it for consumption or investment. But one thing is certain: its *total* is not decided by these people. They decide how to spend what income they have, but their income is decided for them and they have to spend it all. Once they have decided how much to spend on all the products but one they have no choice but to spend what is left on the last. Effectively, then, they decide $(n-1)$ components of y. Final demand, that is to say, determines the remaining $(n-1)$ unknowns of our system.

I shall formalize this by means of **demand functions** for the products. The demand for each product will, or may, depend on its own price and those of other products, and also on the wage and rate of profit since these determine what people have to spend. So demand is a function of the wage, the rate of profit and prices.

$$y_1=d_1(w, r, p),$$
$$y_2=d_2(w, r, p)$$

and so on. The symbols, d_1, d_2 etc. stand for the separate demand functions. The equations may all be put together in vector notation:

$$y=d(w, r, p). \tag{3.4.5}$$

Here d stands for a vector function.

Equation (3.4.5) amounts to n separate equations. Our system now consists of (3.4.1), which is also n separate equations, (3.4.2), (3.4.3), (3.4.4) and the n

equations of (3.4.5). This comes to $(2n+3)$ equations altogether. The unknowns are w, r, the n components of p and the n components of y, making $(2n+2)$ altogether. At first sight, then, there is one equation too many. However, the point of what I was saying about the total of demand is that demand functions are linked together in a special way: the spending on the various goods has always to add up to the given total of income. Total spending is

$$p_1 d_1(w, r, p) + p_2 d_2(w, r, p) + \ldots + p_n d_n(w, r, p),$$

that is, $pd(w, r, p)$. Total income is $wL + rK$, the sum of the incomes of the two classes. So

$$pd(w, r, p) = wL + rK. \tag{3.4.6}$$

This fact is an *a priori* restriction upon the demand functions. They have, automatically, to be of a form that always satisfies (3.4.6), for all values of w, r and p. The important consequence is that the equations in our system (3.4.1)–(3.4.5) are not entirely independent of each other. For example, (3.4.4) can be deduced from the others, in the following way. We know already that (3.4.1) can be turned into the form

$$p = wl^* + rk^*$$

(see (3.3.10) on p. 54). In other words

$$p = wl(I-A)^{-1} + r(pA + wl)(I-A)^{-1}.$$

Postmultiply by y:

$$py = wl(I-A)^{-1}y + r(pA + wl)(I-A)^{-1}y.$$

Now substitute from equations (3.4.3) and (3.4.5):

$$pd(w, r, p) = wL + r(pA + wl)(I-A)^{-1}y.$$

But we know that $d(w, r, p)$ satisfies (3.4.6), so the left hand side may be replaced with $wL + rK$:

$$wL + rK = wL + r(pA + wl)(I-A)^{-1}y.$$
$$\therefore K = (pA + wl)(I-A)^{-1}y.$$

And this is (3.4.4). We have successfully derived it from the other equations in the system, bearing in mind what we know about the form of the demand functions. The system, then, has one redundant equation. Whereas we appeared to have one equation too many for determining the unknowns, it now turns out that we have just the right number. Our model, then, is complete.

Aggregate Capital and the Distribution of Income

From (3.4.4)

$$K = pA(I-A)^{-1}y + wl(I-A)^{-1}y.$$

$$\therefore w = \frac{K}{l(I-A)^{-1}y} - \frac{pA(I-A)^{-1}y}{l(I-A)^{-1}y}.$$

$$\therefore w = \frac{K}{L} - \frac{pA(I-A)^{-1}y}{l^*y}, \tag{3.4.7}$$

substituting (3.4.3) and the definition of l^*. The second term on the right of this equation may be written in various forms:

$$\frac{pA(I-A)^{-1}y}{l^*y} = \frac{pA(I-A)^{-1}y}{L} = \frac{pAx}{L} = \frac{pAx}{lx}.$$

The top of all these fractions is the total cost of the materials used in all industries. The bottom is the labour force. The fractions are the ratio of the cost of materials to the labour employed, in other words the average cost of the materials supplied to a worker. Equation (3.4.7) corresponds very closely to (2.4.6) on p. 26 of Chapter 2. Both equations say that the wage is what is left, on average, out of the capital available for employing a member of the labour force after he or she has been equipped with materials.

Because the cost of materials per worker is different in different industries, movements of capital and labour between industries will alter the economy's average. The second term on the right of (3.4.7) will alter, and so, therefore, will the wage. Alternatively, we may look at this effect by integrated segments of the economy: the cost of materials per worker is different between segments, so movements of capital and labour between segments will alter the wage. Tables 3.4.1 and 3.4.2 give information about the cost of materials per worker in each segment.

I have discussed earlier in this section the effect on the wage of the sizes of different segments. Now I want to discuss the effect of the other term on the right of (3.4.7): K/L. Obviously this, the over-all quantity of capital per worker in the economy, is the primary determinant of the wage (but see Section 3.5 for qualifications).

For simplicity, since I have already dealt with changes in the composition of final demand, I shall now keep it constant. That is to say, the components of net production y (which in equilibrium is the same as final demand) I shall keep in constant proportions: $y_2/y_1, y_3/y_1, \ldots y_n/y_1$ are all constant. If we suppose for a moment that the labour force does not change, then this means that not just the proportions but the actual net output of each product will be constant. For the labour force will always be divided in the same way between the industries. Each industry will employ a constant amount of labour.

Neither the gross nor the net output of each good will vary. So far as production is concerned, nothing in the economy alters. Changes in the stock of capital will affect distribution and prices but not production. And of course, it does not really matter in this whether the labour force varies or not; *per worker* production will always be the same. The vector y/L—net production per worker—is constant.

It does not follow, however, that we can rely on the constancy of the cost of materials per worker. Certainly, because production does not change neither will the actual materials used, per worker, throughout the economy. But their cost probably will. Alterations in K/L alter w and hence p. So the second term on the right of (3.4.7), which may be written $pA(I-A)^{-1}y/L$, is likely to change even though y/L does not. Table 3.4.5 illustrates the sort of thing that can happen. Compare it with Table 3.4.2. They both show the same economy (whose technology is (3.1.1)), and in both the labour force and final demand are the same. The difference between them is simply that the stock of capital is different. This has its effect on the cost of the materials used in each industry and segment.

Table 3.4.5

Technology 3.1.1; $L=1\,000\,000$; $K=1\,131\,868$; $y_1/y_2=4$.
$w=0\cdot57143$; $r=0$; $p_1=1$ (numeraire); $p_2=1\cdot57143$.

| | Industries | | |
	Corn	Fertilizer	Total
Gross production	769 231	230 769	
Labour employed	769 231	230 769	1 000 000
Capital employed	769 231	362 637	1 131 868
Workers' income	439 560	131 868	571 429
Capitalists' income	0	0	0
Total income	439 560	131 868	571 429

| | Segments | | |
	Corn	Fertilizer	Total
Net production	410 256	102 564	
Value of net production	410 256	161 172	571 429
Labour employed	717 949	282 051	1 000 000
Capital employed	776 557	355 311	1 131 868
Workers' income	410 256	161 172	571 429
Capitalists' income	0	0	0
Total income	410 256	161 172	571 429
Integrated requirement of labour	1·75	2·75	
Integrated requirement of capital	1·89286	3·46428	
Integrated capital/labour ratio	1·08163	1·25974	
Integrated requirement of materials	0·89286	1·89286	
Integrated materials/labour ratio	0·51020	0·68831	

Notice in passing that capital cannot increase beyond the amount shown in Table 3.4.5 or the rate of profit would become negative.

So the amount of capital that needs to be spent on materials is liable to vary. The consequence is that what is left over for paying wages is a little complicated to calculate. The relationship between w and K/L is not so straightforward as it was in, for instance, Fig. 2.3.2 on p. 21. It is not generally linear. All the same it can be worked out, and we can draw up a distribution diagram like Fig. 2.3.2. Figure 3.4.1 shows one for technology (3.1.1). The graphs depend on the pattern of final demand, of course, and the diagram shows the effects of two different patterns. The solid lines represent the case where demand is for corn alone (as in Table 3.4.1), the dotted lines where it is divided between corn and fertilizer in the ratio 4:1 (as in Tables 3.4.2 and 3.4.5). A vertical line in the diagram marks an aggregate capital/labour ratio of 0·8, which corresponds to Tables 3.4.1 and 3.4.2.

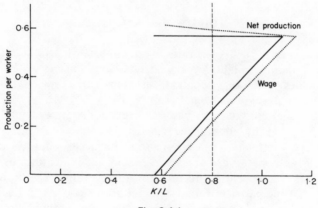

Fig. 3.4.1

The case shown by the solid lines in Fig. 3.4.1 is easy to understand. The economy is there producing corn only, in a constant quantity unaffected by the quantity of capital. The corn is divided between workers and capitalists. But the other case is more difficult. Net production consists of two different goods. They are only reduced to a single quantity of total income available for distribution by a process of **valuation**. Corn and fertilizer are both valued in terms of corn, and their value constitutes total income. Valuations, however, can change even though there are no real changes in the quantities. Increasing quantities of capital increase the wage and this, as it happens in our example, brings down the price of fertilizer in terms of corn. Therefore, increasing capital decreases the value of net production. That is what the dotted line shows. A superficial look at the diagram might lead one to think that capital actually makes a negative contribution to production. But there is no significance in that; it is merely one of the confusing effects of valuation. What is really happening in this model is that production is staying exactly the same; capital has no influence on it. (This, too, is rather a lot to swallow. It is a consequence of one of the model's simplifying assumptions — namely, that there is no choice of technique — and it will be dealt with in Chapter 4.)

Valuation effects are a constant danger to the unwary. The next section has something more to say about them.

Section 3.5   Economic Growth and the Quantity of Capital

Proportional Growth

We can now, with the help of our discoveries in Section 3.4, think about how our model economies might develop as their capital accumulates. There are some difficulties ahead, but we can at least start with a type of growth that is quite easy to analyse: **proportional growth**.

In proportional growth every part of the economy grows equally quickly. Let us suppose that the labour force is growing at some given rate, say 3% per year. Then every industry — its output and all its inputs — must be growing at 3%. Obviously the pattern of gross and net production cannot be changing. This means that an essential precondition for making proportional growth possible is that the pattern of final demand does not change. Each year the demand for every product must increase by the same amount, in our case 3%.

What makes proportional growth easy to analyse is that it allows us to assume that each year the economy is effectively in **equilibrium**. All the formulae we have worked out in earlier sections of this chapter depend on the economy's being in equilibrium. If it is growing, though, strictly it is not. But if the growth is proportional it can maintain the equilibrium wage, rate of profit and prices without changing, just as though it is. Each year the economy will be just as in the previous year but on a larger scale. Each year the supply of labour will be equal to the demand, and the supply of each product equal to its demand. We have no need to worry about the length of time it would take to come to the equilibrium (see p. 45) because the economy is never away from it.

Because the economy is growing, each year more materials are used up than in the year before. Each year a part of net production must be added to the stock of materials. Take as an example our standard economy with technology (3.1.1). Suppose one year it happens to be in the state shown in

Table 3.4.2 on p. 64. The labour force, growing at 3% annually and being 1 000 000 this year, will be 1 030 000 the next. The corn used as input is 358 974 tons this year (its gross minus its net production), and must be greater next year by 3% or 10 769 tons. Similarly the input of fertilizer must increase by 3846 tons. These amounts must be taken out of net production. Not all of net production, then, goes to consumption; some supplies the materials for growth. The stock of subsistence for the workers must also be growing each year, and that too must come out of net production.

The stock of materials and subsistence are together the economy's capital. Adding to them constitutes capital accumulation. Capitalists must be **saving** a part of their income — adding it to capital instead of consuming it. We can work out what fraction of their income they are saving. The total value, in terms of corn, of the addition to materials is

$$10\,769 + 1 \cdot 79061 \times 3846 = 17\,656,$$

since 1·79061 is, from Table 3.4.2, the equilibrium price of fertilizer in terms of corn. At the same time the total value of wages, which is initially 211 460 in terms of corn, grows by 3% or 6344. Capital grows altogether by the sum of these amounts, i.e. 24 000. This is exactly 3% of the initial total of capital, as of course it has to be. The 24 000 tons added to capital is a fraction 0·06275 of the capitalists' income. That, then, is the capitalists' rate of saving.

To generalize, if the labour force is growing at a rate g and the economy's growth is proportional, capital must grow at that rate too. But if r is the rate of profit and s the fraction of profit that is saved, rs is the proportion by which capital grows each year. So

$$rs = g.$$

Once we know g and s then we know what r must be to permit proportional growth. It must be g/s. This much is no different from the single-product economy (see p. 22). And if we also know the pattern of final demand, then we will know all about the state of the economy provided it is growing proportionally. Of course, nothing says an economy necessarily does grow proportionally.

Look at the distribution diagram Fig. 3.4.1 on p. 71. For each pattern of final demand, a higher rate of profit appears as a point farther over to the left. A high rate of growth, then, or a low rate of saving on the part of capitalists, will lead, if the economy happens to be growing proportionally, to a position towards the left of the diagram. Here the distribution of income favours capitalists against workers.

Here also, towards the left of Fig. 3.4.1, the aggregate capital/labour ratio is low. Now this corresponds well with natural expectations. If capitalists save rather little in comparison to the rate of growth of the labour force it is reasonable to expect the capital/labour ratio to be low. And if we compare proportional growth paths that is exactly what our diagram shows. A low s makes for a high r which corresponds to a low K/L.

There is, however, a snag. The correspondence between a high r and a low K/L is less universal than one might think. My next example illustrates.

A Peculiar Example

Let the technology be

$$3/4 \text{ corn \& 1 labour} \longrightarrow 1 \text{ corn}$$
$$1 \text{ corn \& 4 labour} \longrightarrow 1 \text{ cake.}$$

Let final demand for corn and cake be in the proportion $1:1$. Gross production, it is easy to calculate, must then be in the proportion $8:1$. Suppose that the labour force is constant at 1200 people. (For this example we shall not be concerned with growth.) Then gross production of corn must be 800 tons, and of cake 100 tons.

What capital is required to finance this production? It depends on the wage, of course. Let our numeraire be corn, and take first the extreme case when the wage is nought. Capital supplies materials only, evidently 600 tons of corn in the corn industry and 100 in the cake industry, making 700 altogether.

This quantity of capital is the minimum that could employ all the labour force. Further accumulations thereafter will pull up the wage. How much is needed, let us ask, to bring the wage up to $1/8$ ton of corn per year? The wage fund — the part of capital that finances wages — is then 150 tons for the 1200 workers. Together with the cost of materials this makes capital 850 tons.

All this is straightforward. The economy is a particularly simple one in that it has only one basic good, corn. It seems natural to adopt corn as the numeraire. But let us see what would happen if instead we adopted cake.

The first thing to notice is that capital, being a *value*, is measured as a quantity of the numeraire. The choice of numeraire therefore makes a difference to the behaviour of capital as we measure it. How much capital is there in the economy, measured in cake, when the wage is nought? The price of cake relative to corn is given by the ratio of their costs of production:

$$\frac{(1+4w)}{(3/4+w)}$$

where w is the wage *in terms of corn*. When w is nought, this price is $4/3$. We have already calculated that capital in terms of corn is 700 tons when the wage is nought. In terms of cake it is therefore $700/(4/3)$, or 525 tons.

Now, for comparison, take the situation we have already looked at where the wage has risen to 1/8 ton *in terms of corn*. The price of cake relative to corn is then

$$\frac{1+4(1/8)}{(3/4+1/8)}$$

by the formula above. This comes to 12/7. So the wage in terms of cake is $(1/8)/(12/7)$, or 7/96. Total capital in terms of corn we found was 850 tons. In terms of cake it is $850(12/7)$ or $495\frac{5}{6}$ tons. So it is *less* than the capital required when the wage is nought.

Figure 3.5.1 is the distribution diagram for this economy when cake is numeraire. It is plainly odd. An increase in the wage can correspond to a decrease in the quantity of capital per worker. That is the peculiar feature of the example. It offends against what we have believed so far about the working of capital in our model. Capital is spent on two things: materials and wages. If the pattern of production does not alter then the quantity of materials does not alter. So additions to capital should go into paying higher wages. That is how we have thought so far. But this example contradicts it. What is going on is this. We are dealing with values. Although the actual quantity of materials does not alter their value will (see p. 70). In the example, from the point of view of someone who values things in terms of cake, an increase in wages causes such a drop in the value of materials that the total capital needed to finance wages and materials together actually declines. The reason is that the increase in wages brings down the price of corn very sharply relative to cake.

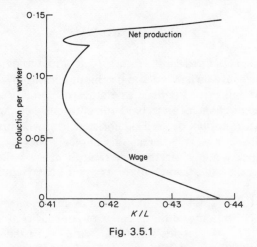

Fig. 3.5.1

No such paradox appeared when corn was the numeraire. But cake is not necessarily a silly numeraire to choose. Measuring value in terms of cake may represent the point of view of capitalists. If capitalists consume mainly cake they will be inclined to think of capital that way. Measuring capital in terms of cake shows what it is worth to the capitalist—what he or she would get by selling up the business in exchange for the consumer good he or she wants. It shows what it would cost a new capitalist to set up in business—how much consumption must be forsaken to buy the materials and labour required. In our strange example an increase in the wage does genuinely make it cheaper to get into business; the capital required for any given output is less in terms of what the capitalist values.

There is some point, then, in measuring capital in terms of the good capitalists consume. So, in comparing the situations where the wage is nought and where it is 1/8 (in terms of corn), are we to say capital has grown or shrunk? In terms of the good used in production it has grown. In terms of the good capitalists ultimately value it has shrunk. Both points of view are valid and have a purpose. We can learn from them that in measuring quantities of capital there is not some single unambiguous concept of capital we are aiming at. Capital can be looked at from different standpoints. We shall want to measure it differently for different purposes. However, we can learn from the example something more. For the purposes of economic analysis there is a clear advantage in using corn as numeraire. There is one clear sense in which the economy needs more capital to pay a wage of 1/8 than one of nought, and our measure of capital ought to show it. To explain why, I need to say something about the nature of capital.

What is Capital?

In Chapter 2 (p. 12) I defined capital as the stock of materials and subsistence that a capitalist needs to own in order to pay his or her employees and carry on the business. Capital, then, I defined as a stock of goods.

But in the present chapter things have surreptitiously changed. The goods needed as inputs for production, and as subsistence for workers, are no longer necessarily all the same sort, whereas in Chapter 2 they were all corn. To collect all the different goods together and treat them as a unitary quantity of capital we took their *value*. Capital in this chapter I have regularly treated as a quantity of value.

Nevertheless, there is still merit in the idea of **capital as a stock of goods**, now of course a collection of different sorts of goods. From a technological point of view it is the goods—materials and subsistence—that make production possible. The special character of capitalism is that these goods are owned by capitalists; they constitute their capital. Suppose it happens in an economy that there is no change in the actual quantity of materials and subsistence used but because of a change in prices their total value alters. Then we might very reasonably want to say that "in real terms" capital has not altered; the apparent change is a mere effect of valuation.

On the other hand, there is at least equal merit in the idea of **capital as value**. As I have said, for one thing it gives us a unitary measure of the quantity of capital. But most important is that it is on that basis that profit is received. The rate of profit, which dictates capitalists' income, is a rate of return on the value of capital. Evidently, therefore, all the calculations we have made, of prices, the wage–profit curve and so on, are all based on the notion of capital as value. In particular, if we were to identify capital with goods we should have difficulty over Wicksell effects and their consequences (see p. 56).

Indeed, the idea of a stock of goods used in production is not itself perfectly straightforward. Materials get used up and subsistence goods get consumed. There is a "stock" only in so far as they are replaced each year. If we were to insist too strictly on treating capital as the actual goods, we should have to say that capital is constantly going out of existence and being recreated. It is much better to say that capital changes its form during the course of the year. At one stage it consists of materials and wage-goods, later of work in progress and later still of the finished product. Then, by exchange the finished product is converted back to materials and wage-goods for the next round. What all these things have in common—what stays constant during the year—is their value. It is natural to think of the capital as value, embodied in different forms during the year.

It is best not to try and adjudicate between the two rival notions of capital. Let us say that capital has two different aspects: capital-as-goods and capital-as-value. We shall certainly want to continue measuring capital by its value because that is essential if we are to understand the workings of the rate of profit, prices and so on. But that leaves us some choice—the choice of numeraire. If possible we shall want to select a numeraire so that the value of capital, measured in terms of the numeraire, is a good reflection of the stock of materials and subsistence. It should not be too much subject to capricious valuation effects that have nothing to do with "real" changes.

The Selection of a Numeraire

Now look again at the peculiar example. We assumed a constant labour force and a constant pattern of final demand. That means that production is constant in every industry. The quantity of materials therefore does not change. But a higher wage obviously demands a greater stock of subsistence goods. Capital viewed as goods is therefore unambiguously greater when the wage is 1/8 than when it is nought. Cake, then, is a poor numeraire, for the economist though perhaps not for the capitalist, because it gets the change in capital the wrong way round.

Let us generalize again. The model economies of this chapter permit no change in the methods of production. Therefore, once the pattern of final demand (hence of production) is given, the quantities used of all the different sorts of materials, per worker, are fixed. The only change there can be in capital-as-goods, per worker, is in the stock of subsistence. An increased wage must mean increased capital per worker. Indeed we may take an increase or decrease in the wage as a *criterion* of an increase or decrease in the amount of capital per worker. We ought to make sure that we measure capital in a way that conforms to that criterion. Then at least our measure will accurately indicate the direction of changes in capital-as-goods.

This, then, is a requirement that limits our free choice of numeraire. We do not want one, like cake, that gets the direction of changes wrong. Goods that actually serve as materials in production, basic goods, are likely to be satisfactory in this respect (though this cannot be strictly guaranteed). Remember, a suitable numeraire is one that associates a high capital/labour ratio with a high wage.

The lesson to draw from all this is that, provided the numeraire is picked sensibly, an increasing capital/labour ratio will always go along with an increasing wage and a declining rate of profit. Figure 3.4.1 is a typical distribution diagram, not Fig. 3.5.1. Different numeraires will yield distribution diagrams of different shapes, even for the same economy and the same pattern of demand. But unless the numeraire is unsuitable the basic form of the diagram will always be the same. And the basic form is what we chiefly need to worry about when comparing patterns of economic growth. We can go back to the discussion of proportional growth secure now in the knowledge that a high rate of saving will, in proportional growth, correspond to a high capital/labour ratio (because we know already that it corresponds to a low rate of profit — see p. 73). And that conforms to intuition.

Growth that is Not Proportional

Look again at Fig. 3.4.1 (p. 71) and the discussion of proportional growth (p. 73). Suppose now that the economy happens to have a particular capital/labour ratio, say 0·8 in the diagram, but that the rate of saving is too high to maintain this ratio in proportional growth. Naturally we should expect that K/L will increase over time and the economy will move to the right in the diagram. We do indeed know, as I have just explained, that with this high rate of saving the appropriate K/L is bigger than the present one. So it is reasonable to suppose that the economy will drift in that direction.

But we must be careful. If the economy is not in proportional growth the wage is changing, the rate of profit too, and prices. All these things will be altering from one year to the next. In proportional growth it was acceptable to assume that markets all stayed in equilibrium, keeping prices constant. That is not acceptable now. The assumptions we used earlier in this chapter to derive formulae for prices, the wage–profit curve and so on, are none of them valid. Outside proportional growth none of the work in this chapter is strictly applicable. So what are we to do?

Only one thing, I think, if we are to say anything at all about the situation. We shall have to assume that the changes are so slow that the economy always manages to stay more or less in equilibrium. What this means is that the capital/labour ratio changes slowly compared with the time it takes for markets to move towards their equilibriums. If the rate of saving is not appropriate for the existing capital/labour ratio the ratio will change. What we assume is that, whatever the ratio happens to be, prices, the wage, etc. are all as they would be if the economy were in equilibrium with that capital/labour ratio. Then as the ratio changes the economy moves through a succession of states of equilibrium. The advantage of the assumption is that we already know all about these states, so we can trace the economy's development. We can use a distribution diagram such as Fig. 3.4.1, derived from the analysis of equilibrium, to follow what will happen.

Let us suppose, then, that the economy is shifting to the right in the diagram because, the rate of saving being high, capital is accumulating faster than the labour force is growing. The rate of profit will decrease and the rate of capital accumulation with it. Eventually, if the rate of saving, s, and the rate of growth of the labour force, g, stay constant the economy should settle down to proportional growth with a rate of profit g/s. But it may be a long time before that happens.

A Constant Quantity of Capital

So far in this section we have faced one problem over the measurement of capital and, I believe, overcome it. We have discovered that, provided only that a decent choice is made of a numeraire, the value of capital will serve as an index of the economy's development. The idea of capital accumulation is unambiguous. More saving leads to more capital, just as it should do.

In all this I have been comparing states of the economy with different quantities of capital (per worker), and thinking about the progress from one to another. But we also ought to think about different states of the economy having the *same* quantity of capital. In Section 3.4 we did some comparative statics along those lines. We looked at different patterns of final demand, keeping the quantity of capital constant. Now we have discovered there is some arbitrariness in our measure of capital. Its value can be measured in terms of alternative numeraires. That means that the notion of a constant quantity of capital is not clear-cut. Suppose we found two equilibriums having different patterns of demand but the same quantity of capital as measured in terms of, say, corn. Relative prices will be different in the two equilibriums and therefore they would certainly not have the same quantity of capital as measured in terms of some other good (unless by chance its price relative to corn is the same in both). What counts as keeping capital constant, then, depends on the numeraire we happen to have chosen. So we ought to think again about the legitimacy of our comparative statics.

One purpose of comparative statics is to investigate causal relations. We aimed to answer the question: if demand changes but other things stay the same, what effects will that cause? What distinguishes comparative statics from studying the dynamics of changes is that we are looking for the long-term effects — the effects that persist once equilibrium is re-established. The difficulty we are now facing is in interpreting the condition "but other things stay the same". Our intention was to isolate a single causal factor. The wage, the rate of profit and prices form a system of variables that in Section 3.4 we took to be determined by outside causes, specifically the labour force, the total quantity of capital and the pattern of final demand. We wanted to isolate the influence of the last of these by keeping the other two constant.

If this is what we want from the comparative statics, unfortunately it gives us no warrant for keeping capital constant in terms of one numeraire rather than another. Indeed it really gives us no warrant for keeping capital constant at all. It might seem sensible, say, to adopt the point of view of the capitalists. They will value their capital in terms of the goods they happen to consume. If, when things change, capital measured this way increases they will feel they now own more capital than they did before. Perhaps, if we are to isolate the effects of demand it is best to keep capital constant as it appears to the capitalists. But now, changes in demand can themselves cause a change in the value of capital as it appears to the capitalists. They hold their capital in the form of goods of one sort and another, or work in progress, at different times of year. Changes in demand change prices, and that changes the value of these goods. There will be capital gains and losses. Even if they take no initiative of their own capitalists will end up owning a different value of capital from the one they started off with. And this is *caused* by the change in demand. It can happen whether the numeraire is capitalists' consumption goods or anything else.

Our project was misconceived. We had planned to separate the causal influence of demand by holding capital constant. But demand can itself causally influence capital. So we must think again. Evidently we ought to keep constant, not some arbitrary quantity like capital measured in some way or other, but only things that are genuinely not themselves affected by demand. In Section 3.4 I treated the quantities of labour and capital as exogenous variables, but capital it now appears is not really exogenous. What is really exogenous — not affected by demand — is, perhaps, capitalists' dispositions to act in certain ways. When demand changes what we really ought to do is follow out what will actually happen: how will capitalists decide how much capital to hold, bearing in mind the price changes that occur and the gains and losses they are making? Conceivably, they might decide to keep their capital constant in terms of some numeraire. That would imply saving and dissaving just enough to cancel out their losses and gains. If they did, then it would be correct for us to treat capital as constant in terms of that numeraire. But it is much more likely that it will not stay constant in terms of anything.

The serious difficulty is not that capital might alter but that how it alters will probably depend on the actual sequence of events that follows the initial change of demand. The speed and timing of price changes are likely to make a difference. To do our work properly we should have to trace the course of events. That means, though, abandoning comparative statics. It would take us far beyond the capacity of this book's analytical methods. So what are we to do?

One possibility is to recognize that our worry about the full causal consequences of changes in demand was in any case rather pointless. I said we should have to take account of how capitalists are disposed to act; that will tell us what will happen to capital after demand alters. However, capitalists' dispositions are very unlikely to lead eventually to any static amount of capital. Economic growth will be going on anyway, whatever happens to demand. The question "What will happen when demand alters, other things staying the same?" only makes sense if we abstract from the continuing process of growth and imagine the economy held in a static limbo. Even to ask the question, then, we have to imagine away the normal motivations of capitalists that cause accumulation. It is silly to try and reinstate them when tracing the effects of demand. The very staticness of comparative statics precludes our thinking of it as a causal investigation even if we want to, because what stays constant — capitalists' dispositions — leads to growth rather than a static state. We must interest ourselves, not in causes, but in comparisons for their own sake. An economy may develop with one pattern of demand or with a different one. To compare the two possible developments we can pick an instant out of each and set them beside one another. The two instants will of course have the different patterns of demand, but we shall want them to be comparable in other respects if the comparison is to be interesting. In particular they ought to be at equivalent stages of development, which means having equal quantities of capital. But now that it is only comparisons, not causes, that interest us, how we choose to define the equality of capital is up to us. It will depend, perhaps, on precisely what is our purpose in making the comparison. In any case it will make no difference to our conclusions, because the results in Section 3.4 do not depend on which product we select as numeraire. What mattered in the analysis was the relative size of different industries' capital/labour ratios when capital moved from one to another, and whatever numeraire capital may be measured in the relative size of capital/labour ratios will always be the same.

This, then, is an interpretation of the comparative statics that escapes the problem. I am not, however, very happy with it. For one thing I do not know quite what the point of comparative statics can be if it has nothing at all to do with what will actually happen in an economy when something changes. Also, it is open to the following rejoinder. Let us run over again the argument that led to it. We were wanting to isolate the consequences of a change in demand. It turned out to be wrong to try and do that by keeping capital constant, because one consequence of a change in demand is likely to be a change in the quantity of capital. So instead we thought we should pay attention to what capitalists will actually decide to do. But then we noticed that capitalists' decisions will almost certainly lead to continuous growth rather than a static state. So comparative statics will be useless unless we give up trying to interpret it causally. That is where the argument led. But now, the method of comparative statics is not quite powerless in the face of economic growth. We have seen that it can compare states of proportional growth just as easily as static states, because an economy growing proportionally is, to all intents and purposes, in equilibrium. To do comparative statics we do *not* have to imagine away capitalists' normal motivations just because they lead to growth. Indeed we can incorporate them explicitly in the theory. Let us suppose capitalists are motivated to save a fraction s of their income. This rate of saving is what we shall hold constant, rather than capital, when demand changes. Then, assuming the labour force grows at a steady rate g, there is only one rate of profit that will maintain the economy in proportional growth: g/s. The composition of final demand can make no difference to this. Whatever happens to final demand, in the long run, once the economy has returned to proportional growth, this rate of profit must always be restored. Of course, if the rate of profit always ends up the same, so do all prices and the wage.

Here, then, is a line of reasoning that leads to the conclusion that the work of Section 3.4, where we held capital constant, was all wasted. We were looking for the effects of demand, but in proportional growth—the only situation where comparative statics is applicable—there are no effects of demand. At least, there are no effects on prices, the rate of profit or the wage. I am not, however, happy with this argument either. Achieving proportional growth is bound to take a very long time. Certainly, comparative statics is to do with the long-term effects of changes, but it would be uninteresting if they were as long term as that. Is there not some intermediate period we can look at? Think of an economy where there has just been an alteration in the pattern of demand. There will be, first of all, various dynamic consequences that are certainly beyond the scope of our methods. Eventually they should work themselves out and markets should find their way back to equilibrium. It should be possible for us to decide what the economy will be like then, even though it will not yet be in proportional growth. The aggregate capital/labour ratio will still be out of balance with the rate of saving, and there will be a further, very long, period of adjustment while that sorts itself out. In the end the economy will be in proportional growth having the same rate of profit as it had originally. My suggestion is that we apply our theory to the intermediate period, when markets are in equilibrium but the capital/labour ratio has yet to adjust. After all, I did say on p. 79 that the theory can be used outside proportional growth, provided we assume that the process of growth changes the aggregate capital/labour ratio only slowly; slowly enough to keep markets continuously in equilibrium. So let us make that assumption.

Take an economy initially in equilibrium, which then experiences a shift of demand. A new equilibrium will in time emerge, where the effects of the shift have worked themselves out, but where the processes of growth have not had time to alter the capital/labour ratio. This does not mean that the ratio is necessarily what it was initially, because the shift in demand may have altered it. But *only* the shift in demand can have altered it; the continuous processes of growth have not yet had an effect. Capital must be measured in terms of some numeraire or other. However it is measured, in going from one equilibrium to the other it may have increased, decreased or stayed the same, and that will be a causal result of the shift in demand. Now, we have worked out in Section 3.4 what the shift in demand would do to prices, the wage and the rate of profit *if* capital were to stay constant. I am now going to argue that all that remains valid, so far as the directions of the effects are concerned, even if capital actually changes.

The argument depends on this: if capital does alter, it will not be directly because of the shift in demand but indirectly because of the shift's effects on the wage, the rate of profit and prices. Suppose that according to our calculations done with a constant quantity of capital the wage would be raised. Along with the rise in the wage go changes in the rate of profit and prices. Because of all these, the quantity of capital may alter. It may alter in such a way as to raise the wage further, or push it back towards its original level. But it most certainly cannot push it back fully as far as its original level. For if the wage went back to its original level so would the rate of profit and prices, and there would be nothing to alter the quantity of capital in the first place. It is impossible, then, for a change in the quantity of capital to cancel out or reverse any change in the wage that would have occurred without it. Since prices and the rate of profit are rigidly tied to the wage the same applies for them.

This is an argument that has its limits in extreme circumstances, but for our purposes it is adequate. It vindicates our assumption, in Section 3.4, of a constant quantity of capital.

Section 3.6   The Influence of Consumers' Demand

The Variables

It is time to look back over this long chapter. We have analysed in detail the workings of our model economies. Let us now try to get a broad view of how they hold together, of what influences what, of what is important and what unimportant. To give the discussion a focus I want to ask, particularly, how significant is the part played by consumers' demand.

What does the model consist of? It has, first of all, a framework supplied by the technology. This we have always taken as given. Other parts of the model that can roughly be called exogenous are: the size of the labour force, the quantity of capital and the composition of consumers' demands. Then there are variables that the analysis has treated as endogenous. These come in two classes: one the **quantity variables**, namely the inputs and outputs in each industry, the other the **price and income variables**, namely the wage, the rate of profit and the prices of goods.

The separation of exogenous and endogenous is not a very strict one. We have allowed for a fair amount of mutual interaction, especially in the course of economic growth. The quantity of capital, for instance, though I have listed it as exogenous, changes through time in a way that probably depends on the rate of profit. The size of the labour force will doubtless depend on the wage. Certainly the demand from consumers for a good will depend on prices and the distribution of income. And so on.

Among the variables I have called endogenous there are some close links that will simplify our discussion. On the quantity side, once we know each industry's output we know its inputs directly from the technology. So we only need to worry about what determines outputs. By the same token, gross outputs and net outputs determine each other rigidly. On the price and income side we have a tight system that rigidly links all the variables together, leaving just one degree of freedom.

No Net Production

Now, to investigate the role of demand, let us start with a static economy. All of net production in this case goes to consumers. An interesting extreme situation, which will help to clarify things, is when there is no net production anyway. This technology provides an example:

$$
\begin{array}{lll}
1/8 \text{ corn} & 1/2 \text{ manure \& 1 labour} \rightarrow 1 \text{ corn} \\
1/2 \text{ corn} & \text{\& 1 labour} \rightarrow 1 \text{ chicken} \\
1/4 \text{ corn \& 3 chicken} & \text{\& 4 labour} \rightarrow 1 \text{ manure.}
\end{array}
$$

It is exactly on the borderline of being unproductive (see p. 39). Its fertility, that is to say, is nought. If an economy employing this technology is not to contract, every single unit of one year's production is needed as input for the next.

An economy like this has only one possible pattern of production. Suppose one million tons of corn are to be grown (gross). Half a million tons of manure will be needed. The production of that will in turn require 3/2 million tons of chickens, and use up 1/8 million tons of corn. The chickens' feed will take up 3/4 million tons of corn. But this is all that is left over out of the crop of corn after deducting its own seed (1/8 million tons) and the corn used by the manure industry. There is thus no room for varying the proportions of production in the three industries. Gross production will always have to be in the proportions $1 : 3/2 : 1/2$. There is no net production at all, of course.

These proportions are, in fact, a self-reproducing vector for the technology (see p. 37). That is simply because the economy has no scope for doing anything but reproducing itself from year to year.

Just as there is only one pattern of production there is only one set of prices possible for the economy. Because there is no net production there can be neither wages nor profit. Each product's price must just cover the cost of its materials. Evidently that means, if we take corn as numeraire, that the price of chicken is 1/2 and of manure 7/4.

Doubtless the example seems rather odd because there is nothing for workers to live off. We may assume, if we wish, that their subsistence requirements have been included among the inputs of materials, in the manner described on p. 33. But in any case the example is only designed to illustrate one point: at the extreme the needs of the production system alone will determine both the economy's structure and its prices. In any economy, even though it is nowhere near the extreme, a great deal of production serves the needs of production itself. Production is to a large extent circular. It serves itself — and consumers only indirectly. So one must expect a good part of the economy to be determined by the technology of production. What I have just illustrated is only a limiting case where production is *entirely* circular, and technology determines everything (except, to be precise, the scale of production as opposed to its structure; the scale will presumably be fixed by the size of the labour force).

Positive Net Production

It is only over net production that there is any choice. Consumers, in fact, can directly choose its composition. The larger is net production, then, the larger is the scope for consumers to affect things. A measure of net production in relation to gross production is the economy's fertility. The greater is fertility the more important is consumers' demand.

To illustrate demand's influence on **quantities**, take an economy whose fertility is positive but quite small. This one's is 1/9:

$$1/2 \text{ corn } \& \ 2/5 \text{ fertilizer } \& \ 1 \text{ labour} \rightarrow 1 \text{ corn}$$
$$1 \text{ corn } \qquad\qquad \& \ 1 \text{ labour} \rightarrow 1 \text{ fertilizer}$$
$$1 \text{ corn } \qquad\qquad \& \ 2 \text{ labour} \rightarrow 1 \text{ bread.}$$

If consumers' demand in this economy were for corn only, gross outputs would be in the proportions 10 : 4 : 0. If the demand were for fertilizer only the proportions would be 10 : 5 : 0. If it were for bread only they would be 10 : 4 : 1. The structure of production, then, is not drastically affected even by total transfers of demand from one product to another. Most of this economy's effort goes into maintaining its productive power — reproducing itself. Gross production can never diverge very far from the proportions of the self-reproducing vector, which happens to be 10 : 4·344 : 0. Technologies that are less circular, less bound up with their own production, have more freedom.

The simple two and three product examples used in this chapter are unrepresentative of real economies in one respect. There is in practice usually quite a definite segregation between basic industries and consumer-goods industries. Basic industries rarely supply consumers. Consumers' demand will affect the size of the various industries that produce consumer goods, and to some extent its influence will penetrate into basic production, but if the technology's fertility is quite small, the penetration will be unimportant.

The greater is the fertility, the greater is the opportunity for demand to affect the price and income variables too. But here things are more complicated because even if demand is given this opportunity, its effect may be limited by another factor: the similarity of the capital/labour ratios in the industries.

Think first about the *wage* and the *rate of profit*. We have seen in Section 3.4 that consumers' demand does influence these things because it helps determine the distribution of capital among the industries. That is to say, demand affects the structure of production (to an extent limited by fertility, as I have just explained) and hence the distribution of capital. If there are differences in the industries' capital/labour ratios the distribution of capital affects the demand for labour and the wage. Demand's capacity to influence the distributional variables, then, depends on fertility and the degree of disparity in capital/labour ratios. The primary determinant of distribution is the aggregate quantity of capital per worker in the economy.

Now think about *prices*. Prices, we know, cannot change at all unless the distributional variables do. Any effect consumers' demand may have on prices can only be through its effect on distribution. And precisely how prices are related to distribution we have investigated quite thoroughly in Section 3.3. We found there that if all industries happen to have the same capital/labour ratio then prices never change at all. They are fixed by the technology alone, specifically by the labour embodied in the products. Differences in capital/labour ratios permit some movements in prices. The same condition, then, as allows demand to affect distribution allows distribution to affect prices.

Because the channel of influence from demand to prices is so indirect we may reasonably expect the eventual effect to be small. The examples in Section 3.4 illustrate that.

A question of special interest is how far a good's price is influenced by the demand for itself. The answer is that the demand for a good is no more intimately connected with its own price than with any other. The link between demand and price is the distribution of income, which affects all prices impartially. And as I say the link is in any case probably a weak one. We have also seen (p. 65) that it may be perverse: an increase in the demand for a product may reduce its price.

All this may seem rather implausible. It seems natural that there should be some more direct connection between demand and price. Our model, though, prevents that because all prices are too tightly linked together. When we take account of scarce resources in Chapter 5 we shall find prices varying more flexibly, and we shall see then whether that leads to a closer connection between demand and price.

Growing Economies

Everything I have said so far about consumers' demand in a static economy applies to final demand as a whole in a growing economy. But then not all of final demand is consumers' demand. The other part consists of goods to satisfy the economy's needs for increased inputs to production. What these needs depend on is the nature of the economy's growth — the rate at which the various industries are expanding. We do not have to go into details. The only point I want to make is that the role of consumers' demand is smaller than in a static economy. A part of final demand is determined not by consumers but by the requirements of expanding industry. The faster is growth, the greater is the fraction of final demand that supplies inputs and the smaller is the importance of consumers' demand.

In the extreme the whole of net production is taken up by growth. There is no room for consumers' demand at all. This is the case of maximum growth mentioned on p. 37. Production will have to be in the proportions of the self-reproducing vector and prices will be fixed, as in the unproductive economy described on pp. 84–85, by the needs of production alone.

There is one last point. In the very long run an economy that is not growing at its maximum rate should move towards a state of proportional growth. Its rate of profit will then be g/s, where g is the rate of growth and s the fraction of their income that capitalists save (see p. 73). The pattern of consumers' demand is irrelevant to this long-run rate of profit. Changes in demand may alter the rate of profit for a while, but only until proportional growth is established again (which may not be for a very long time). Of course, since the rate of profit in proportional growth is independent of demand, so are prices.

Questions on Chapter 3

1. Take this technology:

$$A = \begin{pmatrix} 0 & 1/4 \\ 1/3 & 1/3 \end{pmatrix}$$

$$l = (2 \quad 1).$$

Work out the two products' integrated requirements of labour, and break them down into sequence of dated labour inputs. Show that

$$\begin{pmatrix} 1 \\ 2 \end{pmatrix}$$

is a self-reproducing vector for this technology. What is the technology's fertility? Is it productive?

2. Assuming that the technology of question 1 is adopted by a capitalist and competitive economy, draw up the wage–profit equation. Use product 1 as numeraire first, then product 2, then the self-reproducing vector.

3. Take the general technology described by A and l. Let its self-reproducing vector e be the numeraire. Show that its wage–profit equation is

$$1 = (1+r)\left(\frac{1}{1+R} + w l e\right).$$

(Hint: postmultiply (3.3.2) by e.) Compare this equation with (2.4.5) on p. 26. Do you see any similarity? If so, can you explain how it comes about?

4. How should (3.3.2) be modified if labour is paid in arrears out of production rather than out of capital. Take the technology of question 1 and assume now that labour is paid in arrears. Draw the wage–profit curve using the self-reproducing vector as numeraire. What is notable about it? Do the same for the general technology described by A and l.

5. Take the technology

$$A = \begin{pmatrix} a_{11} & a_{12} \\ 0 & 0 \end{pmatrix}$$

$$l = (l_1 \quad l_2).$$

What is special about it? Prove that the first product's integrated capital/labour ratio is greater than the second's if and only if a_{11}/l_1 is greater than a_{12}/l_2. Hence prove that an increase in the rate of profit will, in this economy, increase the relative price of the product with the greater integrated capital/labour ratio.

6. Equation (3.3.8) expresses prices as functions of the wage and the rate of profit (given the technology). Express them as functions of the rate of profit only, taking a vector z of products as numeraire. Do the same taking labour as numeraire.

7. From (3.3.9) find the slope dw/dr of the wage–profit curve. Is it definitely negative?

8. Consider an economy with this technology:

$$A = \begin{pmatrix} 2/3 & 1/4 \\ 0 & 3/4 \end{pmatrix}$$

$$l = (1 \quad 1).$$

Which of the products are basic? Taking product 1 as numeraire, draw the wage–profit curve. What is the maximum rate of profit? Find the price of product 2 when the rate of profit is 2/5. What is peculiar about this technology?

9. Take an economy that employs the technology of question 1. Suppose all final demand is for product 1 and suppose the labour force is 105. Show that the industries' gross productions are 42 and 21. Take product 2 as numeraire and assume that the supply of capital in terms of product 2 is 38. Show that the rate of profit is 1/2. Draw up a table like Table 3.4.1 showing the state of the economy.

10. Some industries may produce more than one product. We can accommodate this "joint production" into our model as follows. Specify the technology by a labour vector l, an input matrix A and an output matrix B. If the level of "activity" in the j'th industry is one unit, its input of labour is l_j, its input of product i is a_{ij} and its output of product i is b_{ij}. Changing an industry's activity levels changes inputs and outputs proportionally. Show that the model of this chapter is a special case of this new model having the output matrix B equal to the identity matrix I. In general need the matrixes A and B be square? If the industries' activity levels are given by the vector x, what is the economy's net output, and what is its employment of labour? If some given vector y of net production is needed, can you calculate what the industries' activity levels need to be? If the economy is capitalist and competitive, what can you say about prices? Is there any reason to think that some industries might not produce at all?

11. If some industries had barriers to entry that prevented their rate of profit from being lowered to the general level, how would you modify the model?

12. Prove that if the numeraire is either the economy's gross output vector x or its input vector Ax then an increase in the wage implies an increase in the aggregate capital/labour ratio.

13. Take an economy in the equilibrium described in question 9. Suppose now that international trade becomes possible; the two products can be exchanged for each other on equal terms (at a relative price of one) on the world market. What will happen? What will be the effect on the total of national income and its distribution?

4.

CHOICE OF TECHNIQUE

Section 4.1   Single Product Technologies

Techniques and their Mixtures

Till now our model economies have allowed only one technique for each product. In this chapter we shall see what difference it makes to the model's working if several techniques are available. For simplicity we shall start off with an economy that has only a single product.

Let this technology be our example:

$$
\left.
\begin{array}{ll}
\alpha: & 1/4 \text{ corn \& } 1 \quad \text{labour} \longrightarrow 1 \text{ corn} \\
\beta: & 1/3 \text{ corn \& } 2/3 \text{ labour} \longrightarrow 1 \text{ corn} \\
\gamma: & 1/2 \text{ corn \& } 1/3 \text{ labour} \longrightarrow 1 \text{ corn} \\
\delta: & 5/8 \text{ corn \& } 1/4 \text{ labour} \longrightarrow 1 \text{ corn} \\
e: & 2/3 \text{ corn \& } 1/5 \text{ labour} \longrightarrow 1 \text{ corn.}
\end{array}
\right\}
\qquad (4.1.1)
$$

These are all alternative ways of growing corn. I assume that each has constant returns to scale. Also—a new assumption—they may be employed together in any proportions. For example, techniques α and β may be mixed to produce 4 tons of corn from 5/4 tons of seed cultivated by 3 people. One person would work with technique α and grow one ton of corn from 1/4 ton of seed. The other two would work with technique β and grow 3 tons of corn from one ton of seed. By a convenient and obvious piece of notation, we may call the mixed process $\alpha + 3\beta$. Its make-up can be displayed like this:

$$\alpha: \quad 1/4 \text{ corn \& } 1 \text{ labour} \rightarrow 1 \text{ corn}$$
$$3\beta: \quad 1 \quad \text{corn \& } 2 \text{ labour} \rightarrow 3 \text{ corn}$$

$$\overline{}$$

$$\alpha + 3\beta: \quad 5/4 \text{ corn \& } 3 \text{ labour} \rightarrow 4 \text{ corn.}$$

This is like an addition sum; the bottom line is the sum of the two above.

Isoquants

In (4.1.1) are listed various combinations of the inputs corn and labour that will yield one ton of gross output. We may mark them on a diagram that has quantities of the inputs on the axes. Figure 4.1.1 shows the techniques α, β, γ, δ and ε marked in this way.

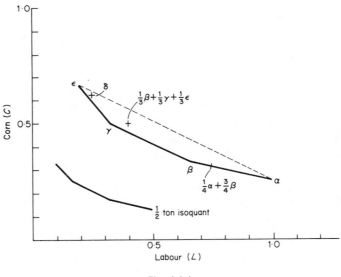

Fig. 4.1.1

Besides these five, other combinations of inputs can be made to produce the same one-ton output by mixing techniques together. There is, for instance, this process:

$$(1/4)\alpha + (3/4)\beta: \quad 5/16 \text{ corn \& } 3/4 \text{ labour} \rightarrow 1 \text{ corn,}$$

which is just the process $\alpha + 3\beta$ shown above on a quarter of the scale. The pair of inputs 5/16 of corn and 3/4 labour is also marked in Fig. 4.1.1, labelled $(1/4)\alpha + (3/4)\beta$. It lies on the straight line between α and β, three quarters of the way along it. The mixture $(1/2)\alpha + (1/2)\beta$ is at the middle of the line, and so on. It is easy to see that any combination of inputs lying on this line will produce a ton of output if techniques α and β are mixed in appropriate proportions.

Similarly, mixing techniques β and γ will produce a ton of corn from inputs on the line $\beta\gamma$ in the diagram. Likewise for the line $\gamma\varepsilon$. Three or more techniques may also be mixed together, and in that way we can get a ton of output from any inputs in the quadrangle $\alpha\beta\gamma\varepsilon$. For instance the following combination is marked in the diagram:

$$(1/3)\beta: \quad 1/9 \text{ corn \& } 2/9 \text{ labour} \rightarrow 1/3 \text{ corn}$$
$$(1/3)\gamma: \quad 1/6 \text{ corn \& } 1/9 \text{ labour} \rightarrow 1/3 \text{ corn}$$
$$(1/3)\varepsilon: \quad 2/9 \text{ corn \& } 1/15 \text{ labour} \rightarrow 1/3 \text{ corn}$$

$$(1/3)\beta + (1/3)\gamma + (1/3)\varepsilon: \quad 1/2 \text{ corn \& } 2/5 \text{ labour} \rightarrow 1 \text{ corn.}$$

Although any point in the quadrangle will yield a ton of corn, most only do so wastefully. A process of production is defined as **inefficient** if the same output can be produced in an alternative way that uses less of one input without using more of any other. An **efficient** process is one that is not inefficient. Technique δ, among others, is inefficient because, as Fig. 4.1.1 shows, a suitably chosen mixture of γ and ε will produce the same one-ton output with less of both inputs.

The collection of points representing *efficient* ways of producing one ton of output is called the one-ton **isoquant**. In Fig. 4.1.1 it consists of the lines $\alpha\beta$, $\beta\gamma$ and $\gamma\varepsilon$.

To produce half a ton of corn efficiently one obviously has to apply on half the scale the efficient processes for producing one ton. The half-ton isoquant therefore has the shape of the one-ton isoquant, shrunk down half way towards the origin. It is also shown in Fig. 4.1.1. There is, in fact, a whole pattern of isoquants, one for each level of output. Some are shown in Fig. 4.1.2. Clearly it is the assumption of constant returns to scale that makes each isoquant similar to all the others. Each "ray" from the origin, such as the ones labelled α, β, γ and ε, shows a particular technique applied on different scales.

The production function

One could draw an isoquant representing some level of output through any point in Fig. 4.1.2, provided it lies between the rays α and ε. That is to say, to any combination of inputs between those rays there corresponds a definite quantity of gross output, the output that would emerge if those inputs were efficiently used by selecting a suitable mixture of techniques. Gross output,

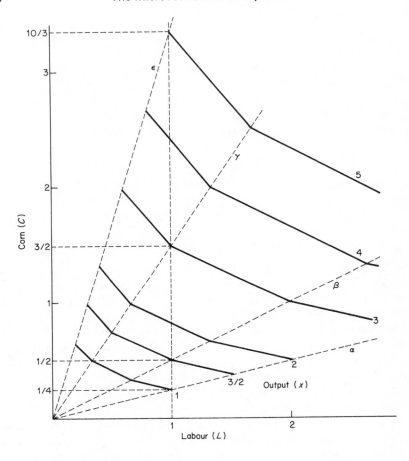

Fig. 4.1.2

then, is a *function* of the inputs. This function is known as the **production function**. If the input of corn is C and of labour L, and if the corresponding gross output of corn is x we may write

$$x = f(C, L).$$

Here f is the production function.

It is hard to specify the production function in algebraic terms for a technology like the one we are discussing, consisting of a few basic techniques and their combinations. But we shall soon come across a different type of technology — "continuous" I shall call it — for which specifying the production function may actually be the most convenient way of defining the technology.

Substitution

Movement upwards from right to left along an isoquant represents a **substitution** of corn for labour. The input of labour is reduced and production maintained at a constant level by using more corn instead. Continuous substitution of one input for another is made possible by varying the mixture of techniques. At the lower end of the isoquant technique α is used on its own. Corn can be substituted for labour by mixing with technique α progressively more of β until finally β comes to be used on its own. Further substitution requires mixing γ with β, and so on.

The slope of the isoquant (strictly—the slope being negative—minus the slope) is known as the **marginal rate of substitution of corn for labour**. It is the rate at which the input of corn has to be increased to make up for a decrease in the input of labour. At kinks in the isoquant, which occur where one technique is used on its own, the marginal rate of substitution is undefined.

Marginal Productivities

So much for substitution along an isoquant, where output is held constant. Let us now see what happens if one input is held constant and the other varied. Output will vary as a result, of course. Let us, say, fix the input of labour at one unit. The vertical dotted line in Fig. 4.1.2 is drawn at this level of labour input. We want to see what happens as we move along this line.

Figure 4.1.3 is a graph of output against the input of corn, labour being constant at one unit. It can be constructed from Fig. 4.1.2 and it is easy enough to see from Fig. 4.1.2 that it must be made up of straight line segments. The kinks in the graph occur where a single technique is in use. Elsewhere techniques are mixed so as to allow different quantities of corn to be combined with the one unit of labour.

The graph in Fig. 4.1.3 shows, in fact, a section of the production function. Its slope is the production function's partial derivative with respect to corn, $\partial x/\partial C$. This derivative is known as the **marginal productivity of corn**. It is undefined at kinks where a single technique is in use.

We can similarly draw a graph of output against the input of labour, holding constant the input of corn. Its slope, $\partial x/\partial L$, is the **marginal productivity of labour.**

There is a simple connection between the inputs' marginal productivities and their marginal rate of substitution (where these things are defined). Suppose the input of labour were to be decreased by some amount dL. Then, if the input of corn did not change, output would fall by roughly

$$\frac{\partial x}{\partial L}\,\mathrm{d}L.$$

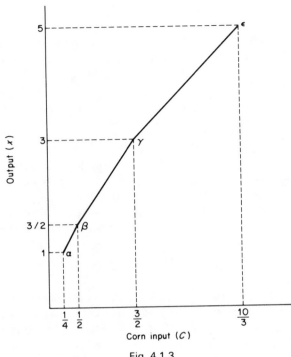

Fig. 4.1.3

If corn input is to be substituted for labour it will have to be increased by just enough to make up for this fall. If it were increased by dC, output would rise again by roughly

$$\frac{\partial x}{\partial C}\, dC,$$

and this will exactly cancel out the original decline if

$$\frac{\partial x}{\partial C}\, dC = \frac{\partial x}{\partial L}\, dL,$$

i.e. if

$$\frac{dC}{dL} = \frac{\partial x/\partial L}{\partial x/\partial C}.$$

Here dC/dL is the rate at which C must grow to make up for a decline in L. It is, in other words, the marginal rate of substitution of corn for labour. The maginal rate of substitution, then is the ratio of the marginal productivities.

A Continuous Technology

Technology (4.1.1) consists of a number of basic techniques quite distinct from each other. It has, nevertheless, some sort of continuity because the techniques can be mixed together. A continuous range of mixed processes is available, linking one basic technique with another. But a technology may also have another sort of continuity. It may be made up of infinitely many basic techniques each only a little different from others.

Here is an example of what I mean. The technology contains the technique

$$C \text{ corn \& } L \text{ labour} \rightarrow x \text{ corn}$$

whenever

$$x = 4C^{2/3} L^{1/3}. \tag{4.1.2}$$

That is to say, for instance, that all the following are techniques within the technology, as well as many others:

$$1/8 \text{ corn \& } 1 \quad \text{labour} \rightarrow 1 \text{ corn}$$
$$1/4 \text{ corn \& } 1/4 \text{ labour} \rightarrow 1 \text{ corn}$$
$$3/8 \text{ corn \& } 1/9 \text{ labour} \rightarrow 1 \text{ corn}.$$

Clearly what I have done in defining this technology is simply to specify its production function (4.1.2). An advantage of doing it this way is that the assumption of constant returns to scale is built into the definition. The definition says, for example, that the technology also includes these techniques:

$$1/4 \text{ corn \& } 2 \quad \text{labour} \rightarrow 2 \text{ corn}$$
$$1/2 \text{ corn \& } 1/2 \text{ labour} \rightarrow 2 \text{ corn}$$
$$3/4 \text{ corn \& } 2/9 \text{ labour} \rightarrow 2 \text{ corn},$$

which are the ones above on twice the scale.

Isoquants for technology (4.1.2) are shown in Fig. 4.1.4. Each point on an

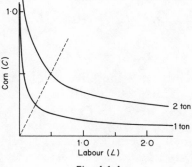

Fig. 4.1.4

isoquant represents a separate technique. No mixing of techniques will ever be efficient. If inputs are to be substituted for one another, it is done by selecting a slightly different technique, not by changing the mixture of techniques.

Another advantage of specifying the production function algebraically is that the marginal productivity of the inputs may then be found simply by differentiating. From (4.1.2)

$$\frac{\partial x}{\partial C}=\frac{8}{3}\left(\frac{L}{C}\right)^{1/3}$$

and

$$\frac{\partial x}{\partial L}=\frac{4}{3}\left(\frac{C}{L}\right)^{2/3}.$$

These are the marginal productivities. Their ratio is the marginal rate of substitution of corn for labour.

$$\frac{\partial x/\partial L}{\partial x/\partial C}=\frac{(4/3)(C/L)^{2/3}}{(8/3)(L/C)^{1/3}}=\frac{1}{2}\frac{C}{L}.$$

Because this continuous technology has no kinks in its isoquants, the marginal productivities are defined for any inputs C and L, and so is the marginal rate of substitution.

A ray from the origin in Fig. 4.1.4 shows a particular technique used on different scales. A technique may be identified by its ratio of C to L, which is the slope of its ray. Every isoquant has the same slope where it meets a particular ray, which means that a given technique, whatever its scale, always has the same marginal rate of substitution. It always has the same marginal productivities of corn and labour too.

Section 4.2   Distribution and the Choice of Technique

Profit Maximizing and the Choice of Technique for a Discrete Technology

Let us now look at the working of a competitive capitalist economy employing a technology of the sort I have been describing. To begin with we shall take as our example technology (4.1.1) and see what determines which of the available techniques is actually adopted. Let corn be the numeraire.

For each technique in (4.1.1) we may draw a wage–profit curve, showing what the relationship would be between the wage and the rate of profit if that were the economy's only technique. We need only apply the method described in Chapter 2 (pp. 14–15). In fact, since technique α is just the example I used in Chapter 2 we already have its curve in Fig. 2.2.1 on p. 15. It is drawn again, labelled α, in Fig. 4.2.1. If, instead, β were the only technique, then when the wage is w the rate of profit would be

$$r = \frac{1-(1/3+(2/3)w)}{(1/3+(2/3)w)}.$$

This is β's wage–profit equation; its graph is also drawn in Fig. 4.2.1. So are the curves for γ, δ and ε.

The decision which technique to employ is naturally in the hands of the capitalists. We shall assume that they always select the technique that gives them the greatest possible rate of profit. This is a natural extension of the assumption we made earlier (p. 44) that capitalists always invest their capital in the most profitable industry. Now we are assuming that within an industry they adopt the most profitable technique. They are profit maximizers generally.

From Fig. 4.2.1 we can now see at once which technique will be chosen. It depends on the wage. When the wage is below 1/4 it will be α. For a wage between 1/4 and 1/2 it will be β. For one between 1/2 and 5/4, γ. And for a higher wage, up to a maximum of 5/3, ε. Technique δ will never be selected.

The wages 1/4, 1/2 and 5/4, the borderlines between one technique's dominance and another's, are known as **switch points**. If the wage were to rise gradually, when it reached one of these points there would be a switch to a new technique. The switch points are easy to find algebraically. Between α and β, for instance, the switch-point wage is the one that makes both techniques equally profitable. For any wage, technique α's rate of profit is (see equation (2.2.1) on p. 14)

$$\frac{1-(1/4+w)}{(1/4+w)}.$$

And we have just worked out that the rate of profit from β is

$$\frac{1-(1/3+(2/3)w)}{(1/3+(2/3)w)}.$$

For these to be equal requires of course that

$$1/4+w = 1/3+(2/3)w$$

(i.e. that each technique has the same cost of production per unit produced), which implies that $w = 1/4$. This is the switch point.

At a switch point two techniques are equally profitable. Capitalists will

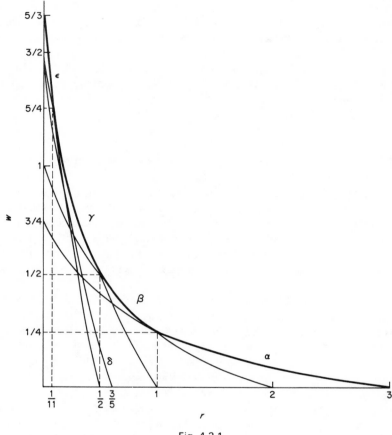

Fig. 4.2.1

indifferently choose either. Or they may choose to mix the two in any proportions; it makes no difference to them. Later on we shall see what actually determines the proportions of the mixture.

When the wage increases through a switch point there is a switch to a technique that has a greater net production per worker than the one it replaces. It also requires more materials and hence more capital. Any switch in a single-product economy must be like this; I leave you to work out why. It seems perfectly natural that an increase in the cost of labour should induce capitalists to substitute materials for labour, and if they do use more materials per worker they must certainly obtain a greater output per worker. The techniques adopted as the wage rises will, of course, be progressively less fertile in the sense defined on p. 9. We shall see that for economies with several products these rules do not necessarily apply.

Isoquants and the Choice of Technique

There is an alternative way of visualizing the choice of techniques. Think about a capitalist who has a certain amount of capital ready to spend on buying inputs. To take a simple example, suppose his capital is 3/2 tons and the going wage is 3/4. He could if he chose use all the capital to employ labour (though of course he would not), and if he did it would get him two workers. Alternatively he could use all 3/2 tons as seed corn. Or he could divide the capital between corn and labour. The whole range of his options for using his capital is shown by the sloping solid line in Fig. 4.2.2, which is known as his **budget line**. Its slope (strictly, minus its slope), is evidently 3/4; the slope of a budget line like this will always be equal to the wage. So, the capitalist has available all these ways of dividing his capital. He will actually choose the one that will bring in the greatest profit. Clearly this will be the one that produces the greatest output; for a given quantity of capital the more the output the more the profit. It is the isoquants that tell us how much output can be raised from any particular combination of inputs. Some isoquants are drawn in the diagram. What we are looking for is the "highest" isoquant—the one

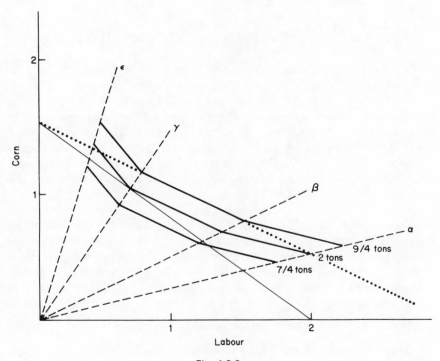

Fig. 4.2.2

representing the greatest output — that the capitalist can get to on his budget line. It must evidently be the isoquant that just touches the line, in our case the 2-ton isoquant. In order to reach it the capitalist will have to adopt technique γ and choose his combination of inputs accordingly (actually one ton of corn and 2/3 units of labour). We have found, then, that γ is the profit-maximizing technique when the wage is 3/4, which confirms what we already knew from Fig. 4.2.1. Of course every capitalist will choose the same technique; the size of his or her capital makes no difference.

Suppose now instead that the wage is 1/2. Then the budget line will have a slope of 1/2, and if our capitalist still has 3/2 tons of capital it will be the dotted line in Fig. 4.2.2. This time the highest isoquant he can attain has a flat face touching the budget line. Any mixture of techniques β and γ will be equally profitable. This wage of 1/2 is the switch point between the techniques.

At the profit-maximizing process the budget line is tangential to the isoquant. So it has the same slope, provided the isoquant has a slope and is not kinked at that point. The budget line's slope is the wage. The isoquant's slope is the marginal rate of substitution of corn for labour. Whenever, then, this marginal rate is defined for the profit-maximizing process it is equal to the wage.

The Choice of Technique for a Continuous Technology

For a continuous technology the choice of technique is just the same in principle. Take technology (4.1.2) as our example. Figure 4.2.3 shows representative wage–profit curves for some of its techniques. There are really an infinite number of these curves. The technique selected at any wage will be the one out of all the infinity whose curve is furthest to the right at that wage. Because the techniques are not sharply distinct a slight change in the wage is bound to bring into use a slightly different technique; no single technique will be applied at more than one wage. To put it another way, every wage is a switch point.

As before the choice of technique can be alternatively illustrated by means of an isoquant diagram. Figure 4.2.4 shows an isoquant for the technology. Because it is smoothly curved there is a properly defined marginal rate of substitution everywhere. So at the technique selected the marginal rate must be equal to the wage. The diagram shows a budget line with a slope of 1/2, corresponding to a wage of 1/2. The technique selected is where it touches the curve, actually this one:

$$1/4 \text{ corn } \& \ 1/4 \text{ labour} \longrightarrow 1 \text{ corn.}$$

Algebraically, we know from p. 98 that the marginal rate of substitution of

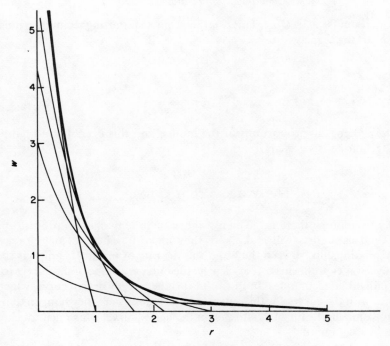

Fig. 4.2.3

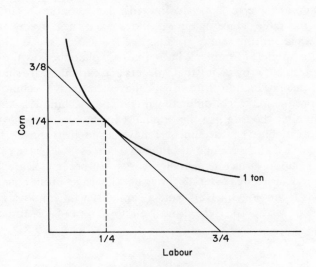

Fig. 4.2.4

corn for labour is $(1/2)(C/L)$. This, for the profit-maximizing technique, must be equal to the wage w. So

$$w = \frac{1}{2}\frac{C}{L},$$

or
$$C/L = 2w. \tag{4.2.1}$$

We know, then, the proportions of the inputs, and this is enough to tell us which technique is selected.

The Wage–Profit Curve

For any technology there is, given a wage, a definite maximum profit to be made. And capitalists will make sure they make it. There is, therefore, a definite relationship between the wage and the rate of profit. Its graph is the **economy's wage–profit curve**. It is, clearly, the outer envelope of the curves for all the individual techniques. In Fig. 4.2.1 it is the heavily drawn curve, which coincides with the curves for the separate techniques where they happen to be profit maximizing.In Fig. 4.2.3 it is again the heavy curve, which just touches each individual curve.

There can be no doubt that the economy's wage–profit curve slopes downwards. Everywhere on its whole length it either touches or coincides with the curve for a technique. And we know from Chapter 2 (p. 14) that the techniques' curves have to slope downwards. The economy's curve must therefore do the same. Once again we find a fixed, negative relationship between the wage and the rate of profit.

In the simpler model of Chapter 2 I was able to explain the downward slope of the wage–profit curve by saying that workers and capitalists are sharing in a fixed total of net production. But now we have alternative techniques and workers' net production will be different with different techniques. A switch in technique will alter the total, so the original explanation of the downward slope is not available. The argument I have given just above—that the wage–profit curve is the envelope of individual curves—will have to suffice. How the distribution of income actually works will become clearer later.

As an exercise, let us work out algebraically the wage–profit equation for the continuous technology (4.1.2). Take a capitalist who employs L people working on C of seed corn. Her output we know from (4.1.2) to be

$$4C^{2/3}L^{1/3}$$

tons of corn. Her costs, and the capital she needs, are

$$C + wL$$

tons, where w is the wage. So her rate of profit is

$$r = \frac{4C^{2/3}L^{1/3} - (C + wL)}{(C + wL)}$$

$$= \frac{4(C/L)^{2/3} - ((C/L) + w)}{((C/L) + w)}$$

(dividing top and bottom by L). But we already know from (4.2.1) that she will select a technique for which

$$C/L = 2w.$$

So
$$r = \frac{4(2w)^{2/3} - 3w}{3w}.$$

$$\therefore \quad r = \frac{2^{8/3}}{3} w^{-1/3} - 1. \tag{4.2.2}$$

This is the wage–profit equation.

The Determination of the Wage

Once the wage is settled, so is the rate of profit. So also is the technique in use, with one qualification, namely that in a discrete technology when the wage is at a switch point there will be a mixture of techniques and we do not yet know the mixture's proportions. Let us assume as usual a **competitive market for labour**. We shall find that it determines not only the wage but also the mixture of techniques at a switch point.

Take technology (4.1.1) as our first example. For each of the techniques α, β, γ and ε there is a range of the wage where it is dominant. Within one of the ranges the economy is exactly as it would have been if the technique in use were the only one available. It would have been a single product economy with a single technique, and we have dealt with economies like that in Chapter 2. We found there (pp. 19–20) that the wage depends on the economy's aggregate capital/labour ratio. More specifically, it is equal to the amount of capital available per worker less the quantity of materials he or she needs to be supplied with:

$$w = \frac{K}{L} - \frac{a}{l}$$

(equation (2.4.6) on p. 26), where a/l is the ratio of materials (seed corn) to labour for the technique in question.

Each of the techniques α, β, γ and ε has a different ratio of materials to labour: 1/4, 1/2, 3/2 and 10/3 respectively. For each I have drawn a graph in

Fig. 4.2.5 of *w* against *K/L* according to the above equation; the graphs are the four sloping dotted lines. Each has, of course, a slope of one. Each one applies, in the economy with a choice of technique, only where the technique it corresponds to is actually chosen. Therefore the economy's graph of *w* against *K/L* is the one drawn in solid lines. It incorporates the appropriate piece out of each of the sloping lines: technique α where the wage is below 1/4, β where it lies between 1/4 and 1/2, γ where it lies between 1/2 and 5/4, and ε where it is above 5/4.

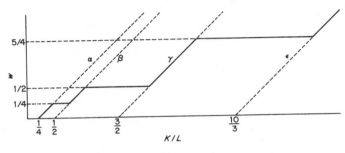

Fig. 4.2.5

The graph's most interesting sections are the horizontal ones that join the sloping pieces. They occur at the switch points between techniques, and show that a change in *K/L* does not necessarily change *w*. To understand what is happening, imagine *K/L* increasing. Suppose, for example, that initially technique β is in use but then capital grows faster than the labour force and brings the wage up to the switch point between β and γ. Initially capitalists are all employing β but by the time the wage goes beyond the switch point they must all have switched to γ. However, the switch cannot happen instantaneously. Technique γ requires more capital per worker employed; as I mentioned on p. 100 the technique brought into use by a rise in the wage must, in a single-product economy, require more capital per worker. Extra capital must be accumulated before all the labour force can be employed on the new technique. In the meantime some people must continue to work with β and as capital grows they will gradually be transferred to γ. For the whole period of the switch the wage will have to stay constant, because there is only one wage that allows both techniques to be used at once. During the course of the switch the economy will have a mixture of techniques. Some capitalists will still have their labour force using technique β, some will have moved on to γ, and some perhaps will operate a mixture themselves. The exact proportions of the economy's mixture will be determined by the amount of capital that has accumulated. When in the diagram *K/L* has progressed, for example, half way along the horizontal section, then half the labour force will be working each technique. This does not mean, as one might imagine, that the mixture is $(1/2)\beta + (1/2)\gamma$; actually it is $(1/3)\beta + (2/3)\gamma$ (as is easily checked). The point is, though, that the mixture is determined.

Once we know K/L we know what the wage must be. We also know what technique is in use, and if the technique happens to be a mixture we know its proportions.

Net Production and its Distribution

The techniques α, β, γ and ε in technology 4.1.1 each deliver a different amount of net production per worker: respectively 3/4, 1, 3/2 and 5/3. Since K/L determines the technique in use it determines net production per worker. The latter is graphed against K/L in Fig. 4.2.6. Figure 4.2.6 also shows the graph of wages reproduced from Fig. 4.2.5. It is a **distribution diagram**, showing production and its division between the classes. Compare it with the distribution diagrams of earlier chapters, especially Fig. 2.3.2 on p. 21, which also describes a single-product economy. In the new diagram there are several points to notice.

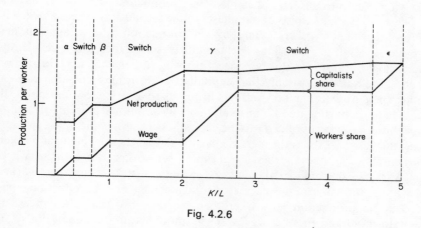

Fig. 4.2.6

First, the general progress of income distribution is much the same as before. There is a minimum quantity of capital that can employ all the labour force, even at a wage of nought. If we imagine capital accumulating beyond that point it has the effect of pulling up the wage at the expense of the rate of profit. Eventually the workers obtain the whole of net production.

However, one new thing that happens during this progress is that production grows. More capital leads to a greater output per worker. One of the less plausible features of the models we dealt with in earlier chapters was the fact that accumulating capital did nothing for production. Now we have introduced into the model an intelligible way in which capital can add to output: the greater is the supply of capital per worker the more productive is the technique that can be employed, because each worker can be supplied with more materials to work on. I shall have a little more to say about this in a moment.

When we look at the economy's progress more closely we see that it has phases of two different sorts. One sort occurs when the wage is not a switch point. Then there is no change of technique, and net production is static. In these phases capital contributes nothing to output. All it can do, as it did in Chapter 2, is pull up the wage. Eventually the wage reaches a switch point and then a phase of the second sort begins. Now it is the wage that is static. Capital now gives workers no benefit but instead equips them to operate a more productive technique. The technique must be more productive because of the rule (p. 100) for single product economies that the technique brought into use by an increase in the wage has more net production per worker than the one it replaces. So while the workers are being equipped output rises. When eventually they are all working the new technique a new phase of the first sort begins. The alternating process ends when, during some phase of the first sort, the wage comes to absorb the whole of net production.

There is one slight puzzle about phases of the second sort, where a switch is in progress. The workers' share of net production is constant but net production itself is increasing. The capitalists' share, therefore, is evidently increasing. But how can this be, since if the wage is constant so is the rate of profit? The answer is simply that capitalists are getting a constant rate of return on a growing capital. And this brings us to a very important point. If the rate of profit is r, and r is constant, then any additional amount of capital must bring in a rate of return r to the capitalists. Their income, that is to say, must increase by r times the increase in capital, and their income per worker they employ by r times the increase in capital per worker. But during a switch the wage is constant, so the increase in capitalists' income per worker constitutes the whole of the increase in total income — or net production — per worker. Net production per worker, then, increases by r times the increase in capital per worker. In other words, the graph of net production in Fig. 4.2.6 has a slope of r. This is true, of course, only during a switch, and the r in question is the rate of profit prevailing at the time. That is why the right-hand sloping sections of the graph slope less steeply; here the rate of profit is smaller.

The graph of net production, then, sometimes has a slope of nought and sometimes a slope equal to the rate of profit. I shall discuss later (p. 135) the significance of this observation.

The Distribution of Income for a Continuous Technology

For a second example of a distribution diagram I shall use the continuous technology defined in (4.1.2). We can find the diagram's shape by simple algebra. Let the total amount of corn used as seed throughout the economy be C, and the total employment of labour L. Then the total of capital must be

$$K = C + wL.$$

$$\therefore \quad \frac{K}{L} = \frac{C}{L} + w.$$

But (4.2.1) on p. 104 tells us that for the technique selected C/L is $2w$. Therefore

$$\frac{K}{L} = 3w.$$

$$\therefore \quad w = \frac{1}{3}\frac{K}{L}. \tag{4.2.3}$$

The graph of w against K/L, therefore, is a straight line with a slope of $1/3$. It is drawn in Fig. 4.2.7.

Net production y is gross production x less the input of corn

$$y = x - C.$$

Using the production function (4.1.2)

$$y = 4C^{2/3}L^{1/3} - C.$$

$$\therefore \quad \frac{y}{L} = 4\left(\frac{C}{L}\right)^{2/3} - \frac{C}{L}.$$

From (4.2.1) C/L is $2w$, which from (4.2.3) is $(2/3)(K/L)$. So

$$\frac{y}{L} = 4\left(\frac{2}{3}\frac{K}{L}\right)^{2/3} - \left(\frac{2}{3}\frac{K}{L}\right). \tag{4.2.4}$$

The graph of this equation is shown in Fig. 4.2.7.

In a continuous technology the switching phase of progress and the non-switching phase are collapsed into one. At every level of the capital/labour ratio there is a switch of technique, but on the other hand no two techniques are ever mixed. So the distribution diagram shows everywhere a sort of fusion of the two phases. The wage graph is a fusion of the flat sections of the discrete case with the sloping sections whose slope is one. So its slope is between

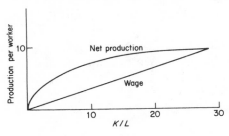

Fig. 4.2.7

nought and one, actually in our example 1/3. Also the graph of net production is a fusion of the flat sections of the discrete case with the sloping sections whose slope is the rate of profit. Its slope, therefore, lies between nought and the rate of profit; certainly it must be less than the latter.

Let us work out the slope of the net production curve. Differentiate (4.2.4):

$$\frac{d(y/L)}{d(K/L)} = \frac{16}{9} \left(\frac{2}{3} \frac{K}{L} \right)^{-1/3} - \frac{2}{3}$$

$$= \frac{16}{9} \cdot 2^{-1/3} \, w^{-1/3} - \frac{2}{3} \qquad \text{using (4.2.3)}$$

$$= \frac{2}{3} \{ \frac{2^{8/3}}{3} \, w^{-1/3} - 1 \}$$

$$= \frac{2}{3} r \qquad \text{by (4.2.2) on p. 105.}$$

The slope, then, is indeed less than the rate of profit.

Section 4.3   The Choice of Technique in Economies with Several Products

Systems of Techniques

Now we come to the multi-product economies described in Chapter 3. What happens if some or all of their industries have a choice of technique?

Our model now, then, contains several industries each producing a single product. Each has one or more techniques available to it. In some industries or

all there may even be a continuous range of techniques. All techniques are of
the sort we are used to: the product is made by labour working on materials
that are themselves some industry's product. All have constant returns to
scale, and they may be mixed together if required. A simple example of such a
technology is:

$$\left.\begin{array}{lll} 1/6 \text{ corn} & \& \ 2 \text{ labour} \to 1 \text{ corn} \\ 1/6 \text{ corn } \& \ 1/6 \text{ fertilizer} \& \ 1 \text{ labour} \to 1 \text{ corn} \\ 1 \text{ corn} & \& \ 2 \text{ labour} \to 1 \text{ fertilizer} \\ 1 \text{ corn} & \& \ 7 \text{ labour} \to 1 \text{ bread} \\ 2 \text{ corn} & \& \ 3 \text{ labour} \to 1 \text{ bread.} \end{array}\right\} \quad (4.3.1)$$

The first thing we must do is sort the techniques into **systems**. To make
up a system of techniques we simply pick one technique from each industry.
Technology (4.3.1) has four systems:

$$\alpha_1 : \left\{\begin{array}{ll} 1/6 \text{ corn} & \& \ 2 \text{ labour} \to 1 \text{ corn} \\ 1 \text{ corn} & \& \ 2 \text{ labour} \to 1 \text{ fertilizer} \\ 1 \text{ corn} & \& \ 7 \text{ labour} \to 1 \text{ bread,} \end{array}\right.$$

$$\alpha_2 : \left\{\begin{array}{ll} 1/6 \text{ corn} & \& \ 2 \text{ labour} \to 1 \text{ corn} \\ 1 \text{ corn} & \& \ 2 \text{ labour} \to 1 \text{ fertilizer} \\ 2 \text{ corn} & \& \ 3 \text{ labour} \to 1 \text{ bread,} \end{array}\right.$$

$$\beta_1 : \left\{\begin{array}{ll} 1/6 \text{ corn } \& \ 1/6 \text{ fertilizer} \& \ 1 \text{ labour} \to 1 \text{ corn} \\ 1 \text{ corn} & \& \ 2 \text{ labour} \to 1 \text{ fertilizer} \\ 1 \text{ corn} & \& \ 7 \text{ labour} \to 1 \text{ bread,} \end{array}\right.$$

$$\beta_2 : \left\{\begin{array}{ll} 1/6 \text{ corn } \& \ 1/6 \text{ fertilizer} \& \ 1 \text{ labour} \to 1 \text{ corn} \\ 1 \text{ corn} & \& \ 2 \text{ labour} \to 1 \text{ fertilizer} \\ 2 \text{ corn} & \& \ 3 \text{ labour} \to 1 \text{ bread.} \end{array}\right.$$

Each system can be thought of as a possible complete technology for the
economy. Therefore, once we have chosen a numeraire we can draw a
wage–profit curve for each. Figure 4.3.1 shows the wage–profit curves for our
example, where corn is taken as the numeraire. For the sake of another
illustration, Fig. 4.3.2 shows the curves for some imaginary economy. (There
is no reason why, in multi-product economies, wage–profit curves should
always be convex to the origin.)

When two systems of techniques differ only in the techniques of non-basic
industries their wage–profit curves will be identical (unless one of these
industries happens to be the numeraire industry; to avoid that possibility I
shall assume that the numeraire is basic). The reason is that the wage–profit
curve is determined by the basic industries and the numeraire industry only

(see p. 48). That is why Fig. 4.3.1 contains only the two curves α and β, despite its·four separate systems of techniques. In the difficult arguments that follow I want to be able to forget about choices of technique within non-basic industries. So for the time being I shall suppose that all these industries possess only one technique each.

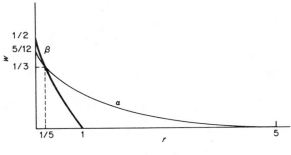

Fig. 4.3.1

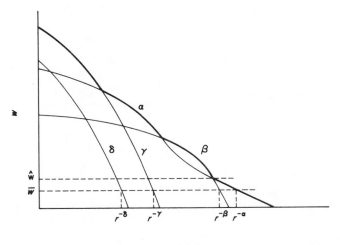

Fig. 4.3.2

The Choice of Technique in Basic Industries

Given a wage, say $\bar{w}$ in Fig. 4.3.2, each system will determine a corresponding rate of profit, marked $\bar{r}^{\alpha}$, $\bar{r}^{\beta}$, $\bar{r}^{\gamma}$ and $\bar{r}^{\delta}$ in the diagram. Each will also determine corresponding prices for all the products: $\bar{p}^{\alpha}$, $\bar{p}^{\beta}$, $\bar{p}^{\gamma}$ and $\bar{p}^{\delta}$. (Each $\bar{p}$ is a vector with one component for each product.) All this is thoroughly discussed in

Chapter 3. Generally the prices corresponding to a given wage will be different for each system; there is no reason to think otherwise.

For any wage the system of techniques that will actually be selected for use is one that leads to the greatest rate of profit, the one whose wage–profit curve lies farthest to the right. This is not as obvious as it sounds. The choice of technique is made, not by the capitalist class as a whole deciding what is best for them, but by individual capitalists competing with each other within the various industries. They will select the most profitable techniques in their own industries but it is not obvious that that will lead to the greatest profit over all.

Let me be more specific. Suppose in Fig. 4.3.2 that the wage is $\bar{w}$ but the system of techniques in use happens to be δ, say. Can we be sure that capitalists will switch to α, which is, over all, the most profitable system? The prices at present prevailing are $\bar{p}^\delta$. The capitalists in any industry will look at the techniques available to them and decide which is the most profitable — which, to put it another way, has the lowest cost per unit produced. Which technique that is naturally depends on the prices of the inputs. Capitalists will evaluate the costs at the existing prices $\bar{p}^\delta$. No doubt if everyone in an industry switched to a different technique prices would change. But capitalists in competition cannot reckon on that; they are price takers deciding only whether to switch themselves. It would be foolish to switch to a technique that is more costly than the present one in the hope that everyone else will make the same switch and thereby alter prices enough to make it less costly; there is no reason to expect everyone else to do that. So capitalists at present employing the δ techniques will only switch to α techniques if they are more profitable when evaluated at the prices $\bar{p}^\delta$. We know they would be more profitable once prices had altered to $\bar{p}^\alpha$ because α is, over all, more profitable than δ. But can we be sure they are more profitable at $\bar{p}^\delta$?

A similar question comes up in reverse. Suppose the economy is actually employing the most profitable system α. Could it happen that capitalists in some industry, calculating costs at the prevailing prices $\bar{p}^\alpha$, might find some other technique more profitable? If they were to adopt that technique prices would change and they would end up with less profit than before, but each individual capitalist can only make his or her best decision taking prices as given. So can we be sure that once system α is selected there will be no move away from it?

The answer to both questions is that we *can* be sure; both these difficulties over the choice of technique turn out to be imaginary. That is what I shall now set out to prove. The argument is, I am sorry to say, quite complicated.

The first thing I shall show is this. Suppose some system or other — ε to give it a name — is established. The corresponding prices $\bar{p}^\varepsilon$ prevail and the rate of profit is $\bar{r}^\varepsilon$. And suppose capitalists in one or more (basic) industries now find that some alternative technique is more profitable, evaluated at $\bar{p}^\varepsilon$. Then if they adopt the new technique or techniques, so that a new system is established with new prices, then the new rate of profit will be higher than $\bar{r}^\varepsilon$. The proof is as follows. After the capitalists have made the switch, but before prices change, the rate of profit will be above $\bar{r}^\varepsilon$ in industries that have switched and still $\bar{r}^\varepsilon$ in others. Then prices will change to equalize the rates of profit between industries. I proved on p. 50 of Chapter 3 that when an equalization like this occurs the final rate of profit must lie strictly between the previous highest and lowest rates. It must, therefore, be more than $\bar{r}^\varepsilon$. That ends the proof.

Consequently if the most profitable system α were in use and some alternative techniques (in basic industries) proved more profitable at prices $\bar{p}^\alpha$, switching to them would raise the over-all rate of profit. But actually there is no system of techniques with a higher over-all rate. Therefore there can be no techniques more profitable at the α prices than the α techniques. That removes one of our difficulties.

The other difficulty needs, first of all, to be defined more precisely. Imagine that, say, system ε is established but that in some (basic) industry the ε technique turns out to be less profitable at prices $\bar{p}^\varepsilon$ than some other. Then the other technique will be adopted, a new system will become established and a new over-all rate of profit will emerge. This rate will, I have just proved, be greater than $\bar{r}^\varepsilon$. Under the new system it might again turn out that there is some more profitable alternative technique for some industry. Then there will be another switch, to a system with a still higher rate of profit. The chain of switches may continue, each link raising the rate of profit. There can never be a return to a system earlier in the chain because that would cause a reduction in the rate of profit. Eventually the chain must stop, therefore, at a system where no industry finds it has any more profitable technique to switch to. If this system at the end of the chain is α, the most profitable of all, all is well; the economy has selected the system it ought to select. But could the chain end at some different system? That is our difficulty, now more sharply defined: is it possible that in some system — call it δ — other than the most profitable one, no industry has available an alternative technique more profitable than the one it is using, when evaluated at the prices $\bar{p}^\delta$?

Well, suppose that does happen. System δ differs from α in one or more industries. Imagine that, starting from an initial state where δ is in use and prices are $\bar{p}^\delta$, these industries were to adopt the α techniques. Our supposition is that none of these α techniques is more profitable, at prices $\bar{p}^\delta$, than the original δ techniques. Adopting them, then, either reduces the rate of profit in those industries or leaves it the same. (Of course, capitalists would not actually make the switch we are imagining, but there is nothing to stop us following up what would happen if they did.) Prices will adjust to equalize the rate of profit, and by the proposition on p. 50 the rate of profit cannot end up above the original one $\bar{r}^\delta$. But by now it is system α that is in use, and system α does actually have a higher rate of profit than $\bar{r}^\delta$. So we have reached a contradiction. Our supposition was evidently impossible, and that removes the second of the difficulties that troubled us.

We have finally established the single point that at any wage the system of techniques actually selected is the most profitable. The economy is always on the outside envelope of the individual wage–profit curves — on the heavily drawn curve in Fig. 4.3.2.

Some Facts about Switch Points

There are levels of the wage that constitute switch points between systems. Switch points need some examining. Take, for the sake of discussion, the wage $\hat{w}$ in Fig. 4.3.2, which is a switch point between systems α and β.

Let the wage be $\hat{w}$ and suppose the system actually in use is α. Prices, then, are $\hat{p}^{\alpha}$. Evaluated at these prices, the β technique in any (basic) industry where it differs from the α technique must be exactly as profitable as the α technique. This needs proving. If any industry found the β technique *more* profitable than the α technique it would adopt it and thereby (as we know) raise the over-all rate of profit. But we know that no system of techniques exists with a higher rate of profit at this wage, so that is impossible. If, on the other hand, no industry found that β technique more profitable than the α technique but one or more found it less profitable, than if all industries switch to β techniques the over-all rate of profit would be reduced. But this change is simply a switch to system β, which actually has the same rate of profit at this wage, so that is impossible too.

Evaluated at $\hat{p}^{\alpha}$, then, the β techniques offer exactly the same rate of profit, $\hat{r}^{\alpha}$, as the α techniques. So they bring in exactly the same rate as each other. To put it another way, if the β techniques were all adopted — if the β system were adopted — but α prices remained in force, all industries would still be equally profitable. The α prices equalize profit for the β system. They are, that is to say, equilibrium prices for the β system. Indeed, they must be the β prices. At the switch point α and β prices are identical.

At a switch point between two systems of techniques the wage and rate of profit are the same for each. So, we have just discovered, are all prices.

One consequence is that whenever two systems of techniques, like α and β, have a mutual switch point — whenever, that is to say, their wage–profit curves meet on the outer envelope of wage–profit curves — they normally only differ in one of their industries. The easiest way to see this is by counting equations. Let there be n industries altogether. For each of the two systems of techniques there are n equations, one for each industry, relating the wage, the rate of profit and prices (see p. 46). One further equation is required to fix the numeraire, so that makes $(2n+1)$ altogether. At the switch point both systems have the same wage, rate of profit and prices. Therefore all the $(2n+1)$

equations are actually relating the same $(n + 2)$ unknowns: one wage, one rate of profit and n prices. This can normally only mean that most of the equations are identical; the techniques in most industries must be the same in both systems so as to produce the same equation. There is room only for one industry to have two different techniques — two equations. For then we shall have two equations from this industry, one from each of the $(n - 1)$ others and one for the numeraire. That makes $(n + 2)$ altogether, which is just enough to fix the unknowns.

A second consequence is that capitalists in the industry where the α technique differs from the β technique are impartial between them. Both are equally profitable. They equally happy to employ one, the other or a mixture of the two. At a switch point, then, systems of techniques may be mixed.

The Direction of Switches

For a single-product technology we found (p. 100) that as the wage rises through a switch point the new technique brought in always has a higher requirement of materials, and hence of capital, per worker than the one thrown out. That seems natural; as labour becomes more expensive it seems a good idea to use other inputs instead. Does an equivalent rule apply to economies with several products?

The first problem is to decide just what an equivalent rule would be. At a switch a new technique is introduced, which may be more or less capital intensive than the old. But also the new technique may make use of different inputs from the old, and these might be more or less capital intensive in their production. It would be possible for a switch to raise the capital/labour ratio in the economy as a whole even though the ratio in the new technique itself is lower than before; the new technique might use inputs with a very high ratio. Evidently it is the products' *integrated* capital/labour ratios we should look at. There is a convenient fact that simplifies things here: all products will, when a switch occurs, have their integrated capital/labour ratios shifted in the same direction; if one ratio falls, or rises, they all will. The proof is in the Appendix to this chapter. Bearing this in mind one would most naturally expect that an increase in the wage, when it causes a switch of techniques, will raise the integrated capital/labour ratios of all the products, or at least not reduce them. If this were true the economy's aggregate ratio would certainly be raised, or at least not lowered. So is it true? The answer is: not necessarily. Here is an example where an increase in the wage causes a switch that reduces the products' integrated capital/labour ratios:

$$
\left.
\begin{array}{lll}
\alpha\colon & 8/25 \text{ yoghurt} & \& \ 18/25 \text{ labour } \rightarrow 1 \text{ yoghurt} \\
\beta\colon & & 1/18 \text{ culture } \& \ 1 \text{ labour } \rightarrow 1 \text{ yoghurt} \\
& 2 \text{ yoghurt} & \& \ 1 \text{ labour } \rightarrow 1 \text{ culture.}
\end{array}
\right\} \ (4.3.2)
$$

There are two systems of techniques in this technology, each consisting of the sole technique in the culture industry together with either technique α or β in the yoghurt industry. Their wage–profit curves are drawn in Fig. 4.3.3. There are two switch points:

$$r = 1; \quad w = 1/4$$

and $$r = 5/4; \quad w = 14/81.$$

Concentrate on the second of these. From the diagram it is clear that a wage increase at this switch point brings in technique β to replace α. Now the price of culture here in terms of yoghurt is its cost of production raised by the rate of profit:

$$
\begin{aligned}
&(1+r)(2+w) \\
&= (9/4)(2+(14/81)) \\
&= 44/9.
\end{aligned}
$$

Given this we may calculate yoghurt's integrated capital/labour ratio from the formula $(pA + wl)(I - A)^{-1}$ (see p. 44). For system α it turns out to be ·6173 and for β ·5354. Culture also has a smaller ratio under system β. Yet β is the system introduced by an increase in the wage.

This rather surprising phenomenon is known as **capital reversing**. It calls for an explanation. I shall not try to give a complete account — that would take too long — but I shall try to indicate how it happens. In the example above yoghurt produced by system β, which I shall call β yoghurt, has a lower integrated capital/labour ratio than α yoghurt. Wage costs, then, constitute a larger part of the cost of producing β yoghurt than α yoghurt. Normally, therefore, one would expect an increase in the wage to raise β yoghurt's costs faster than α yoghurt's. Since the two sorts of yoghurt are actually identical that would incline capitalists towards using the α method, and since at the switch point they are indifferent between the methods, at a slightly higher wage one would expect them to use system α. However, on p. 55 of Chapter 3 we came across the surprising possibility that an increase in the wage can reduce the price of a product with a lower integrated capital/labour ratio relative to one with a higher one. Since prices are proportional to costs, reducing the relative price comes to the same thing as reducing the relative costs. Now, this discovery we made in Chapter 3 applied to two different products within one system of techniques. But it does not strain one's credulity to think it might also apply to two alternative methods of making the same product. And indeed that is what has happened in the example. The increase in the wage actually reduces the relative costs of making β yoghurt, despite its lower integrated capital/labour ratio. So we can see that the unexpected direction of the switch is closely connected with the unexpected direction of price changes in Chapter 3. They spring from the same cause: ultimately, Wicksell effects.

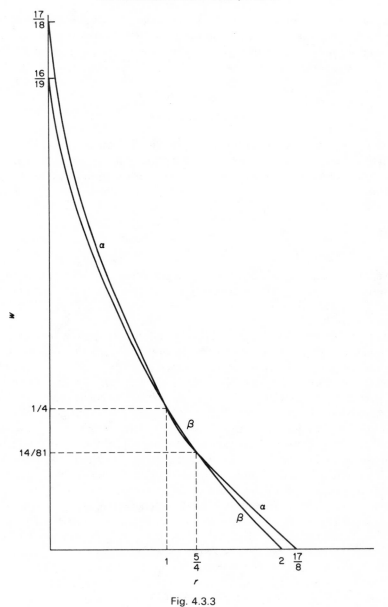

Fig. 4.3.3

Another point to notice is the possibility of **reswitching**. Figures 4.3.2 and 4.3.3 both show it. System α is selected at low wages and again for a range of higher wages, but in between another system is selected. Some people have been surprised by this possibility and, as I shall explain in Section 4.5 (p. 141), it causes difficulties for a theory of income distribution that has been quite popular amongst economists.

Neither capital reversing nor reswitching is possible in a single-product economy. I leave you to work out why.

The Choice of Technique in Non-basic Industries

Given the wage, the rate of profit and the prices of basic goods are all determined without reference to non-basic industries. I have described how; the choice of technique in basic industries is part of the process. We did, remember, assume that the numeraire is a basic good.

For a technique within a non-basic industry the costs of production consist of materials (all of which we assumed on p. 33 to be basic) and wages. Given the wage these costs are strictly determined. All that capitalists are called on to do is survey the available techniques and select the cheapest. The price of the product will then be this cheapest cost raised by the rate of profit, which is again given from elsewhere. There will be no reaction on the rest of the economy. Naturally the technique selected is likely to depend on the wage.

For an example look back to technology (4.3.1), whose wage–profit diagram is Fig. 4.3.1. The cost of production, measured in corn, of a unit of bread is $(1 + 7w)$ and $(2 + 3w)$ in the two techniques. When w is less than $1/4$ the first of these is the smaller; when w is more than $1/4$ the second. So the bread industry has a switch point at $1/4$. There is, remember, a switch from the α system to the β system in the basic industries at a wage of $1/3$. So, for a wage below $1/4$ system α_1 is in use, for a wage between $1/4$ and $1/3$ system α_2, and above $1/3$ system β_2.

Section 4.4   Production and Distribution

The Wage, the Rate of Profit and Prices

Given the wage we know how to determine what system of techniques is in use (except that at a switch point we do not yet know the proportions in which techniques are mixed). Following from that we also know the rate of profit and prices, because within any system the economy works just like the ones we investigated in Chapter 3. Switch points create no difficulty in this because both the systems that meet at a switch point determine the same rate of profit and prices.

The wage is negatively related to the rate of profit: the economy's wage–profit curve slopes downwards. It is the envelope of the curves for the separate systems, and they certainly all slope downwards.

About the relation between prices and the wage there is nothing definite to say. It is unpredictable, we know, even without a choice of techniques. And when a change in the wage may bring about a switch of technique, which may itself be in an unpredictable direction, prediction is even less possible.

The fact that the wage alone is enough (given the technology) to determine the system of techniques selected, and hence all prices, is known as the **non-substitution theorem**. The theorem's special point is that *unless it affects the wage* the pattern of final demand has no effect on techniques or prices; it can cause no substitution amongst the inputs to production. Of course nothing says that final demand will actually not affect the wage; normally it will to some extent because it affects the distribution of capital among industries (see Section 3.4). It can, therefore, influence techniques and prices to some extent. The lesson to draw from the non-substitution theorem is not that the demand for goods makes no difference to their prices, but that it makes no more difference when there is a choice of technique than when there is not. The introduction of a choice of technique gives demand no extra leverage.

Net Production and its Distribution

What remain to be settled are the wage and, at switch points, the mixture of techniques. We can set about settling them exactly as we did for the single product economy in Section 4.2, assuming a competitive market for labour. Each system of techniques gives the wage as a particular function of the economy's aggregate capital/labour ratio. We can draw a graph for each system and pick out from each graph the appropriate section where that system is actually in use. The only difference is that we now have to take account of the pattern of final demand, because we know that demand can influence the wage even for a given capital/labour ratio. Our graphs have to be drawn with a particular pattern of demand in mind.

Example 1

As an example take technology (4.3.1), take corn as numeraire and assume that final demand is for corn alone. The bread industry will not then exist, so we have only the two systems α and β to worry about. Under system α, indeed, the fertilizer industry will not exist either since in that system fertilizer is non-basic. The system reduces to the single-product technology

$$1/6 \text{ corn } \& \text{ } 2 \text{ labour } \rightarrow 1 \text{ corn.}$$

For this the graph of the wage w against the aggregate capital/labour ratio K/L is the left-hand dotted straight line in Fig. 4.4.1. System β is

$$1/6 \text{ corn } \& \text{ } 1/6 \text{ fertilizer } \& \text{ } 1 \text{ labour } \rightarrow 1 \text{ corn}$$
$$1 \text{ corn } \qquad\qquad \& \text{ } 2 \text{ labour } \rightarrow 1 \text{ fertilizer.}$$

Both industries happen to have the same composition of capital (compare technology (3.3.12) in p. 57). That means (see p. 57) that the price of fertilizer relative to corn is unchanging. There are therefore no valuation effects to complicate things, and for this system too the graph of w against K/L is a straight line with a slope of one. It is shown dotted in Fig. 4.4.1.

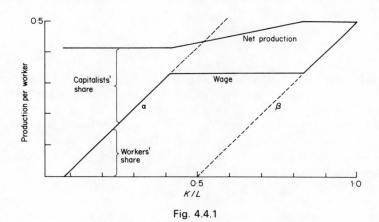

Fig. 4.4.1

The lower of the two solid graphs in Fig. 4.4.1 is the wage graph for the economy. It follows the α line for wages below the switch point of $1/3$ and the β line above it. The diagram also includes a graph of net production. It is, in fact, a standard distribution diagram. It looks just like the diagrams for single-product economies, such as Fig. 4.2.6 on p. 107, because the technology is so simple.

Example 2

Let us now continue with the same technology (4.3.1), and keep corn as the numeraire, but this time assume that final demand is for bread alone. The bread industry will be operating and we shall have to take account of the technique it employs. We discovered on p. 119 that the systems of techniques in use are α_1 when w is less than $1/4$, α_2 when w lies between $1/4$ and $1/3$ and β_2 when it is more than $1/3$.

For each system we can, as before, draw a graph of w against K/L, bearing in mind that all net production consists of bread. Let us do the calculations, as an illustration, for system β_2. If the gross productions of the three industries are x_1, x_2 and x_3 and their net productions y_1, y_2 and y_3, then for system β_2

$$y_1 = x_1 - (1/6)x_1 - x_2 - 2x_3$$

$$y_2 = x_2 - (1/6)x_1$$

$$y_3 = x_3.$$

If we now make $y_1 = y_2 = 0$ and $y_3 = 1$, the solution is

$$x_1 = 3$$

$$x_2 = 1/2$$

$$x_3 = 1.$$

That is to say, if net production consists only of bread then the industries, gross productions must be in the ratios $3:1/2:1$. Knowing this it is easy to work out that to produce, net, a ton of bread will require seven workers altogether, and as materials three tons of corn and $1/2$ ton of fertilizer. The price of fertilizer relative to corn is 2, so that the value of the materials comes to 4. The value of materials per worker employed, then, is $4/7$. The wage paid in these circumstances must be

$$w = K/L - 4/7,$$

the quantity of capital available per worker less the part of it that has to be laid out on materials. The graph of this equation is shown as a dotted line in Fig. 4.4.2, together with those for the other systems, which can be worked out in much the same way. As in Example 1, and for the same reasons, wage graphs are all straight lines. The economy's wage graph is picked out in solid lines.

Following our usual procedure, we can complete the distribution diagram by putting net production into it. We found just now that to produce, net, one ton of bread takes seven workers altogether when system β_2 is employed. So net production per worker is $1/7$. In the same way a worker's net production can be calculated for the other systems. It is actually $5/47$ for α_1 and $5/39$ for α_2. Thus the progression from α_1 to α_2 to β_2 as K/L grows consistently increases net production per worker. However, all these are quantities of bread, and our numeraire is corn. It happens that bread's price in terms of corn declines with increasing wages. The resulting graph of net production's value is shown in Fig. 4.4.2.

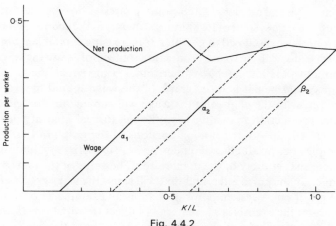

Fig. 4.4.2

It is worth comparing Figs 4.4.1 and 4.4.2. The only difference between the economies they represent is in final demand: for corn in one and bread in the other. The demand for bread calls the baking industry into existence, and that brings some noticeable changes. The most striking consequence, apart from the introduction of valuation effects, is the creation of a whole new switch point. Because baking is not a basic industry its choice of techniques makes no difference to the economy's wage–profit curve, and it received very little attention in Section 4.3. But a non-basic industry may be very important all the same. It may be the home of a large part of the economy's capital, and in switching its technique it may absorb a lot more. While it re-equips, the wage will be held at a switch point determined by the non-basic industry itself.

Example 3

My last example is from technology (4.3.2), which has both reswitching and capital reversing. Let yoghurt be the numeraire, and let final demand be for yoghurt only. The distribution diagram is Figure 4.4.3. It is put together in the usual way; I shall not go through the details. The diagram's peculiar features I shall comment on in a moment.

General Characteristics

Let us survey the examples and see what generalizations can be made. Imagine K/L growing; what will happen in the economy as a consequence?

First of all, the economy's progress obviously has phases of two types:

switch-point phases and non-switch-point phases. Look at the latter first. During these a single system of techniques is in use, so the economy is really no different from those discussed in Chapter 3. Increasing capital per worker will "in real terms" do nothing to net production, but simply raise the wage by the whole amount of the increase. So, other things being equal, the graph of net production should be flat and the graph of the wage should have a slope of one. However, with the change in the wage will come valuation effects. The value of net production may alter even though its real quantity does not — hence the curved, downward sloping portions of the graph in Fig. 4.4.2. (In other examples net production happens not to suffer from valuation effects because it consists entirely of the numeraire.) The value of the materials used up in production may also alter, and that will cause the wage graph to deviate from its slope of one — system β in Fig. 4.4.3 is an example. (For none of the other systems in the examples are materials subject to valuation effects, either because they consist only of the numeraire, or because the basic industries have the same composition of capital as each other.) We know from Chapter 3 (p. 75) that in extreme situations valuation effects may even cause the wage graph to slope downwards. But we found that if they do it points to an

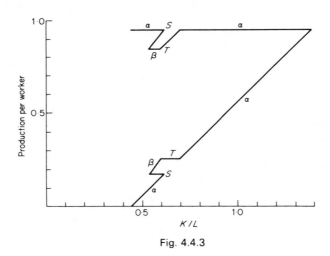

Fig. 4.4.3

unsuitable choice of numeraire, one that allows capital-as-value to decline without any decline in capital-as-goods. We need to be sure again now that our numeraire does not have that failing; a basic good, we decided, will almost certainly do all right. The only difficulty now we have a choice of technique is that in different systems different goods may be basic. Conceivably there might not be one that is basic in all. That, though, is such a distant possibility I think we may ignore it.

Now attend to the switch-point phases of the growth in K/L, and for the moment ignore Example 3. For these phases we can say straight away that the wage is constant; the wage graph is flat. Increasing capital goes to increasing production; the net production graph slopes upwards. We can actually be more precise about it: its upward slope is equal to the rate of profit r. The reason is exactly the same as for the single product case. Since the rate of profit is constant, any increase in capital must return to the capitalists that same rate of profit. Their income, that is to say, increases by r times the increase in capital. And because workers' income is constant the increase in capitalists' income constitutes the whole of the increase in net production. The same argument may be put into symbols. The value of net production is the sum of capitalists' and workers' incomes (see p. 61):

$$Y = rK + wL.$$

Y is the value of net production, the scalar product py of the price vector p and the net production vector y.

$$\frac{Y}{L} = r\frac{K}{L} + w.$$

$$\therefore \quad \frac{d(Y/L)}{d(K/L)} = r + \frac{K}{L}\frac{dr}{d(K/L)} + \frac{dw}{d(K/L)}.$$

At a switch point r and w are constant as K/L varies, so the last two terms on the right are nought. Therefore

$$\frac{d(Y/L)}{d(K/L)} = r.$$

The derivative $\dfrac{d(Y/L)}{d(K/L)}$ is the rate at which net production per worker increases in response to increases in K/L. It is, in fact, the slope of the net production graph, and we have just proved it to be r.

The most important thing to remember about switch points is that there are no valuation effects. Prices, the wage and the rate of profit are all constant.

Capital Reversing

Now we can look again at Examples 3. Figure 4.4.3 which depicts it conforms perfectly to the rules I have described. At switch points the wage is constant and the graph of net production has a slope of r. What makes the diagram peculiar is that at the switch from α to β the graphs go backwards.

The explanation is that this particular switch is the one with capital reversing. I defined capital reversing on p. 117 in terms of the products' integrated capital/labour ratios. Capital reversing means that an increase in the wage introduces a system of techniques where all the products have lower integrated capital/labour ratios than before. The aggregate capital/labour ratio for the economy as a whole depends on the pattern of demand. But because *every* product has a reduced ratio, we know that the aggregate ratio must be reduced, whatever the pattern of demand may be.

System β, then, requires less capital per worker than α. It follows, incidentally, that it must have less net production per worker than α. The net production graph must have a positive slope of r at the switch, and this is the only way that can happen. Here, then, is another discovery worth recording: where there is reversing of capital there is reversing of net production; increasing the wage introduces a system of techniques having less net production per worker.

Capital reversing is a "real" phenomenon and not in any way a mere valuation effect. When on p. 75 we discovered a downward sloping wage graph — another instance where a higher wage corresponds to a smaller quantity of capital per worker — we decided it was a consequence of measuring capital badly and could be put right by changing the numeraire. But that is not true now. At a switch point, after all, there are no valuation effects. A capitalist operating system α at the switch point wage (14/81) would have more than enough capital to transfer all his or her workers to system β. He or she could even do it without recourse to the market by dividing his or her labour force between yoghurt production and culture production. He or she would have more than enough capital to pay wages and supply the workers with yoghurt to set the process going. Also, of course, the reduction in net output that coincides with capital reversal is no valuation effect. The actual quantities of goods produced decline, not just their value.

Over a certain range of the aggregate capital/labour ratio (between 0·5354 and 0·6173 in the example) an economy with capital reversing has three possible equilibrium levels for the wage. If the economy's capital/labour ratio is growing slowly, the wage will increase until it gets to the switch point and then jump to a higher equilibrium, because capitalists will all switch to system β and then find they have some capital left over. The spare capital must pull up the wage. In the diagram the economy will jump from S to some point such as T. The jump cannot be a sudden one because it involves altering the structure of the economy, and while it is in progress prices and the wage will change in ways our static theory cannot predict. There will be capital gains and losses. There is therefore no knowing exactly what K/L will be once the economy settles down again in its new equilibrium. The point T in the diagram is just a guess.

Continuous Technologies

I have not, for multi-product economies, given examples of continuous technologies. They are no different in principle. Their special feature is that they have no sharp distinction between switch points and others. Their distribution diagrams, for instance, will show everywhere a mixture of the two sorts of phase I have been describing.

Economic Growth

Growth needs a mention only to say that there is almost nothing to add to the discussion in Chapter 3. Some level of K/L will lead to proportional growth: the one where the rate of profit is g/s (g is the labour force's rate of growth and s the capitalists' rate of saving). Notice that the correspondence we found in Chapter 3 (p. 78) between a high rate of saving and a high capital/labour ratio in proportional growth will be disturbed by capital reversing if it occurs. And if g/s happens to coincide with the rate of profit at a switch point there will be a range of capital/labour ratios that can support proportional growth.

Outside proportional growth I have already made an informal use of a growing capital/labour ratio in explaining the distribution diagrams. For this to make sense we must implicitly assume that the change is slow enough to keep the economy constantly in equilibrium. The choice of technique makes no difference to that.

Section 4.5 Distribution and Marginal Productivities

The Production Function for an Industry

Sections 4.1 and 4.2 contained a certain amount of what may be called **marginal analysis**. I defined marginal productivities and marginal rates of substitution, and later on related them to the wage. The first thing I want to do in this section is extend that analysis, in quite general terms, to economies with several products.

We begin by defining a **production function** for each product. For the time being let us concentrate on the first product only. Assuming it can be made by several different techniques and the techniques can be mixed, the inputs may be applied in various different combinations. We could if we chose draw isoquants, each one showing all the combinations of inputs that will, when applied efficiently, produce some particular quantity of output. (The diagram would probably require more dimensions than two — one for each input.) And given a particular combination of inputs there is some definite quantity of output they will produce if used efficiently. The output, that is to say, is a function of the inputs:

$$x = f(c_1, c_2, \ldots c_n, L). \qquad (4.5.1)$$

Here x is the first product's (gross) output, $c_1, \ldots c_n$ are the quantities of each of the n products used as input and L is input of labour. The function f is the product's production function. I have included all n products as inputs simply for the sake of generality. Many of them may not actually be used at all in the first industry; in that case the function is only defined when their quantities are nought.

Because there are constant returns to scale, the same function serves equally well for the industry and for a capitalist enterprise within it. It tells us what the industry can produce from given inputs, and what an enterprise can produce from given inputs.

As we did in Section 4.1 we can define marginal productivities for the inputs. They are the production function's partial derivatives. The derivative $\partial x/\partial c_i$ is the marginal productivity of the i'th product, and $\partial x/\partial L$ is the marginal productivity of labour. Marginal productivities need not always exist. With a discrete technology the production function will have kinks in it, and at the kinks its partial derivatives — marginal productivities — will be undefined.

Where marginal productivities are defined, though, we can also define marginal rates of substitution. They are the ratios of marginal productivities.

$$\frac{\partial x/\partial L}{\partial x/\partial c_i}$$

is the marginal rate of substitution of product i for labour, and

$$\frac{\partial x/\partial c_j}{\partial x/\partial c_i}$$

is the marginal rate of substitution of product i for product j.

Any particular technique or mixture of techniques will always have the same marginal productivities and marginal rates of substitution whatever scale it is applied on, and whether it is seen from the point of view of the industry or of an individual capitalist.

The Profit-maximizing Technique

In Section 4.2 we found that the technique or mixture of techniques that maximized profits has a marginal rate of substitution of corn for labour equal to the wage, provided that the marginal rate of substitution happens to be defined at that point. I now want to generalize that conclusion and the proof that led to it.

The generalized conclusion is that for the profit-maximizing technique or mixture the price ratio of any pair of inputs is equal to the marginal rate of substitution if it is defined. Precisely:

$$\frac{p_j}{p_i} = \frac{\partial x/\partial c_j}{\partial x/\partial c_i} \text{ for any } i \text{ and } j \tag{4.5.2}$$

and

$$\frac{w}{p_i} = \frac{\partial x/\partial L}{\partial x/\partial c_i} \text{ for any } i. \tag{4.5.3}$$

Now for the proof. Take a capitalist in the industry, Christine, who is working out which technique is the most profitable. Suppose she happens to use some technique that has products i and j as inputs but does not conform to rule (4.5.2), so the marginal rate of substitution is defined but not equal to the ratio of prices. Suppose for the sake of argument that

$$\frac{p_j}{p_i} > \frac{\partial x/\partial c_j}{\partial x/\partial c_i}.$$

I shall explain how Christine may increase her profits by adopting another technique. She should substitute some of product i for j. Suppose she decreases the input of j by a little bit dc_j, then in order to maintain the same output she will have to increase the input of i by this amount times the marginal rate of substitution:

$$\frac{\partial x/\partial c_j}{\partial x/\partial c_i} \, dc_j.$$

The quantity of product i will cost her

$$p_i \frac{\partial x/\partial c_j}{\partial x/\partial c_i} \, dc_j,$$

which is (by our assumption) less than

$$p_i \frac{p_j}{p_i} \, dc_j = p_j dc_j,$$

less, that is, than what she has saved on product j. By making the substitution, then, Christine has got the same output at a lower cost, which is obviously a gain. If the price ratio p_j/p_i were less than the marginal rate of substitution she would gain by substituting in the opposite direction. Only when they are equal can she be maximizing profits. We have proved, then, that (4.5.2) is true of the profit-maximizing technique, and the same proof obviously applies to (4.5.3).

Prices and Marginal Productivities

Marginal rates of substitution are ratios of marginal productivities. Our rules (4.5.2) and (4.5.3) say, put differently, that the prices paid for inputs are in proportion to their marginal productivities, when these are defined:

$$\left.\begin{array}{c} p_1 = \lambda \dfrac{\partial x}{\partial c_1}, \\[2mm] p_2 = \lambda \dfrac{\partial x}{\partial c_2}, \\[2mm] \vdots \\[2mm] p_n = \lambda \dfrac{\partial x}{\partial c_n}, \end{array}\right\} \qquad (4.5.4)$$

and
$$w = \lambda \frac{\partial x}{\partial L}. \qquad (4.5.5)$$

The number λ is the constant of proportionality—the same for all inputs. Our next job is to find out its value.

The best approach is to look at our capitalist Christine's total revenues and outlays. We shall have to make use of a simple fact about marginal productivities that relates them to total output. It is a consequence of the technology's contant returns to scale. Suppose the first input c_1 is increased by θc_1, some small fraction of itself. Other things being equal output would increase by θc_1 times the input's marginal productivity

$$\theta c_1 \frac{\partial x}{\partial c_1}.$$

But suppose that every input is simultaneously increased by the same fraction θ. The total effect on output will be the sum of all the individual effects

$$\theta c_1 \frac{\partial x}{\partial c_1} + \theta c_2 \frac{\partial x}{\partial c_2} + \ldots + \theta c_n \frac{\partial x}{\partial c_n} + \theta L \frac{\partial x}{\partial L}.$$

We know, though, because of the constant returns to scale, that output will actually increase by the same fraction θ of itself, by θx in fact. So

$$\theta x = \theta c_1 \frac{\partial x}{\partial c_1} + \theta c_2 \frac{\partial x}{\partial c_2} + \ldots + \theta c_n \frac{\partial x}{\partial c_n} + \theta L \frac{\partial x}{\partial L}.$$

$$\therefore \quad x = c_1 \frac{\partial x}{\partial c_1} + c_2 \frac{\partial x}{\partial c_2} + \ldots + c_n \frac{\partial x}{\partial c_n} + L \frac{\partial x}{\partial L}. \tag{4.5.6}$$

This is the simple fact I mentioned. (It is known as **Euler's Theorem**.)

Now go back to Christine. Her total costs are

$$p_1 c_1 + p_2 c_2 + \ldots + p_n c_n + wL,$$

which by (4.5.4) and (4.5.5) come to

$$\lambda \left(c_1 \frac{\partial x}{\partial c_1} + c_2 \frac{\partial x}{\partial c_2} + \ldots + c_n \frac{\partial x}{\partial c_n} + L \frac{\partial x}{\partial L} \right),$$

and by (4.5.6) to

$$\lambda x.$$

The revenue raised by selling the product is px, where p is its price. The rate of profit r is (Revenue–Cost)/Capital, i.e.

$$r = \frac{px - \lambda x}{\lambda x}.$$

$$\therefore \quad \lambda = p/(1+r).$$

Now we have our constant of proportionality. Put it back into the equations (4.5.4) and (4.5.5):

$$\left. \begin{aligned} p_1 &= \frac{1}{(1+r)} p \frac{\partial x}{\partial c_1} \\[2mm] p_2 &= \frac{1}{(1+r)} p \frac{\partial x}{\partial c_2} \\ &\quad\vdots \\ p_n &= \frac{1}{(1+r)} p \frac{\partial x}{\partial c_n} \end{aligned} \right\} \tag{4.5.7}$$

$$w = \frac{1}{(1+r)} p \frac{\partial x}{\partial L}. \tag{4.5.8}$$

The terms $p \dfrac{\partial x}{\partial c_1}$, $p \dfrac{\partial x}{\partial c_2}$ and so on, including $p \dfrac{\partial x}{\partial L}$, are the values of the inputs' marginal productivities, the rate at which increasing the inputs would increase revenue. The equations say that, once the profit-maximizing technique is selected, the price paid for an input is equal to the value of its marginal productivity discounted by the rate of profit. All this applies, naturally, only if the marginal productivities are defined.

So far in this section we have been dealing with the first industry only, but of course everything I have said is equally true in every industry. Equation (4.5.1), which specifies the first product's production function, ought really to be written with an extra index on the variables tying them down to the first product:

$$x_1 = f^1(c_{11}, c_{21}, \ldots c_{n1}, L_1).$$

There are similar functions for each product. Here is the j'th:

$$x_j = f^j(c_{1j}, c_{2j}, \ldots c_{nj}, L_j).$$

We can define marginal productivity in each industry as before. The marginal productivity of product i in industry j is $\partial x_j / \partial c_{ij}$ and the marginal productivity of labour in industry j is $\partial x_j / \partial L_j$. There are marginal rates of substitution in each industry:

$$\frac{\partial x_k / \partial c_{jk}}{\partial x_k / \partial c_{ik}} \quad \text{and} \quad \frac{\partial x_k / \partial L_k}{\partial x_k / \partial c_{ik}}.$$

In every industry equations equivalent to (4.5.2) and (4.5.3) apply for the profit-maximizing technique whenever the appropriate marginal rates of substitution are defined. So do equations equivalent to (4.5.7) and (4.5.8). In fact

$$p_i = \frac{1}{(1+r)} p_j \frac{\partial x_j}{\partial c_{ij}} \text{ for all } i \text{ and } j \tag{4.5.9}$$

and

$$w = \frac{1}{(1+r)} p_j \frac{\partial x_j}{\partial L_j} \text{ for all } j. \tag{4.5.10}$$

For the profit-maximizing system of techniques, that is to say, the price of each input including labour is equal to the value of its marginal productivity in any industry discounted by the rate of profit. Its marginal productivity, then, has the same value anywhere and we can speak without ambiguity of *the* value of its marginal productivity. Discounted by the rate of profit it is equal to its price.

This finding is easy to account for. Capital can earn the going rate of profit r. A capitalist in any industry divides his or her capital between the various inputs required, and has the option of spending a little more or a little less on any particular input. If spending a little more earns a return greater than r— what capital can earn elsewhere—he or she will take the opportunity of doing so. On the other hand, if the last unit of capital spent on this input gets a lower return than *r* the capital will be withdrawn and applied elsewhere. In equilibrium the return "at the margin" to capital spent on the input must be *r*. The cost of buying a unit of the input is its price; its contribution to revenue is the value of its marginal product; so the latter must exceed the former by the rate of profit. That is what (4.5.9) and (4.5.10) say.

The Contributions to Production of Labour and Capital

Economists have shown a lot of interest in the relationship between the price paid for an input and its marginal productivity. The wage and the marginal productivity of labour have concerned them especially, because the wage constitutes the income of the working class and labour's marginal productivity tells us something about the contribution that class makes to the economy's production. Are workers paid the equivalent of what they contribute?

According to a standard argument in economics, in a competitive economy workers should receive as wages exactly the value of their marginal contribution. The wage, that is to say, should be equal to the value of what an extra worker would produce. The argument is that if an employer found the wage to be less than the value of what an extra worker would add to his or her enterprise's production he or she would employ the extra worker. And he or she would lay off workers if the wage was more than the value of the marginal contribution. Only when the two are equal can there be an equilibrium.

Against this argument has to be set what we have just established: that the wage is less than the value of labour's marginal productivity, by a discount equal to the rate of profit. How can these things be reconciled? I shall describe one popular reconciliation and its ramifications, and discuss whether it is valid.

It claims that labour's marginal productivity does not really represent what labour contributes at the margin to production. The marginal productivity is defined as the increase in production that would result from employing an extra worker without increasing any other input. But to employ this extra worker requires more capital; his or her wage has to be financed. So capital and labour both increase together. The extra production that results cannot be attributed solely to the labour; some of the credit is due to the capital. Marginal productivity is a technical concept defined from technology alone. It consequently misses the contribution capital makes to production because the need for capital to finance production is not specified in the technology. Therefore the marginal productivity of labour overstates labour's real contribution. Although the wage is less than the marginal productivity, the standard argument above adequately demonstrates that it must be equal to the true marginal contribution. So the argument goes:

This view identifies a marginal contribution of capital as well as of labour, and a corollary of it is that capital's marginal contribution must, in competition, be equal to the rate of profit. Suppose a capitalist, George, adds some small amount of capital δK to his enterprise, without increasing his labour force. What will the extra capital contribute to production? Evidently it must be spent on materials rather than labour, but however it is spent we know that it must bring in a return equal to the prevailing rate of profit r. The extra materials will cost δK, so the value of the extra output must be $(1+r)\delta K$ so as to yield the required return r. The economy's net production will be increased by the extra output and diminished by the extra materials; the value of the net increase is

$$(1+r)\delta K - \delta K = r\delta K.$$

The rate, then, at which capital contributes to the value of net production is the rate of profit r. It is, of course, this contribution to *net* production we are interested in.

So there is an outline of the opinion I want to discuss: labour and capital both earn the value of their marginal contributions. To assess it properly we shall have to define the marginal contributions more carefully, and then see what they come to.

What lies behind this way of thinking is something called the **aggregate production function**. Labour and capital are the two basic requirements of production—the two "factors of production" as they are often called. Given the technology, it is the amounts of labour and capital in the economy that determine how much it can produce. Production, then, must be a function of labour and capital:

$$Y = F(K, L).$$

K and L are the aggregate quantities of capital and labour. Y is the economy's net production; for the time being we shall measure it as usual by its value py where p is the vector of prices and y the vector of net productions of the individual goods. F is the aggregate production function.

The derivatives $\partial Y/\partial K$ and $\partial Y/\partial L$ are the **marginal contributions of capital and labour**. They are more commonly known as marginal productivities, but I prefer to keep that term for the purely technical marginal productivities defined earlier in this section (p. 128). Labour's marginal contribution is different from its marginal productivity; the former is defined by keeping capital constant, the latter by keeping constant the input of materials.

The aggregate production function cannot possibly be determined from the technology alone. Capital, which comes into it, is not a technical concept. The amount of capital needed for any amount of production depends not just on technology but also on the prices of inputs.

Now, unknown to ourselves we have in fact been discussing the aggregate production function in much of this chapter. We know very well that net production can be determined from K and L. The aggregate capital/labour ratio K/L fixes the value of net production per worker; the graphs of net production in all the distribution diagrams show this. Then from the total number of workers L we know the total value of net production. Obviously there are constant returns to scale in the aggregate production function: increasing K and L by the same proportion will increase Y by that proportion too because K/L remains constant.

Look back to Fig. 4.1.3 on p. 96. It shows a section of a *technical* production function, a graph of output against the input of corn when the input of labour is kept constant. The graphs of net production in Figs 4.2.6, 4.2.7, 4.4.1, 4.4.2 and 4.4.3 are the equivalent for the *aggregate* production function; if the labour force is constant they show net production determined by the quantity of capital. On their vertical axes they have Y/L and on their horizontal axes K/L so their slope is

$$\frac{\mathrm{d}(Y/L)}{\mathrm{d}(K/L)}$$

which, for a constant L, is the same as the marginal contribution of capital $\partial Y/\partial K$.

We have, then, already discussed capital's marginal contribution. We found that it depends on whether or not the economy is in the course of switching its system of techniques. When a switch is in progress increasing capital contributes to production by transferring more of the labour force to a more productive technique. We did indeed find that in these circumstances the marginal contribution of capital is the rate of profit r (see p. 125). But at other times capital serves only to increase the wage. It contributes nothing at all to net production in real terms, although there may at these times be valuation effects that alter the value of net production in one way or another. It is certainly only at switches that $\partial Y/\partial K$ is equal to r.

An interesting case is the example worked out in Section 4.2 (pp. 109–110) of a single-product economy with a continuous technology. The switch-point states of this economy are conflated with the non-switch-point states and the result is that the marginal contribution of capital is persistently below the rate of profit.

As for the marginal contribution of labour we can apply to it the method we used for capital on p. 125. Start again from the fact that the value of net production is the sum of capitalists' and workers' incomes.

$$Y = rK + wL.$$

Differentiate with respect to L, keeping K constant:

$$\frac{\partial Y}{\partial L} = \frac{\partial r}{\partial L} K + \frac{\partial w}{\partial L} L + w.$$

Labour's marginal contribution $\partial Y/\partial L$, then, is equal to w only if $\partial r/\partial L$ and $\partial w/\partial L$ are both nought. Changing L (with K constant) will only leave r and w unchanged if there is a switch of techniques in progress. So, once again, the claim that the marginal contribution is equal to the wage is confirmed only at switch points.

What, then, is wrong with the arguments I presented? Their mistake is to concentrate on what happens in a single enterprise and forget the reper- cussions elsewhere in the economy. Let us reconsider the argument about George and the marginal contribution of capital. It turned on working out what would be the addition to production in George's enterprise if he added a bit to its capital. So as to keep the aggregate labour force constant we assumed that he spent the extra capital on materials only. Now, if the wage happened to be a switch point he might indeed do that; he might use the capital to equip workers for applying the new technique. But at other levels of the wage George would want to continue with the same technique as before. That means dividing his additional capital between buying more materials and employing more workers, so as to keep the proportions constant. If the aggregate labour force is unchanged, then, the result will be an increased demand for labour against a fixed supply. The wage will have to rise. The rise must be insignificant for George's enterprise because by the definition of competition the enterprise's actions cannot alter prices significantly; George is a price taker. But the insignificant effects on every enterprise in the economy will add up to something important. Every capitalist finds labour costs increased a little. Therefore with the same capital he or she can produce less than before. There is a reduction in output throughout the economy which has to be set against whatever increase there is in George's enterprise. That is what the original argument ignored, and as a result it overestimated capital's marginal contribution except at switch points. There is a similar mistake in the argument that tried to equate the wage with labour's marginal contribution.

Chain-index Capital

That, however, is not the death of the way of thinking I have been describing. It is really quite happy to concede that the wage and rate of profit differ from the corresponding marginal contributions as I defined them, because I measured capital and net production by their values. In the aggregate production function

$$Y = F(K, L)$$

I took Y and K as values, and that, according to this point of view, is a hopeless confusion of prices and quantities. It is not surprising that the function's derivatives, defined that way, are not what they ought to be. The discrepancy is simply a valuation effect.

We ought, then, this theory insists, to treat capital as a quantity of goods, not a value. We must try to sort out the goods that constitute capital from the price that has to be paid for them. Capital-as-goods is not by itself a precise concept because capital consists of a lot of different sorts of goods. Somehow we have to aggregate them together to make a unitary measure — **index** — of the quantity of capital-as-goods. Correspondingly we shall need a unitary index of the prices of these goods, an aggregate of all their separate prices. If we construct our indexes properly, the value of capital, which is what we start off from, will be the product of the quantity index and the price index. Similarly we shall need to separate the value of net production into an index of its quantity and an index of its price.

Now, we know that as the value of capital grows changes in the economy come in two distinct phases, according to whether or not a switch is in progress. This is the clue to constructing the price and quantity indexes. In a switch-point phase, no prices change at all. Any change in the value of net production or of capital must result from real changes in their quantities. So during a switch-point phase we must make sure that the price indexes stay constant and all changes of value are registered as changes in the indexes of quantity. On the other hand, when the economy is not at a switch point but instead staying faithful to one system of techniques, there are no real changes in production per worker or in the materials used per worker. Here, then, any changes in the value of capital or output are changes in price, not quantity. The quantity indexes must be held constant. The essence of this way of thinking is that to each system of techniques (under a given pattern of final demand) there corresponds a unique quantity of capital per worker and a unique quantity of net output per worker. While the system remains in use these things must not alter.

With all this in mind we can set out to redraw our graphs of net production against capital. Previously they had on their axes the *values* of net production and capital. Now they are to have the *quantities* as measured in the new way. For a simple illustration I shall explain how to convert Fig. 4.2.6 (p. 107), which refers to an economy that employs technology 4.1.1 (p. 91).

At the start of the graph the value of capital per worker stands at 1/4 ton. This is the smallest amount of capital that can employ the whole labour force, and it employs it on technique α. Here at the start is a good point to base our price indexes, so let us arbitrarily call the price of capital here 1 and the price of net production 1 too. Since the value of capital is 1/4 we have to say that the quantity of capital is 1/4, and since the value of net production is 3/4 its quantity is 3/4 too. Thus we fix the first point of our reconstructed graph. 3/4 of net production against 1/4 of capital. The graph appears in Fig. 4.5.1.

As the value of capital increases beyond 1/4 technique α continues in use. So long as it does our principles allow the quantities of neither capital nor net production to alter. The point α in Fig. 4.5.1 stands for the whole interval where that technique is in use. The quantity of capital has to stay constant but

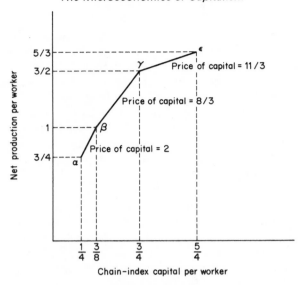

Fig. 4.5.1

its value increases and therefore its price must increase. In fact by the time the switch to technique β begins the value of capital reaches 1/2 (see Fig. 4.2.6), so that the price of capital must reach 2. As for net production, though, Fig. 4.2.6 shows its value to be constant in this interval. Its price is therefore constant too. A simplifying feature of this example, indeed, is that the price index for production never alters, which means we have no need to distinguish the quantity of production from its value.

Now comes the switch to β. Here, as I explained, we keep the price indexes constant and attribute alterations in value to alterations in quantity. During the switch the value of capital grows from 1/2 to 3/4. Its price we have already fixed at 2, so its quantity evidently grows from 1/4 to 3/8. Meanwhile net production goes up to 1. So we find the point marked β in Fig. 4.5.1.

In the next interval of Fig. 4.2.6 technique β is applied on its own. Quantities do not change. The price of capital moves up to 8/3, since its quantity is fixed at 3/8 and we know from Fig. 4.2.6 that its value increases to 1. Then we have another switch, and so on. We can continue constructing Fig. 4.5.1 by alternately keeping prices and quantities constant.

The measure of capital we have just worked out is called a **chain index** for obvious reasons. Other graphs of net production can be converted from value to chain-index quantity terms in just the same way. If we were doing the job on Fig. 4.4.2 where net production is subject to revaluation, net production would appear as a chain index too. A conversion to chain-index terms can also be applied to continuous technologies like the one appearing in Fig. 4.2.7, but I shall excuse myself from explaining the method in such cases.

Figure 4.5.1 is a section of the economy's aggregate production function, now re-expressed in terms of quantities. This function, notice, is no more determined from the technology alone that is the original function expressed in values. Indeed we actually derived the former from the latter as it is presented in Fig. 4.2.6. Both functions depend on assumptions we have made about the society as well as about its technology. In principle any sort of society might use the technology, but the aggregate production functions apply only to a competitive capitalist one. Just because we have now managed to conceive of capital as a quantity rather than a value that does not make it any more like a purely technical concept.

The Marginal Contributions of Chain-index Capital and of Labour

Now compare Fig. 4.2.6 with its *alter ego* Fig. 4.5.1. The latter graph has been purged of all horizontal stretches because they are supposed not to represent changes in real capital. It is left with the sloping sections only, and their slopes have been adjusted. Previously they were equal to the prevailing rate of profit, but now (it is easy to see) they have been multiplied by the price of capital as we have defined it. Had our example contained any changes in the price of net production the slopes would also have been *divided* by that price. The slope of this graph in Fig. 4.5.1 is what now counts as the marginal contribution of capital — the rate at which net production increases in response to increases in chain-index capital. We find, then, that

$$\text{Marginal contribution of capital} = \text{Rate of profit} \times \frac{\text{Price of capital}}{\text{Price of net production}},$$

or, since multiplying capital's marginal contribution by the price of net production gives us the value of the marginal contribution,

Value of marginal contribution of capital = Rate of profit × Price of capital.

If a capitalist owns a unit quantity of capital his or her income from it is its value — price — times the rate of profit. That is what appears on the right of this equation. The equation says, then, that owners of capital receive as income exactly the value of what capital contributes at the margin to production. It is precisely the idea we have been pursuing through these last few pages. It previously appeared in a simpler form, that capital's marginal contribution ought to equal the rate of profit, but the difference is merely that then we conceived of capital and production as values. Now we think of them as quantities they have to be multiplied by an appropriate price before they become values.

Consistently with our redefinition of capital as a quantity we must redefine the marginal contribution of labour as the rate at which increasing the labour force increases net production when the quantity of chain-index capital is held constant. Varying labour without varying chain-index capital, however, cannot be done except by altering the system of techniques in use, because to each system we have insisted that there is a unique capital/labour ratio. Our new definition of labour's marginal contribution therefore only makes sense when the economy is undergoing a switch. And we know already that in the course of a switch the marginal contribution's value is equal to the wage. The definition of capital as a chain index, then, has succeeded in justifying the popular view we set out to investigate: both factors of production receive as income the value of what they contribute, at the margin, to production.

Is there anything wrong with this conclusion?

Faults of the Chain Index

There are, I think, two things wrong. The first is that chain-index capital is not at all a proper measure of capital, even of capital conceived as goods. I discussed capital-as-goods in Chapter 3 (pp. 76–77) and suggested that it is a valid notion to be set alongside capital-as-value. But the goods that constitute capital include wage goods for workers. If workers are paid out of capital, capital however conceived has to include a component for their pay. It is simply wrong, then, to say that each system of techniques requires a unique quantity of capital per worker. It requires a unique quantity of materials per worker, but the total quantity of capital-as-goods per worker depends on the wage. The higher the wage the greater the quantity of capital needed to operate the system.

In any of the distribution diagrams, Fig. 4.2.6 for example, the intervals where capital grows under the dominance of a single system of techniques represent genuine accumulations of real capital. In constructing the chain-index, though, all these expansions of capital are dismissed as mere valuation effects. Certainly there are often valuation effects that occur during these periods, but the underlying growth of capital is not one. We made sure in our choice of numeraire (see p. 78) that a rightward movement in the diagram can only be achieved by saving on the part of capitalists. The example of Fig. 4.2.6 makes this especially obvious because it refers to a single-product economy, which is immune to valuation effects. The capital measured on that diagram's horizontal axis is real capital—capital-as-goods by any standards. In constructing the chain index we simply left out significant phases of the economy's progress. They happen to be the ones where the factors' incomes differ from the values of their marginal contributions. That is how the chain index achieves its aim.

It must be said that none of this constitutes a fair criticism of the chain index itself. It was never intended to be applied to models like mine where wages are financed out of capital. Where capital-as-goods consists of materials only, not wage goods, the idea is more convincing. The conclusion we have to draw is that it makes no sense in circumstances like ours. If workers are paid out of capital, indeed, there is no acceptable way of defining labour's and capital's marginal contributions that makes them equal to their incomes.

The second thing wrong with the chain index is a fault even on its home ground where capital consists of materials only. Figure 4.5.2 shows the chain index version of the net production graph in Fig. 4.4.3. This is the example with reswitching, derived from technology (4.3.2). Because technique α appears here twice in the chain the construction of the chain index has forced us to give it two different capital/labour ratios. This contradicts the whole

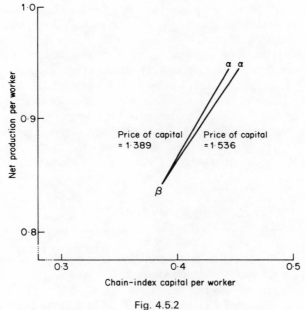

Fig. 4.5.2

principle on which the chain index is based: that each technique has a unique ratio of its own. It is obvious that whenever a technology has reswitching the same problem will arise, and also that it has nothing to do with labour's being paid out of capital. The possibility of reswitching, then, invalidates the chain index. This is reswitching's chief significance.

Conclusion

This section has been a digression. Marginal analysis is not very much help to us in our explorations of the behaviour of economies. When we worked out the determinants of the choice of technique, of the wage, of prices and so on it contributed rather little. (It would have been more useful, however, if more of our examples had been continuous technologies.) I have given space to it because of its importance in the history of economics. We found some valid facts relating prices and the marginal productivities of inputs, which we defined strictly from the technology. We also investigated an idea about the incomes of the factors labour and capital and their marginal contributions to production. In the end it turned out to be rather unsuccessful. The idea's popularity arose, I think, from a misunderstanding about capital. People tried to treat capital as an input into production very much symmetrical to labour. They imagined it is in some way a technical requirement of production and should obey much the same rules as technical inputs. They identified capital with the "capital goods" that capital buys, because these are, of course, technical requirements of production. When difficulties emerged they thought of them as difficulties over aggregating the capital goods to form a unitary quantity of capital. But the fundamental mistake is to treat capital that way in the first place. Capital-as-goods is an important aspect of capital, a form that capital takes sometimes during the course of production, but it is not the same thing as the capital. Capital cannot be separated from prices, those social, not technical, entities. One advantage of working with a model where capital is partly spent on labour is that no one would make the mistake of identifying capital with the things it buys: that would mean identifying capital with labour.

Questions on Chapter 4

1. Explain why, if we assume that techniques have constant returns to scale and can be employed in any combination, isoquants must slope downwards and be convex towards the origin.
2. We found in Section 4.2 that for the profit-maximizing process the marginal rate of substitution of corn for labour will be equal to the wage whenever the former is defined. In places where the marginal rate of substitution is not defined, is there a similar rule about the wage? (Are there limits on what the wage may be?)
3. For a single product economy, the following diagram shows the distribution of income between workers and capitalists. Explain why.

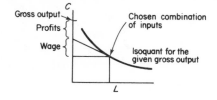

4. A corn economy has a choice between this technique

$$3/8 \text{ corn } \& 1/2 \text{ labour} \longrightarrow 1 \text{ corn}$$

and any technique given by the production function

$$x = 2\sqrt{(CL)}.$$

Draw the economy's wage–profit curve. Why does it have no maximum rate of profit? Draw an isoquant. Draw the distribution diagram.
5. Inefficient techniques will never be adopted at any level of the wage. Of what other techniques may this be true?
6. For a single-product technology prove that an increase in the wage, if it causes a switch in technique, will always bring into use a technique that is less labour intensive and less fertile.
7. Show that the following technology leads to reswitching:

71/144 corn	& 7/8 labour	$\longrightarrow$ 1 corn
1/6 corn & 1/6 fertilizer	& 1 labour	$\longrightarrow$ 1 corn
1 corn	& 1 labour	$\longrightarrow$ 1 fertilizer.

8. An economy has the following technology. In the corn industry there is only this one technique:

$$1/4 \text{ corn } \& 1 \text{ labour} \longrightarrow 1 \text{ corn.}$$

In the glue industry glue is produced according to this production function:

$$x_2 = \sqrt{(C_2 L_2)}$$

where x_2 is the output of glue and C_2 and L_2 are the inputs of corn and labour into the glue industry. Take corn as the numeraire. When the wage is w show that the technique actually selected in the glue industry will be:

$$\sqrt{w} \text{ corn } \& 1/\sqrt{w} \text{ labour} \longrightarrow 1 \text{ glue.}$$

Find the price of glue as a function of the wage. Assume that final demand is for glue only, and let the net production of glue be y_2. Find the gross productions of the two industries. Hence show that if the economy's labour force is L and its stock of capital K then

$$L = \left(\frac{1}{\sqrt{w}} + \frac{4}{3} \sqrt{w} \right) y_2$$

and

$$K = \left(\frac{7}{3} \sqrt{w} + \frac{4}{3} w \sqrt{w} \right) y_2.$$

Find the level of K/L that makes the rate of profit nought. Draw (roughly) a distribution diagram for this economy (i.e. a graph of w against K/L and of $p_2 y_2/L$ against K/L). Does the accumulation of capital increase or decrease the economy's output of glue?

9. Convert the graph of net production in Fig. 4.4.1 into chain-index form.

Appendix: Changes in Integrated Capital/Labour Ratios at a Switch

On p. 116 I postponed to this appendix a proof that when there is a switch from one system of techniques to another, all products will have their integrated capital/labour ratios altered in the same direction.

I shall presume that the switch is one where only a single industry alters its technique. This is the normal case (see p. 115); I shall mention others at the end. We may as well take the affected industry to be the first and we shall take it to be basic because it is only the choice of technique in basic industries that we are concerned with.

Suppose that the switch *reduces* the integrated capital/labour ratio of product 1. I shall show it reduces every product's ratio. Let product 1's integrated requirements of labour and capital be l_1^* and k_1^* before the switch and $\bar{l}_1^*$ and $\bar{k}_1^*$ after. So

$$k_1^*/l_1^* > \bar{k}_1^*/\bar{l}_1^*.$$

First I shall show that $k_1^* > \bar{k}_1^*$ and $l_1^* < \bar{l}_1^*$. At the switch the wage, the rate of profit and prices are the same in both systems. Product 1's price before the switch is

$$w l_1^* + r k_1^*$$

where w and r are the wage and the rate of profit (see (3.3.10) on p. 54). This equals the price after the switch:

$$w l_1^* + r k_1^* = w \bar{l}_1^* + r \bar{k}_1^*.$$

$$\therefore \quad w \frac{l_1^*}{\bar{l}_1^*} + r \frac{k_1^*}{l_1^*} \frac{l_1^*}{\bar{l}_1^*} = w + r \frac{\bar{k}_1^*}{\bar{l}_1^*} < w + r \frac{k_1^*}{l_1^*}.$$

$$\therefore \quad \left(w + r \frac{k_1^*}{l_1^*} \right) \frac{l_1^*}{\bar{l}_1^*} < \left(w + r \frac{k_1^*}{l_1^*} \right).$$

$$\therefore \quad \frac{l_1^*}{\bar{l}_1^*} < 1.$$

$$\therefore \quad l_1^* < \bar{l}_1^*.$$

The proof that $k_1^* > \bar{k}_1^*$ is similar.

Now we know that product 1's integrated requirement of labour is increased I shall show that every product's is increased. I shall use the standard notation of Chapter 3 to represent the system of techniques in use before the switch. Remember that only the first industry alters its technique at the switch, so l_j and a_{ij} are unchanged for all i and for all j except 1.

Take any product j other than the first. I shall break down its integrated requirement of labour into components of progressively more and more indirect labour. To start with, its integrated requirement is the sum of its direct requirement and the integrated requirements of its inputs

$$l_j^* = l_j + a_{1j}l_1^* + a_{2j}l_2^* + a_{3j}l_3^* + \ldots + a_{nj}l_n^*.$$

Now we split up in the same way the integrated requirements of all the inputs except the first:

$$l_j^* = l_j + a_{1j}l_1^* + a_{2j}(l_2 + a_{12}l_1^* + a_{22}l_2^* + a_{32}l_3^* + \ldots + a_{n2}l_n^*)$$
$$+ a_{3j}(l_3 + a_{13}l_1^* + a_{23}l_2^* + a_{33}l_3^* + \ldots + a_{n3}l_n^*)$$
$$+ \ldots$$
$$+ a_{nj}(l_n + a_{1n}l_1^* + a_{2n}l_2^* + a_{3n}l_3^* + \ldots + a_{nn}l_n^*)$$
$$= \{l_j + (a_{2j}l_2 + a_{3j}l_3 + \ldots + a_{nj}l_n)\} + \{a_{1j} + (a_{2j}a_{12} + a_{3j}a_{13} + \ldots + a_{nj}a_{1n})\}l_1^*$$
$$+ (a_{2j}a_{22} + a_{3j}a_{23} + \ldots + a_{nj}a_{2n})l_2^* + (a_{2j}a_{32} + a_{3j}a_{33} + \ldots + a_{nj}a_{3n})l_3^*$$
$$+ \ldots + (a_{2j}a_{n2} + a_{3j}a_{n3} + \ldots + a_{nj}a_{nn})l_n^*.$$

Next we again split up $l_2^*, l_3^*, \ldots l_n^*$ as before. The process is repeated again and again. It leaves us on the right with (a) terms containing the technical coefficients l_2, l_j, etc. and a_{12}, a_{1j}, a_{3j}, etc. but none referring to the first industry, (b) terms containing these coefficients times l_1^*, and (c) a residual containing l_2^*, $l_3^* \ldots l_n^*$ which becomes infinitely small as the dissection is continued. We know that (b) must be positive because all the coefficients are non-negative and because since product 1 is basic it must appear somewhere as a direct or indirect input into product j.

Now comes the switch. The terms in (a) stay the same, (b) increases because l_1^* increases and (c) is insignificant. So l_j^* increases.

An exactly similar argument shows that k_j^* falls. There is no worry about revaluing capital because at the switch there are no price changes. Consequently k_j^*/l_j^* falls, and this applies to every j.

If k_1^*/l_1^* should rise at the switch or stay constant the same proof will show that every integrated capital/labour ratio will do likewise. So we have proved what we wanted.

A word now about switches that involve a change of technique in more than one industry. These are, in effect, two or more switches that happen to coincide. They occur where several wage–profit curves meet on the envelope of wage–profit curves. At these multiple switches it is possible for the integrated capital/labour ratios of different goods to move in opposite directions. What happens to the aggregate capital/labour ratio will then depend on the pattern of final demand.

5.

SCARCE RESOURCES

Section 5.1   A Single-product Economy

A Single Technique

I am now going to incorporate scarce resources into our model. Once more I shall do it in the simplest possible case first. So take the single-product technology we originally worked with in Chapter 2:

$$1/4 \text{ corn \& 1 land \& 1 labour} \rightarrow 1 \text{ corn}. \qquad (5.1.1)$$

All the usual assumptions—constant returns to scale, no alternative techniques and so on—continue to apply. But now we shall pay more attention to the input of land than we did in Chapter 2, because we shall be assuming that it is scarce and needs to be paid for.

We can calculate corn's integrated requirement of land. For a ton of corn let it be m^* acres. Then m^* must be the sum of the direct requirement, 1 acre, and the indirect requirement. The latter is the integrated land requirement of the materials, which is evidently $(1/4)m^*$. So

$$m^* = 1 + (1/4)m^*.$$
$$\therefore\ m^* = 4/3.$$

The economy we shall take to be capitalist. It contains capitalists and workers in the usual relationship, and there will now also be a third class: the **owners of land**. In order to farm, capitalists must rent land from the landowners. Rent is the landowners' source of income. Why they can manage to charge rent, and how much they can charge, is what we shall be studying.

I shall assume that rent has to be paid in advance; a capitalist will not be allowed to farm a piece of land unless he or she has already paid rent for it. It is therefore another call on capital, together with wages and the cost of materials. I could have made the opposite assumption that rent is paid in arrears, and it would have led to some differences in the analysis. I chose this one for neatness and convenience.

Let corn be the numeraire. Let the wage be w and the rent charged for an acre of land t. The rate of profit, r, we can calculate in the usual way:

$$r = \frac{1-(1/4+t+w)}{(1/4+t+w)}.$$

$$\therefore \quad 1 = (1+r)(1/4+t+w). \tag{5.1.2}$$

This is the **wage–profit–rent equation**. It relates the incomes of the three classes. Its graph is the surface shown in Fig. 5.1.1. The coordinates given in brackets in the diagram show (r, t, w) in that order. Like the simple wage–profit curve of Chapter 2 (Figure 2.2.1 on p. 15) it shows how a worker's net production, 3/4 ton of corn, can be divided between the worker, his or her employer and the landlord. The surface slopes downwards, as it were, in each direction; one class can only gain at the expense of one of the others. The diagram shows a section of the surface for a constant rate of profit r. Notice that the section is a straight line because for a constant r (5.1.2) is a linear relationship between t and w. The slope of the line is the technology's land/labour ratio, in this case one.

Whereabouts on its wage–profit–rent surface the economy finds itself I shall

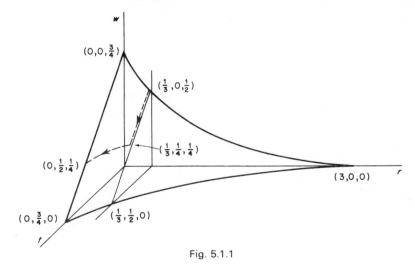

Fig. 5.1.1

assume to be settled by **competitive markets in land and labour**. Let the economy's labour force be L and its supply of land M. For a moment assume that L is less than M. Then not all the land will be farmed because of a shortage of workers; some will have to be left vacant. The owners of vacant land will receive no rent. Consequently no rent can be charged anywhere, because any owner who tried to charge rent would find his or her tenant enticed away by the offer of a presently vacant farm at a lower rent. The situation is therefore exactly the one Chapter 2 dealt with: land is free and plentiful.

Now imagine that the labour force is growing and capital growing with it at the same rate; the economy is in proportional growth (see p. 22). Suppose the wage (which must be constant) is $1/2$. Eventually L will grow to equal M. Then every piece of land will be farmed. Land will become scarce. If the labour force were still to continue growing the wage would have to drop to nought, for the same reason as rent was nought before. It would be silly to suppose that the labour force can increase when the wage is nought, so if we are to squeeze any sense out of our model we shall have to assume that the increase stops at the moment when all the land becomes occupied. The most natural way to set this up would be to suppose that the level of the wage influences the growth of the labour force. As the wage falls towards nought there is some level at which the growth stops. Call this "the subsistence wage", and assume for the sake of argument that it is $1/4$.

At the moment L becomes equal to M the wage will drop to the subsistence level. The way this happens is as follows. Capitalists find themselves suddenly competing against each other for land, and having to pay rent for it. Part of their capital will be directed away from paying wages to paying rent. If K is the economy's stock of capital it must be divided up into: $(1/4)L$ to supply workers with seed corn, tM to pay rent and wL to pay wages.

$$K \quad = (1/4)L + tM + wL.$$
$$\therefore K/L = 1/4 + t + w.$$
$$\therefore t + w = K/L - 1/4. \tag{5.1.3}$$

(Remember that L and M are equal.) Of the capital available per worker, this equation says, a quarter of a ton must be set aside for seed and the rest is divided between worker and landowner. Now that land has become scarce the division moves in favour of the landowner. Meanwhile the rate of profit will not alter.

All this happens instantaneously. The labour force has now stopped growing, but nothing need stop capital from accumulating. If capitalists save some fixed fraction of their income they will presumably still do so. Clearly there is no question of proportional growth any more because land cannot grow. Capital per worker K/L (and capital per acre) will increase. By (5.1.3) rents plus wages will increase. Since the wage has to stay at the subsistence level (if it rose the labour force would grow) all the benefit will be taken by landowners. The accumulation of capital will raise rents and cause the rate of profit to fall. If capital continues to accumulate the rate of profit will eventually reach nought.

The economy's progress is shown by the dotted line in Fig. 5.1.1.

Choice of Technique

We have done what we can with technology 5.1.1, but it is too rigid to be a very instructive example. There is only one proportion of labour to land that allows both to be fully employed. It is more natural to suppose that once all the land is cultivated the labour force might still grow, working the land more intensively. Let us explore that possibility. We need a technology with a choice of less and more intensive techniques:

α: 1/4 corn & 1 land & 1 labour $\rightarrow$ 1 corn

β: 1/3 corn & 1/3 land & 4/3 labour $\rightarrow$ 1 corn. $\left.\right\}$ (5.1.4)

Each technique will have a wage–profit–rent surface. The two are shown in Fig. 5.1.2. They intersect along the heavy curve. At any combination of wage and rent the technique selected will be the one with the higher rate of profit. So the economy's wage–profit–rent surface is the outer envelope of the two individual ones. Obviously it slopes downwards. The intersection is a **locus of switch points**.

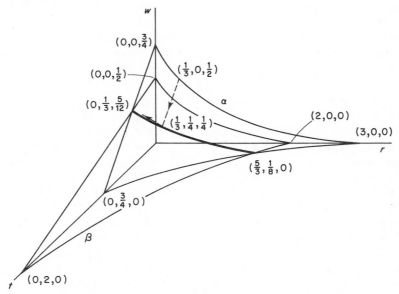

Fig. 5.1.2

Figure 5.1.3 is a section through the diagram at a particular rate of profit (1/3). The switch point at this rate of profit has $w=1/4$ and $t=1/4$. The diagram shows that, given a constant rate of profit, a fall in the wage through the switch point brings in technique β to replace α. Technique β has the lower land/labour ratio (and of course the lower integrated land/labour ratio). So the fall in the wage brings in the less land-intensive technique. This is a general rule for single-product economies. I shall leave you to see why; it is rather obvious if one bears in mind that for a constant rate of profit the sections of the wage–profit–rent surfaces are straight lines. The rule, however, does not hold good for economies with several products.

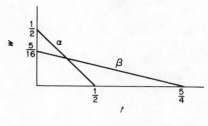

Fig. 5.1.3

Now let us see what we can expect to happen in the economy as the labour force grows and capital accumulates. As in the previous example let us suppose that initially land is plentiful and the rent nought. Then technique α will be in use. We may as well assume that the economy is growing proportionally as before, with a wage of 1/2 and a profit rate of 1/3. The land will all eventually be occupied. The labour force cannot continue growing after that unless technique β comes into use, and that cannot happen unless the wage drops to the switch point. So the wage must drop immediately. The wage will fall to 1/4, and that will make rent 1/4 too (see Fig. 5.1.2 or 5.1.3).

Let us assume for this new example that the labour force continues to grow as before. The extra workers will be accommodated on the land by using the more intensive technique β. The switch to β will take time; how much time depends on how quickly the labour force grows. If, for instance, the area of land is one million acres, then the switch will begin when the labour force reaches one million and be complete when it reaches four million. Meanwhile the economy will have to stay at a switch point. That does not mean, though, that there can be no changes in the wage or rent. During the course of the switch the rate of profit may alter, taking the economy to a different point on the locus of switch points. As an example, we may assume that capital continues to grow at the same rate as the labour force. Then the ratio of capital to labour in the economy as a whole will stay constant. What will happen? We must work out how much capital is required per worker by each of the techniques. When rent is t and the wage w, technique α has a capital/labour ratio

$$1/4 + t + w,$$

and technique β

$$\frac{1/3 + (1/3)t + (4/3)w}{4/3}.$$

At the original switch, where t is $1/4$ and w is $1/4$, these ratios are $3/4$ and $9/16$ respectively. Technique β, then, has the smaller capital/labour ratio. Since β is progressively taking over from α the economy's ratio would, other things being equal, drop. This tendency can only be counteracted by a progressive increase in the wage. So the economy must move upwards and leftwards along the locus of switch points. Rent will progressively increase too, and the rate of profit will fall. The dotted curve in Fig. 5.1.2 shows the economy's progress. Where it will all end up depends on whether capital continues to accumulate at the same rate, on how quickly technique β takes over all the land, and so on. I do not want to pursue the details any further.

Clearly if there were many techniques to choose from a good number of complicated situations might arise. And what happens will depend particularly on the behaviour of the supplies of labour, land and capital. In this introductory section I have tried out some alternative assumptions about the supplies of these things. In a single-product model that is not too hard to do, but when we go on to more general models we shall find the analysis so difficult that we have to make some rather restrictive assumptions about them simply in order to make progress.

Section 5.2   Prices and Distribution

The Basic Equations

Now let us suppose that our economy has n products. Let its technology be represented by an input-output matrix A, a row vector of (direct) labour coefficients l, and a row vector of (direct) land input coefficients m. So we have simply added the vector m to the model we looked at in Chapter 3. All Chapter 3's assumptions are retained.

The vector l^* of integrated requirements of labour turned out to be

$l(I-A)^{-1}$ (p. 40) and for the same reason the vector of integrated requirements of land is

$$m^* = m(I-A)^{-1}. \tag{5.2.1}$$

The products' integrated land/labour ratios are m_1^*/l_1^*, m_2^*/l_2^* and so on.

Assume that the economy is capitalist and competitive, with a class of workers, a class of capitalists and a class of landowners. Assume there are competitive markets in labour and land. Rents and wages are both paid out of capital. Let the prices of products be the row vector p, let rent be t and the wage w. For the moment I shall not specify a numeraire. Let r be the rate of profit. As before (p. 44) we can define a vector of integrated requirements of capital.

$$k^* = (pA + tm + wl)(I-A)^{-1}. \tag{5.2.2}$$

The rate of profit in the first industry is

$$r = \frac{p_1 - (p_1 a_{11} + p_2 a_{21} + \ldots + p_n a_{n1} + tm_1 + wl_1)}{(p_1 a_{11} + p_2 a_{21} + \ldots + p_n a_{n1} + tm_1 + wl_1)}.$$

$$\therefore \quad p_1 = (1+r)(p_1 a_{11} + p_2 a_{21} + \ldots + p_n a_{n1} + tm_1 + wl_1).$$

Similarly

$$p_2 = (1+r)(p_1 a_{12} + p_2 a_{22} + \ldots + p_n a_{n2} + tm_2 + wl_2)$$

and so on. There is a similar equation for each industry. They may all be put in vector notation:

$$p = (1+r)(pA + tm + wl). \tag{5.2.3}$$

The unknowns in these equations are r, t, w and the n components of p. That makes $(n+3)$ unknowns altogether. To fix the level of prices a numeraire needs to be arbitrarily chosen, so we have effectively $(n+1)$ equations. There are two degrees of freedom, then. Once we fix two of the unknowns all the rest will be determined.

To put the equations in (5.2.3) into a more usable form let us solve them for p.

$$p = (1+r)pA + (1+r)(tm + wl).$$
$$\therefore \quad p(I-(1+r)A) = (1+r)(tm + wl).$$
$$\therefore \quad p = t(1+r)m(I-(1+r)A)^{-1} + w(1+r)l(I-(1+r)A)^{-1}. \tag{5.2.4}$$

(The last step assumes that $(I-(1+r)A)$ is not singular; see p. 52 of Chapter 3.) The terms $(1+r)m(I-(1+r)A)^{-1}$ and $(1+r)l(I-(1+r)A)^{-1}$ have a simple meaning. They may be expanded into a series by the method I used on p. 57 of Chapter 3. For instance

$$(1+r)l(I-(1+r)A)^{-1} = (1+r)l + (1+r)^2 lA + (1+r)^3 lAA + \ldots$$

I explained on p. 57 that the terms on the right are the inputs of direct and indirect labour needed in production, compounded forward to the time when the final product emerges. So the vector $(1+r)l(I-(1+r)A)^{-1}$ may be called the vector of **compounded requirements of labour**. I shall write it $\hat{l}(r)$. I show it explicitly as a function of r to remind you that, unlike the simple integrated requirement l^* of labour, the compound requirement is not a constant of the technology. So

$$\hat{l}(r)=(1+r)l(I-(1+r)A)^{-1}. \tag{5.2.5}$$

Similarly

$$\hat{m}(r)=(1+r)m(I-(1+r)A)^{-1} \tag{5.2.6}$$

is the **compounded requirement of land**. Equation (5.2.4) tells us, then, that

$$p=t\hat{m}(r)+w\hat{l}(r); \tag{5.2.7}$$

prices are the compounded cost of land plus the compounded cost of labour.

Profits, Rents and Wages

Equation (5.2.7) shows, for one thing, the relationship between the three distributional variables t, w and r. Let z be the numeraire vector (see p. 43 of Chapter 3) so that by definition

$$pz=1.$$

Postmultiplying (5.2.7) by z gives

$$pz=t\hat{m}(r)z+w\hat{l}(r)z.$$
$$\therefore \quad 1=t\hat{m}(r)z+w\hat{l}(r)z. \tag{5.2.8}$$

This is the wage–profit–rent equation. Its graph will be some surface such as the one shown in Fig. 5.2.1. The economy might find itself at any point on this surface; our equations so far tell us nothing about where. The surface slopes downwards. That is to say, if one of the variables r, t or w increases at least one of the other two must decrease. If rent is constant profit can only be increased at the expense of a declining wage, and if the wage is constant profit can only be increased at the expense of declining rent. We can be sure of this for reasons I shall give in a moment. They are a little complicated but essentially just like the ones given in Chapter 3 (pp. 49–51) for the downward slope of the wage–profit curve.

What causes the complication is that there may be some ambiguity about the direction in which the wage or rent changes. In the model without land we knew (p. 51) that if the wage falls relative to one product it falls relative to them all. So when talking about the direction of changes in the wage we never

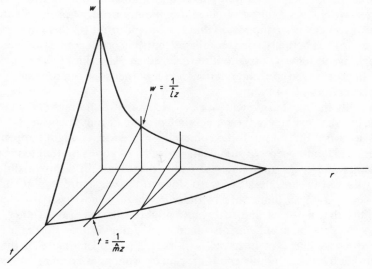

$$w = \frac{1}{\hat{l}z}$$

$$t = \frac{1}{\hat{m}z}$$

Fig. 5.2.1

had to worry about the choice of numeraire. But in our new model the wage may increase relative to some product and simultaneously decrease relative to another. To see that such a thing must be possible, imagine that the rate of profit increases for some reason and that, relative to some product or other, the wage stays constant (so there must evidently have been some change in rent). Except in very unusual circumstances the change will bring about some alteration in the relative prices of products. Relative to the standard we are using, against which the wage stays constant, some products will go up and others down; it would only be mere chance if they all happened to go up or all down. Evidently, then, against some products the wage will rise, and against others fall.

When we say the wage rises or falls, then, we shall always have to say in terms of what. Of course the same goes for rent. With this in mind I shall prove the following. Suppose that the rate of profit rises, and also that, in terms of some product or other, the wage also rises or perhaps stays constant. Then rent falls in terms of *every* product. Here is the proof. The change we are talking about will probably change the relative prices of products. Pick the product that has fallen most, that has declined (or stayed constant) relative to all the others. Since the wage has risen or stayed constant relative to some product or other it has certainly risen or stayed constant relative to this one. So this product has fallen or perhaps stayed constant, relative to every other product, and also the wage. If it had *also* fallen or stayed constant relative to rent it would have fallen or stayed constant relative to every one of the inputs used in its production, since the only inputs are products, labour and land. That, however, would mean that producing it could not be more profitable than it was before. Yet we are supposing that the rate of profit (in this industry and every other) has actually risen. It follows that this product must in fact have risen relative to rent. Relative to it rent has fallen. And since this product has itself fallen or stayed constant relative to every other product, rent has plainly fallen relative to all of them.

Naturally the same argument works if we swap around rent and wages. It establishes that, whatever the numeraire, profit can only increase if rent or wages decrease. But it establishes something more too. It might happen that workers and landowners consume different sorts of goods, so that to measure *real* wages and *real* rent we should want to measure in terms of different standards. Given that, the downward slope of the wage–profit–rent surface, whatever is used as numeraire in drawing it, does not itself prevent the possibility that real rent and real wages might both increase together, even though the rate of profit has also increased. Imagine that horses are our numeraire and that rent in terms of horses is a good measure of the real standard of living of landowners. If the rate of profit goes up and rent goes up in terms of horses, the wage–profit–rent surface shows that the wage falls in terms of horses. But might not the real wage (which should perhaps be measured in terms of pigs) go up? My argument has shown that the answer is no. It would have been extraordinary had it been yes, since that would have meant everybody's real income increasing simultaneously. But it is as well to have this confirmation of what seems obvious.

So much for the complication. It occurs only when the rate of profit alters. If the rate of profit is constant, the connection between rent and the wage is rather simple. A constant rate of profit makes the compounded requirements $\hat{m}(r)$ and $\hat{l}(r)$ of land and labour constant too. Write them $\hat{m}$ and $\hat{l}$. Then (5.2.8) is the equation of a straight-line relationship between t and w. The slope of the straight line is $\hat{m}z/\hat{l}z$ downwards. Of course this slope will normally be different at different levels of r. Figure 5.2.1 shows some sections of the wage–profit–rent surface made at different levels of r.

If the rate of profit stays constant, then when the wage goes up it goes up relative to every product. So there is none of the ambiguity I have mentioned. The same is true for rent of course. I leave you to work out the proof.

Prices and Distribution

What about the influence of the distribution of income on the prices of products? It may be helpful to start by casting the basic equation (5.2.3) in a different form.

$$p = pA + tm + wl + r(pA + tm + wl).$$
$$\therefore\; p(I-A) = tm + wl + r(pA + tm + wl).$$
$$\therefore\; p = tm(I-A)^{-1} + wl(I-A)^{-1} + r(pA + tm + wl)(I-A)^{-1}.$$
$$\therefore\; p = tm^* + wl^* + rk^*.$$

This equation makes explicit the requirement of capital in production whereas in (5.2.7) it was hidden in the compounding of land and labour. Compare it with (3.3.10) on p. 54. Prices, this equation says, are made up of the payments for the land, labour and capital employed directly and indirectly in production. It makes a few facts rather obvious. For instance, if the rate of profit is nought relative prices will be a weighted average of the integrated requirements of labour and land. If m^*, l^* and k^* are all proportional to each other relative prices will be constant, unaffected by the distribution of income. But when it comes to understanding changes in prices the equation can be as deceptive as its counterpart in Chapter 3 (see pp. 54–56). The vector k^* of integrated requirements of capital is not a constant but changes when the rate of profit changes. Unlike m^* and l^*, it is subject to valuation effects. For this reason what happens to prices when the rate of profit changes is unpredictable (see p. 55). But k^* is also likely to alter even if the rate of profit stays constant but the wage and rent alter. The definition of k^* in (5.2.2) makes that clear. Therefore it is not even obvious how prices will change when the distribution of income shifts between workers and landowners. One would naturally expect that a falling wage associated with a rising rent would raise the relative price of products with a high integrated land/labour ratio. But this need not be true. So we have found yet another awkward consequence of valuation effects. An important thing to notice about it is that it is, once again, caused by the existence of capital and profit. It is the revaluation of capital that causes trouble even though it is not the result of a change in the rate of profit. And if the rate of profit happened to be nought, so that

$$p = tm^* + wl^*,$$

the difficulty would not occur; a fall in the wage together with a rise in rent would be guaranteed to raise the relative price of land-intensive products.

However, provided the rate of profit stays constant we can actually come to a definite conclusion about the behaviour of prices when wages and rent alter. We can use (5.2.7) again. The vectors $\hat{m}$ and $\hat{l}$ depend only on r (and the technology) as the definitions in (5.2.5) and (5.2.6) show. If r is constant so are they. Now suppose t goes up with r remaining constant, so that w falls. Then (5.2.7) shows that this puts more weight on $\hat{m}$ in the determination of prices and less on $\hat{l}$. Relative prices are a sort of mixture of compounded land requirements and compounded labour requirements, and as distribution shifts towards landowners the former tend to predominate. It is plain, in fact, from (5.2.7) that the goods whose relative prices will increase are the ones with a comparatively high compounded requirement of land. To be precise, when rent rises and the wage falls in such a way that the rate of profit is unaltered then one product will rise relative to another if it has a greater compounded land/labour ratio.

So there is this one straightforward rule governing the behaviour of prices. It depends on the rate of profit's constancy, of course. If the rate of profit were to change more or less anything might happen; in Chapter 3 (p. 55) we found no rule for that case. But with a constant rate of profit we know that movements in relative prices are governed by compounded land/labour ratios. The crucial point, though, is that these ratios are not the same as the *integrated* land/labour ratios. The latter are technical constants telling us the relative land and labour intensities of the products' production processes. The compounded ratios depend also on the distribution of income. A product may be more land intensive than another — have a greater integrated land/labour ratio — but at some rate of profit have a lower compounded land/labour ratio. If so its price will move in the opposite direction to the one one might expect from the land and labour intensities.

Here is an example. Let

$$A = \begin{pmatrix} 0 & 0\cdot1 & 0 \\ 0 & 0 & 0\cdot1 \\ 0\cdot8 & 0 & 0 \end{pmatrix}$$
$$m = (2 \quad 1 \quad 0)$$
$$l = (1 \quad 1 \quad 1).$$

Then it turns out that m_1^*/l_1^* is $1\cdot11$ and m_2^*/l_2^* is $1\cdot02$. So product 1 is more land intensive than 2. But if the rate of profit is one then $\hat{m}_1/\hat{l}_1$ is $0\cdot79$ and $\hat{m}_2/\hat{l}_2$ is $0\cdot92$. So by (5.2.7) we know that at this rate of profit an increasing rent will raise the price of the less land-intensive product 2 relative to product 1.

The nearer is the rate of profit to nought the nearer will the compounded requirements be to the integrated requirements. Therefore the less likely is this "perverse" behaviour of prices.

Section 5.3   Distribution and the Supply of Resources

Supply Functions

Now we have looked at the relationships amongst prices and incomes the time has come to complete the model by deciding how the variables can be finally determined. Our basic equation (5.2.3), remember, left two unknowns to be settled. I am going to assume that they get settled in *competitive markets for land and labour*.

The demand for both these inputs comes from capitalists and the supply from landowners and workers. I shall be analysing the equilibrium of supply and demand in much the way I did in Section 3.4 of Chapter 3, but there is one problem to deal with first. In any industry the ratio of land to labour is rigidly determined by the technology. In the economy as a whole the ratio also depends partly on the structure of production: the more important are the land-intensive industries, for instance, the higher the ratio will be. But once the structure is determined (by the pattern of final demand) no change in prices or distribution can change that ratio. So unless the supplies of labour and land happen to be in precisely the right proportion they cannot both be fully employed. This is a difficulty for our theory because it would mean that in equilibrium either rent or the wage would have to be nought, and if that is plausible for rent it is certainly not for the wage. We met the problem in Section 5.1 (p. 149) and there I solved it by assuming that there is some wage that causes the labour force neither to grow nor shrink. Then once land is fully employed the wage will have to stay at this level, and the aggregate land/labour ratio will be kept at precisely what technology requires.

I am now going to take an alternative way out of the difficulty. Up to now in this book I have always assumed that the supply of labour in any particular year is given simply by the size the labour force happens to be that year. But I might equally well have assumed that the supply of labour in any year is not fixed but depends on, say, the wage. A higher wage might induce more people to go to work or, alternatively, fewer (because, perhaps, when the wage is high families can afford to have fewer of their members as wage earners). Let us now make this assumption that the wage influences the supply of labour. Then we can leave to the wage the task of adjusting the economy's aggregate land/labour ratio to what technology requires.

Let us try this out in an example. Take this technology:

$$A = \begin{pmatrix} 0 & 1/2 \\ 1/3 & 0 \end{pmatrix}$$

$$m = \begin{pmatrix} 2 & 1 \end{pmatrix}$$

$$l = \begin{pmatrix} 1 & 3 \end{pmatrix}.$$

It is easy to work out that product 1's integrated requirement of land is 14/5 and of labour 12/5. So if we suppose that final demand is for product 1 only the land and labour employed in the economy will have to be in the ratio 14:12. Assume that the quantity of land is a fixed amount, 14 units. And assume that labour is supplied according to the function

$$L = 150w - 1/2$$

where w is the wage measured in terms of product 1. To bring the labour force into the correct proportion to land L must be twelve. According to the supply function w must therefore be $1/12$.

The economy's wage–profit–rent equation turns out to be

$$(1+r)^2(1+2t+6w)+6(1+r)(2t+w)-6=0.$$

Now we know that w is $1/12$ we have to fix t and r together. They will be determined by the relative supplies of land and capital. There are, we assumed, 14 units of land. And let us assume that the supply of capital is $17/3$ units measured in terms of product 1. Then it turns out that the equilibrium rent is $1/12$ and the equilibrium rate of profit $1/2$.

There is a hidden trap in making the supply of labour depend on the wage only. In deciding how much labour to supply workers will pay attention to the wage compared with the prices of the goods they intend to buy with it. It would be more plausible to write the supply function $L(w,p)$ rather than $L(w)$. However, if the numeraire is chosen judiciously the simple form may be acceptable. Suppose the numeraire is a vector of goods in the proportions that workers regularly buy them in. Then w represents the quantity of these goods they can buy. It is the "real" wage. And it is not totally implausible to assume that the supply of labour depends on the real wage only. So for the sake of simplicity we may write the supply of labour as $L(w)$, but we must remember that that commits us to a particular choice of numeraire.

In section 5.1 I arranged to align the supplies of labour and land in the correct proportions by assuming that the labour force grows when the wage is above some subsistence level and shrinks when it is below it. That can be thought of as an extreme version of the new assumption that the supply of labour depends on the wage. It is the case of infinitely elastic labour supply; in the long run any quantity of labour will be supplied at the subsistence wage.

Having made the supply of labour depend on the wage we gain some generality if we also allow the supply of land to depend on rent: $M(t)$. Again, this is a simplified assumption; it would really be better to make it depend on rent and prices: $M(t,p)$. If we use the simple form we are committed to having as numeraire a vector of goods representing the proportions of landowners' consumption, so that t represents the real rent. And if we simultaneously assume that L depends only on w and M depends only on t we are implicitly assuming that workers and landowners consume goods in the same proportions. This, then, is a restrictive assumption.

The Supply Locus

In previous chapters I have described the way the economy's equilibrium is determined and then gone on to some comparative statics: to describing the effects on the equilibrium of changes in the supply of capital, in the pattern of demand and so on. The example above gives an idea of how equilibrium is determined in our new model, and it would be easy enough to try out in the example the effects of shifting demand to product 2, of increasing the supply of land and so on. But beyond such very simple examples the model we have now arrived at is so immensely complicated in its workings that there is no neat and simple way of analysing its equilibrium, and there are scarcely any general conclusions we can draw about its comparative statics. In order to make any headway at all in the analysis we shall have to make a number of special assumptions. Different special assumptions might lead to different conclusions. We might, for instance, assume that the supply of land is inelastic and see what rules of comparative statics emerge from that. But actually I shall make a different set of assumptions. They are not necessarily particularly plausible but they lead to a method of analysis that seems to me useful. It offers quite a comprehensible idea of how the parts of the economy are related together. And it can be generalized (see Section 5.5).

The first thing I shall assume is that there is a fixed pattern of final demand. Whatever the distribution of income and whatever prices may be, the composition of final demand remains the same. The total volume of demand may vary but goods are always bought in the same proportions. To put it algebraically, demand y always has the form $v\bar{y}$ where $\bar{y}$ is a fixed vector and v a scalar. The vector $\bar{y}$ shows the pattern of demand; I shall call it the **standard demand**, or, since in equilibrium final demand is the same as net production, the **standard production**. The scalar v shows the scale of demand and production.

The assumption that the pattern of demand is fixed is one that I have generally made in previous chapters, in Section 4.4 for instance. It is a more serious assumption for the present model because removing it would make a large difference to the analysis. If, for example, we were to suppose that workers and capitalists have different patterns of demand, or that the pattern of demand depends on relative prices, that would have been quite easy to incorporate into the analysis of earlier chapters but rather hard in this one. We shall, all the same, be able to investigate the effects of changes in the pattern of demand.

The purpose of the assumption is to ensure that land and labour have always to be employed in the same proportions. The amount of land employed in the economy is m^*y or $vm^*\bar{y}$, and the amount of labour employed is l^*y or $vl^*\bar{y}$. Land and labour, therefore, are always employed in the ratio $m^*\bar{y}:l^*\bar{y}$.

Now I shall assume that land and labour each have **supply curves** and that each curve slopes upwards, as for instance in Fig. 5.3.1. This is a major assumption. It requires, first, that the supply of land depends on rent only and the supply of labour on the wage only. I have explained that this implies that landowners and workers value their income in terms of the same vector of goods, which must be the numeraire. Fortunately this happens to fit neatly our other assumption that final demand is unaffected by changes in distribution. We may take it that workers and landowners each consume in the proportions of the standard demand $\bar{y}$, that $\bar{y}$ is the numeraire, and that the supplies of labour and land depend only on the real wage and rent as measured in terms of $\bar{y}$. The assumption requires, second, that the supply curves slope upwards. The analysis, actually, will work if one of them should be flat (perfectly elastic), but not if one should be vertical (perfectly inelastic) or slope downwards. This is a serious imposition on the model because in reality the supply curve of labour might easily slope downwards and the supply of land might be perfectly inelastic.

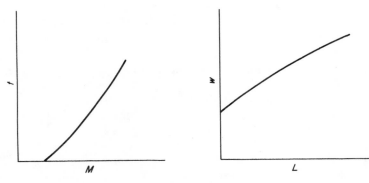

Fig. 5.3.1

Our assumptions imply that only some particular combinations of the wage and rent are possible if the economy is to be in equilibrium. Pick a rent. That determines a supply of land. If this much land is to be employed the employment of labour must be $l^*\bar{y}/m^*\bar{y}$ times as much. Then labour's supply curve determines what the wage must be. Figure 5.3.2 illustrates by means of a diagram with four quadrants. The north-west and south-east quadrants contain the supply curves of land and labour, appropriately oriented. In the south-west quadrant, between the axes showing the quantities of land and labour, is a line that shows what combinations of land and labour can be employed together. Its slope is $m^*\bar{y}/l^*\bar{y}$. For any point on this line we can see from the supply curves what the wage and rent must be to attain it. So we obtain a **supply locus** in the north-east quadrant.

We have found a limit on the variation of the wage and rent. It means that the economy can no longer be anywhere on the wage–profit–rent surface, but is confined to a single curve. Figure 5.3.3 illustrates: the equilibrium is confined to the heavy curve. So we have gone some way towards finding the economy's equilibrium. The problem was, as it were, two dimensional and we

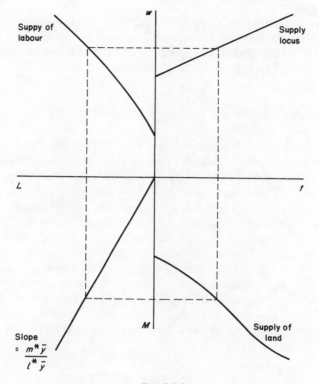

Fig. 5.3.2

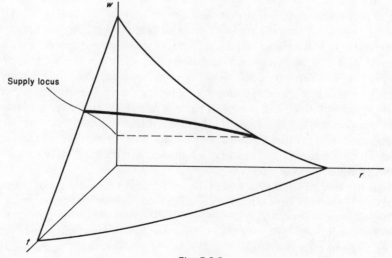

Fig. 5.3.3

have now reduced it to one dimension. We have got this far by comparing with each other the availability of land and labour. To finish the job we must compare the availability of these two inputs with the availability of capital. Again I can supply a diagrammatic method.

Costs and Capital

For each quantity of production v we know how much land is needed to produce it: $vm^*\bar{y}$. From the supply curve we know what rent per acre has to be paid to get this quantity of production; we know rent per acre as a function of v. Now if rent per acre is t the total rent paid to obtain output v is $tvm^*\bar{y}$, so that rent *per unit of output* is $tm^*\bar{y}$. Since t is a function of v we can draw a graph of rent per unit of output against output v. Figure 5.3.4 shows one, labelled "average cost of land." It is really simply the ordinary supply curve of land with its axes rescaled. Similarly we can produce an average labour cost curve from the supply curve of labour, and that is shown in Fig. 5.3.4 too.

The cost of producing, net, an output v is made up of the land cost, the labour cost and the cost of materials. In Figure 5.3.4 we have the first two already. The quantity of materials used is the vector Ax, where x is the economy's *gross* production, and their cost is pAx. The cost may be written

$$pAx = pA(I-A)^{-1}y = vpA(I-A)^{-1}\bar{y}.$$

(I shall call the vector $A(I-A)^{-1}\bar{y}$ the **standard materials**.) Now, if p were a constant these materials cost would simply be proportional to the scale of output v. The cost of materials per unit of output would be a constant, and its graph a horizontal line. But materials are subject to revaluation. Take any given level of v. From the supply curves of land and labour we know what wage and rent will have to be paid to obtain this much output. And we know from (5.2.3) that the wage and rent determine all prices. So for the level of output v we can value the cost of the materials required. At a different level of output their cost will be different because their prices will be different. We can draw a graph of the cost of materials per unit of output, the "average materials cost", and it will deviate from the horizontal line because the materials are being constantly revalued. As usual with valuation effects, there are no general rules about precisely how this graph behaves. Figure 5.3.4 shows a possible average materials cost curve.

In some special circumstances there would be no revaluation of materials. One case is where prices do not vary at all, which happens only when m^*, l^* and k^* are all proportional to each other (p. 157). Another is where the standard materials vector is proportional to the numeraire. Because the numeraire has its value fixed by definition, so in that case has the vector of materials (since materials are always proportional to the standard materials). Now, we have

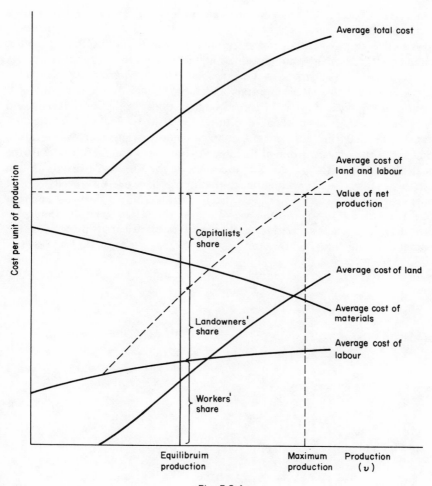

Fig. 5.3.4

seen (p. 162) that the assumptions underlying our analysis are really only acceptable if the numeraire is the standard production $\bar{y}$. So this case only occurs when the economy's inputs of materials are proportional to its net production, and this means (pp. 36–38) that the economy is producing in the proportions of the self-reproducing vector. The circumstances that keep constant the value of materials are therefore extremely special ones. We cannot decently confine our attention to these cases only. On the other hand it is worth remembering that cases without this particular valuation effect do exist. For the sake of analysis it is often convenient to see first of all what happens without the valuation effect and then see what difference this effect can make. Figure 5.3.5 shows a set of curves where the value of materials is constant.

We have graphs of the ιnree components of cost. Putting them together gives us a graph of the total per unit cost of production. It is shown on Figs 5.3.4 and 5.3.5. In Figure 5.3.5 it must plainly slope upwards because it is the sum of two upward sloping graphs and a horizontal one. I have drawn it sloping upwards in Fig. 5.3.4 too, though actually valuation effects could cause the average total cost curve to slope downwards. That would happen if the average materials cost curve were to slope downwards steeply enough to cancel out the upward slope of the other two curves. We can see how that is possible. Suppose the products that constitute the numeraire are not much used as materials for production, and suppose they are produced without much capital. Then as we go rightwards in our diagram, as the wage and rent rise, the numeraire will probably rise in value relative to capital-intensive products. The price of the latter, that is to say, measured in terms of the numeraire, will fall. If, now, the materials used in production are mostly

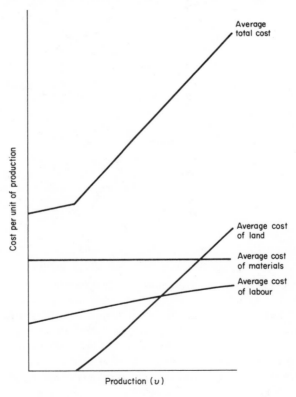

Fig. 5.3.5

capital-intensive products, the average cost of materials will fall. And if, furthermore, the cost of materials is a large fraction of total cost — if, that is to say, the economy as a whole is capital intensive — then average total cost may fall as we move rightwards.

So now we have a cost curve of sorts. Costs, though, are the same as capital in our model since all costs are financed out of capital. So the supply of capital will determine where on the cost curve the economy must be. Moving rightwards along the cost curve requires the accumulation of capital. This is plain enough when the curve slopes upwards because moving rightwards then implies greater output v and also greater cost or capital per unit of output. It is also true when the curve slopes downwards, and this requires some explanation.

Nothing guarantees that the average total cost curve does not slope downwards so steeply that a greater output can actually be produced at a lower cost — not, that is to say, just a lower cost per unit but a lower cost altogether for the whole of output. Greater output requires greater payments to be made to workers and landowners, but materials may be revalued downwards so much that cost as a whole is lower. So greater output requires a smaller value of capital. But this is a possibility I dealt with at length in Chapter 3 (pp. 74–78). The *value* of capital may be smaller for a greater output, but it is plain that the *quantity* of capital conceived as goods is larger. Greater output can only be achieved by giving workers and landowners a greater command over goods — wages and rents that are higher in real terms — and by using a greater quantity of goods as inputs. So it unambiguously requires a greater amount of capital-as-goods. To achieve a greater output capitalists will have to save and add to their capital. Conceivably the value of their capital may actually finish up lower than before, but that is a problem of valuation. The remedy I recommended in Chapter 3 was to choose a better numeraire, one consisting of goods that are used as inputs. We may not be able to do that now because we are already committed to a particular numeraire. But we can at least recognize that real capital accumulation always means a rightward movement in our diagram.

So we can see what its effects are. At any moment output will be a some level such as the one marked by a vertical line in Fig. 5.3.4. The accumulation of capital moves the line right. It increases output, therefore, and it increases the employment of land and labour. It increases both the wage and rent. Consequently it decreases the rate of profit. This result at least resembles previous models; accumulation reduces profit. We can see where the process must end in Fig. 5.3.4. The horizontal dotted line shows the value of net output per unit of net output. It shows, to put it another way, the value of the standard output $\bar{y}$. The line is horizontal, and actually at a height of one unit, because $\bar{y}$ is the numeraire. This value of net output is divided between workers, landowners and capitalists. The sloping dotted curve shows the payments made to workers and landlords (the sum of land costs and labour costs). Where it meets the horizontal line, profit is extinguished. This point is marked in the diagram as the maximum production. (Notice that, although I have marked the shares of the three classes on the diagram, Fig. 5.3.4 is not a distribution diagram comparable to those in previous chapters. It does not have capital on its horizontal axis, and its vertical axis shows incomes per unit of output, not total incomes.)

The accumulation of capital in this model adds to production. It does so, not by allowing more productive techniques to be employed as happened in Chapter 4, but by drawing more resources into production. In this our assumption that the supply curves slope upwards is obviously crucial.

Comparative Statics with a Constant Value of Capital

Suppose the economy possesses some given value of capital K. Then when its output is v it has capital K/v per unit of output. The graph of capital per unit K/v is shown in Fig 5.3.6. The diagram also shows the cost curves reproduced from Fig. 5.3.5, which represents the *special case without valuation effects*. So long as K does not alter the economy's equilibrium is at the intersection of the average total cost curve and the graph of capital per unit. So the equilibrium level of output is v_1.

Now let us try out the effect of changing the supply of a resource. Suppose, say, that the supply of land is increased; its supply curve shifts to the right. Since the graph of the average cost of land comes directly from the supply curve it shifts right too. Its new position is the dotted curve in Fig. 5.3.6. The new equilibrium output is v_2. Evidently it must be greater than before. Consequently the employment of both labour and land increases. Because labour's supply curve has not moved the wage must have increased. The effect on rent is not quite so obvious in the diagram. But actually rent must definitely be less than before for the following reason. Since output has increased and the supply of capital has not there is now less capital available per unit of output. On the other hand more capital per unit of output is being spent on labour. Less is therefore available for rent. Since more land is in use the rent paid per acre must be smaller. It is also possible to be sure that the rate of profit has increased. The rate of profit is:

$$\frac{\text{value of gross production} - \text{capital}}{\text{capital}}.$$

(Remember that costs are the same as capital.) Capital we are assuming to be constant. So the rate of profit goes up or down according to whether the value of gross production goes up or down. The value of gross production is the

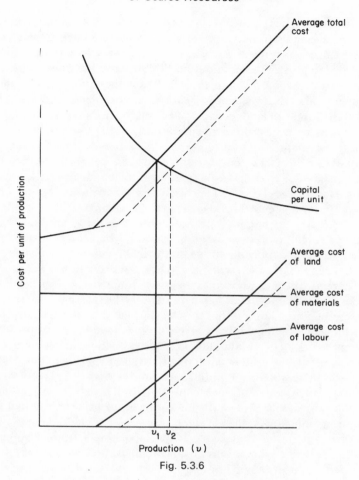

Fig. 5.3.6

value of net production plus the cost of materials. The value of net production *per unit produced* is constant because the unit of net production $\bar{y}$ is our numeraire. And the cost of materials per unit of production is also constant because that is the assumption of the special case we are dealing with. So the value of gross production per unit of output is constant. Since output has increased the total value of gross production has increased. And that proves that the rate of profit has increased.

All this applies only to the special case without valuation effects. The results are much as one might expect: a reduced scarcity of land reduces rent, it increases production and it increases the wage and the rate of profit. Of course changes in the supply of labour will have symmetrical consequences. But when we allow for valuation effects none of these plausible rules is reliable.

Valuation effects appear in two forms. First, as we have seen, the graph of the average cost of materials may deviate from a horizontal line. Second, it may move up or down as a result of changes in the supply of land or labour; the value of materials at any level of output v depends on the wage and rent that would prevail at that output, and an alteration in the supply curves will cause these things to alter. It is quite possible for valuation effects to lead to a rise in rent when the supply of land increases. They may cause an increased supply of land to result in reduced production, and so on. I shall leave it to you to try out the various possibilities.

The analysis, with some modifications, could be taken further to investigate the consequences of changes in the pattern of demand. But it would be an unproductive exercise because almost the only conclusion would be that valuation effects make general conclusions impossible. I do not intend to follow this line any further. For one thing it becomes very complicated as well as inconclusive. But more seriously it is doubtful whether a constant value of capital is a valid basis for comparative statics in this context. In Chapter 3 (pp. 79–83) I argued that there is something to be learnt from holding constant the value of capital, but one important step in my argument (p. 83) is not valid for the model of this chapter. That step depended on the fact that once the rate of profit is given so are all prices and the wage, which was true in Chapter 3 but not any longer. Keeping capital constant means keeping its value constant relative to the numeraire, and in the present model the results might be quite different if the value were kept constant relative to a different numeraire. Yet there is no good reason for making it constant relative to one numeraire rather than another. This difficulty could perhaps be taken care of by keeping constant not the supply of capital but a supply *function* of capital that makes capital a function of the rate of profit and prices. But the analysis would become very hard. For these reasons it is worth trying another approach.

Comparative Statics with a Constant Rate of Profit

What other approach is there? In the discussion in Chapter 3 I said it is not easy to know what one ought to hold constant when doing comparative statics. But one possibility is the rate of profit. The grounds I gave for that idea are that there is normally only one rate of profit that permits proportional growth. To be precise, if capitalists save a fraction s of their income and the labour force grows at a rate g the rate of profit in proportional growth will always be g/s. Since an economy of the sort we were dealing with in Chapter 3 will, given long enough, drift towards proportional growth, this rate will always be re-established in the long run after some change. So there is some point in comparing different states of the economy with the same rate of profit.

Our present model, however, cannot grow proportionally. For it to do so would require its supplies of labour and land to grow at the same rate, which is rather much to ask. It could, I suppose, be made more plausible by talking about a second sort of labour instead of land. But there is a simpler way to justify keeping constant the rate of profit. We may suppose that capitalists supply capital with perfect elasticity. There is some rate of profit they find acceptable. If the rate should drop below this level they will set about withdrawing their capital from production. If it goes above they will save and add to capital. In the long run the rate of profit will only be in equilibrium at its acceptable level. If there is some change like an increased supply of land the rate of profit will eventually return to this same level.

For the models of earlier chapters, comparative statics with a constant rate of profit is rather uninteresting because a constant rate of profit implies constant prices and a constant wage. So rather little can change. In our present model, there is more scope for variation. All the same the analysis is fairly simple, and it reaches some definite conclusions. For these reasons it seems worth pursuing.

We shall keep the assumptions that there is a fixed pattern of demand and that there are upward sloping supply curves for land and labour. Consequently the economy has a supply locus like the one in Fig. 5.3.2. This is one relationship between the wage and rent. And now the rate of profit is fixed, a second relationship between the wage and rent is determined by the wage–profit–rent equation. It was shown in Fig. 5.2.1 (p. 155). By putting the two relationships together, as Fig. 5.3.7 does, we can see the equilibrium at once. The upward sloping curve in the diagram is the supply locus and the

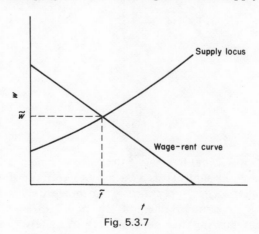

Fig. 5.3.7

downward sloping line the wage–rent relationship from Fig. 5.2.1. The equilibrium wage and rent are marked $\tilde{w}$ and $\tilde{r}$.

What is the effect of increasing the supply of land? Figure 5.3.8 reproduces the curves from Fig. 5.3.7 together with the four-quadrant apparatus that we used in Fig. 5.3.2 to draw up the supply locus. Increasing the supply of land means shifting land's supply curve from the solid to the dotted position. The supply locus is consequently raised. The effect is obviously to raise the wage and lower rent in equilibrium. The diagram also shows that more labour and more land are employed. So output is evidently increased too. All this meets one's natural expectations.

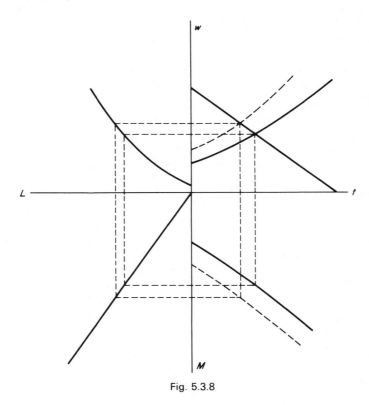

Fig. 5.3.8

Figure 5.3.9 shows what happens if the pattern of demand alters while the supply curves stay the same. (It is a bit fishy to keep the supply curves fixed while demand alters. The supply curves, remember, only make good sense if the numeraire is the standard demand. But now I am altering the standard demand without altering the numeraire. Fortunately, a more thorough method of analysis (pp. 185–190) shows that the conclusions are valid anyway.) The slope of the line in the diagram's south-west quadrant is $m^*\bar{y}/l^*\bar{y}$, where $\bar{y}$ is the standard demand. This slope is, in fact, the economy's land/labour ratio. Changing $\bar{y}$ will change the ratio. For instance, shifting demand from a product with a lower integrated land/labour ratio to one with a higher one will raise the economy's ratio as a whole. That makes the line steeper. The diagram shows that the result is a lower wage and a higher rent than before. The employment of labour is lower and of land higher. Again all this meets ones natural expectations.

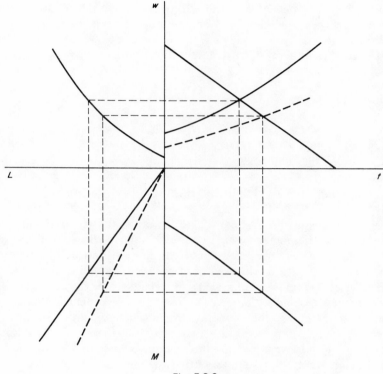

Fig. 5.3.9

We can put this conclusion together with something we discovered in Section 5.2 (p. 158) about the movement of relative prices. We discovered that if the wage goes down and rent goes up in such a way that the rate of profit stays constant, then a product with a higher *compounded* land/labour ratio will rise relative to a product with a lower one. We now know that, under the same condition of a constant rate of profit, the wage will be caused to fall and rent to rise by a shift of demand from a product with a lower *integrated* land/labour ratio to one with a higher one. So, provided the difference between two product's integrated land/labour ratios goes in the same direction as the difference between their compounded ratios, a shift of demand from one product to the other raises the relative price of the latter, which is what one would expect. We saw (p. 158) that there is no guarantee that the compounded and integrated ratios will differ in the same direction, but that it seems quite likely they will if the rate of profit is small. If they do, then the movement of relative prices will probably meet ones natural expectations too.

On the whole, then, comparative statics with a constant rate of profit conforms quite well to intuition. The reason is that fixing the rate of profit does away with a number of valuation effects. But it does not do away with the difference between integrated and compounded land/labour ratios, which leaves open the possibility of perverse behaviour of prices. And of course the analysis relied on other restrictive assumptions too.

Section 5.4   Choice of Technique

Systems of Techniques and Switch Points

Suppose now, in our model where land is scarce, that some or all of the economy's industries have more than one technique to choose from. Most of the arguments and methods of Section 4.3 can be applied without alteration to our new more complex model, so I need only remind you of them.

We may set up a number of **systems of techniques** for the economy, each containing one technique for each industry. Each system amounts to a possible technology for the economy. Each will have a wage–profit–rent surface. Figure 5.4.1 represents an economy with three systems. By the argument on pp. 112–115 we know that the economy will actually adopt, for any given wage and rent, the system that offers the greatest rate of profit. So the wage–profit–rent surface for the economy as a whole is the outer envelope of the surfaces of individual systems. There will be places called switch-points where two, and sometimes three, systems are equally profitable. In the diagram the switch points lie on the heavily drawn curves. If the economy should be moved through one of these switch points by a change in the wage and rent it will change the system of techniques in use. The argument on p. 115 shows that at a switch point the alternative systems have not only the same wage, rent and rate of profit but also the same price for each product. Furthermore (pp. 115–116) if two systems share a switch point they will normally only differ in one industry.

There is one argument that does not carry over to the new model. In the appendix to Chapter 4 (pp. 144–145) I proved that a switch will move every product's integrated capital/labour ratio in the same direction, either up or

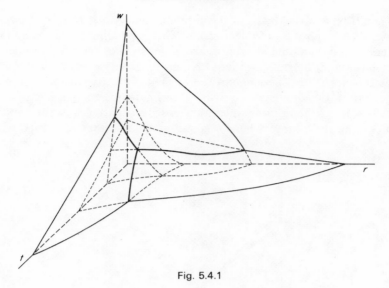

Fig. 5.4.1

down (provided it is a switch of the normal sort that only alters the technique in one industry). That proof is no longer valid. A switch may increase one product's integrated capital/labour ratio and decrease another's. And it may do the same with integrated land/labour ratios. So when we come to talk about the direction of switches, whether in particular they increase or decrease land/labour ratios, we shall have to be careful. I shall, in fact, consider the land/labour ratio *of the economy as a whole*, not the ratio of any individual product. And which of two systems of techniques has the higher land/labour ratio may depend on the composition of the economy's production.

The Direction of a Switch

In this section I am going to confine myself to switches that occur at a constant rate of profit; I shall assume that the wage and rent always change together in a way that leaves the rate of profit unchanged. The point of keeping the rate of profit constant I discussed on pp. 170–171. One advantage is that it concentrates attention on what is really the subject of this chapter: the scarcity of resources and its effects. In particular it is a natural idea that as a resource becomes more scarce relative to others the economy will adopt techniques that economize on its use. We shall see what grounds there are for this idea.

I shall continue to make the assumptions of Section 5.3 that there are upward sloping supply curves for land and labour and a fixed pattern of demand. The standard demand $\bar{y}$ will be our numeraire. It also defines, of course, the composition of the economy's net production.

Since we have a given fixed rate of profit we can take a section through the wage–profit–rent diagram at that rate, and look only at that. Figure 5.4.2 shows such a section. The economy represented in the diagram has, given the rate of profit, two alternative systems of techniques. Each has a wage–rent curve that is a straight line sloping downwards. The slopes of the lines are given by the ratio $\hat{m}z/\hat{l}z$ where $\hat{m}$ and $\hat{l}$ are the vectors of compounded

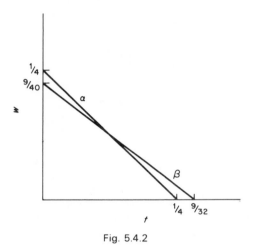

Fig. 5.4.2

requirements of land and labour and z is the numeraire vector. Since the numeraire is $\bar{y}$ the slopes are actually given by $\hat{m}\bar{y}/\hat{l}\bar{y}$. The diagram labels the system α and β. The α system has the steeper wage–rent curve, so

$$\frac{\hat{m}^\alpha \bar{y}}{\hat{l}^\alpha \bar{y}} > \frac{\hat{m}^\beta \bar{y}}{\hat{l}^\beta \bar{y}}. \tag{5.4.1}$$

If the wage declines and rent rises the economy will switch from system α to β. If, besides (5.4.1), it is also true that

$$\frac{m^{*\alpha}\bar{y}}{l^{*\alpha}\bar{y}} > \frac{m^{*\beta}\bar{y}}{l^{*\beta}\bar{y}} \tag{5.4.2}$$

then the economy's aggregate land/labour ratio declines at the switch. That is what one would expect: as rent rises the economy moves to a system of techniques that economizes on land. And as a general rule things probably will work in this direction, at least if the rate of profit is small, because then the vectors $\hat{m}$ and $\hat{l}$ of compounded requirements are not unlike the vectors m^* and

l^* of integrated requirements. But they need not. Here is an example of a technology where the switch goes the other way:

α: 1/4 corn   & 1 land & 1   labour $\rightarrow$1 corn
β: 1/8 corn & 1/2 weedkiller & 1 land & 1/4 labour $\rightarrow$1 corn
     3/32 corn   & 1   labour $\rightarrow$1 weedkiller.

Let final demand be for corn only and let corn be the numeraire. This economy has a switch point where $r = 1$, $t = 1/8$ and $w = 1/8$. Figure 5.4.2, as it happens, illustrates this particular economy, given a profit rate of one. System β is the one selected at a higher rent and lower wage. But corn's integrated land/labour ratio is one under system α and 4/3 under β. So at a higher rent the system selected is the one that uses relatively more land.

Supplies of Land and Labour

Let us put the supplies of land and labour into the model. Figure 5.4.3 shows the wage–rent curves for two systems of techniques, labelled α and β as before. System β has the less steep line, which means that condition (5.4.1) applies to this economy. The diagram also shows the supply locus for each system,

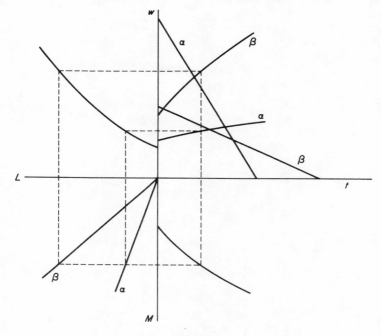

Fig. 5.4.3

together with the diagrammatic apparatus for constructing it. The systems have different loci because they employ land and labour in different ratios. The slopes of the lines in the diagram's south-west quadrant are equal to these ratios. I have drawn the diagram with the α line steeper than the β line, which means that system α has the greater land/labour ratio. That is to say, (5.4.2) applies to this economy. As I explained just above, this represents the most typical situation.

Now suppose that the supply of labour grows progressively; the supply curve in Fig. 5.4.3 moves leftwards. All the time, we assume implicitly, capital adjust to keep the rate of profit constant. Figure 5.4.4 shows what happens. The supply loci move downwards. They move in the diagram from the positions α_1 and β_1 to α_2 and β_2 to α_3 and β_3. Originally the equilibrium is at the point E_1. Then as the α locus moves downwards it carries the equilibrium with it, reducing the wage and raising rent. In time the switch point will be reached. Then the switch to system β begins, but it cannot be instantaneous because system β needs more labour to operate it than does α. So as the supply of labour continues to expand progressively more workers will be put to work on system β instead of α. Meanwhile the wage and rent will be held at the switch point. The switch will be complete when system β's supply locus reaches position β_3. Thereafter the wage will once more fall and rent rise.

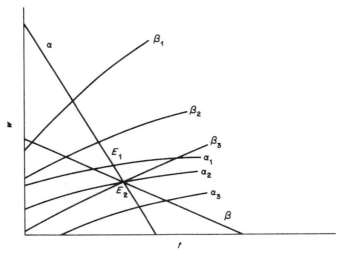

Fig. 5.4.4

That describes the switch for a typical case. Figure 5.4.5, on the other hand, illustrates what happens when the switch is in the perverse direction, to a system that uses more land per worker than before. The inequality (5.4.2) is reversed, the α line in the south-west quadrant is less steep than the β line, and consequently the α supply locus lies above the β one. An increasing supply of labour brings the loci down. Initially equilibrium is at E_1, with system α in use. By the time the loci reach position α_3 and β_3 the equilibrium will have dropped to the switch point. Capitalists will find system β as profitable as α. Before the wage falls any further they must all have converted to the new technique. But

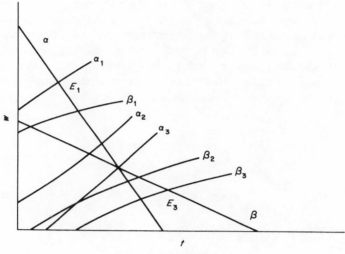

Fig. 5.4.5

the economy already has more than enough workers to operate system β, since system β requires fewer workers than α did. The only way equilibrium can be achieved is for the wage to drop suddenly and thereby encourage some workers to remove themselves from the labour market. The new equilibrium will be at E_3; the economy will jump to this position and all capitalists will switch to system β precipitately. A perverse switch will not be a gradual affair like a typical switch. It is worth noticing that for a range of positions of the supply loci, such as α_2 and β_2, the economy has two possible equilibriums.

Production

It would be nice to know what happens to the economy's output at a switch. But unfortunately not much can be said. From the elementary fact that the value of the economy's net production must be equal to the sum of the classes' incomes, i.e.

$$py = rK + tM + wL,$$

it follows that

$$\frac{py}{L}=\frac{rK}{L}+\frac{tM}{L}+w.$$

On the left of this equation is the value of net production per worker employed. What happens to it when the economy switches from one technique to another? During a switch prices, the rate of profit, rent and the wage all stay constant, so it all depends on the changes in the capital/labour ratio K/L and the land/labour ratio M/L. If they both increase, so does net production per worker. But we cannot tell what happens to net production per worker unless we know the change in *both* the capital/labour ratio and the land/labour ratio. And in this section we have concentrated only on the latter. Obviously there is much more that needs to be found out about these switches, but I shall leave the subject here.

Section 5.5   Economies with Several Scarce Resources

Prices and Incomes

This section will be quite brisk and mathematical. Its purpose is to set out the model of Sections 5.2 and 5.3 in a more formal way and to make it more general by allowing the possibility of several scarce resources. Many of the equations will turn out to be the same as those in Chapter 3, but with some of that chapter's scalars reinterpreted as vectors, and some of its vectors as matrices.

Let the economy have n products and h resources. Amongst the resources I count labour, and if necessary labour of different sorts. The technology is represented by an $n \times n$ input–output matrix A, just as before, and an $h \times n$ matrix l of resource requirements. The component l_{ij} of matrix l is the amount of resource i needed in the production of a unit of product j. (Thus in the model of Section 5.2 the matrix l was a $2 \times n$ matrix whose rows were the vectors that I there called m and l.)

We can define an $h \times n$ matrix l^* of integrated resource requirements:

$$l^*=l(I-A)^{-1}. \tag{5.5.1}$$

The columns of l^* list the products' direct and indirect requirements of resources, their *resource profiles* as I shall call them.

The basic equation connecting prices and the rate of profit is

$$p=(1+r)(pA+wl). \tag{5.5.2}$$

Here p is an n-dimensional row vector listing the prices of the products, r is the rate of profit and w is an h-dimensional row vector listing the prices of resources. The unknowns in the equation are r, the n components of p and the h components of w, making $n+h+1$ altogether. Equation (5.5.2) is really n equations. So once the numeraire is chosen there are h unknowns still to be determined. For instance, we might determine the prices of resources in some way, and then the rest will follow.

The look of (5.5.2) is identical to (3.3.2) on p. 46. It can be solved for p in the same way (p. 51) to give:

$$p=(1+r)wl(I-(1+r)A)^{-1}. \tag{5.5.3}$$

I shall write

$$\hat{l}(r)=(1+r)l(I-(1+r)A)^{-1}. \tag{5.5.4}$$

This $h\times n$ matrix $\hat{l}(r)$ shows the products' compounded requirements of resources. Equation (5.5.3) may be written

$$p=w\hat{l}(r). \tag{5.5.5}$$

Let us postmultiply (5.5.5) by an n-dimensional column vector z of products:

$$pz=w\hat{l}(r)z.$$

If z is the numeraire pz is one. So

$$w\hat{l}(r)z=1. \tag{5.5.6}$$

This equation connects together the economy's distributional variables, namely the rate of profit and the prices of resources. It is the generalized version of the wage–profit–rent equation.

Should the rate of profit happen to be constant $\hat{l}(r)$ is a constant matrix $\hat{l}$. Equation (5.5.5) is simply

$$p=w\hat{l}.$$

One implication is that if a resource goes up in price and another down, in such a way as to keep constant the rate of profit, then products with a higher compounded ratio of the former resource to the latter will rise relatively in price. Under a constant rate of profit (5.5.6) is

$$w\hat{l}z=1. \tag{5.5.7}$$

which is a simple linear relationship between the prices of resources.

Supply and Demand for Resources

To close the model I shall assume as usual that resources are bought and sold in competitive markets. For the sake of generality I shall allow that the supplies of the resources depend on w, r and p, and write them $L(w,r,p)$. L is an h-dimensional column vector. Likewise I shall write the final demands for products as functions of w, r and p: $y(w,r,p)$ where y is an n-dimensional column vector. If the economy is to be in equilibrium its net production must be equal to $y(w,r,p)$. In that case the resources it employs will be $l^*y(w,r,p)$. So in equilibrium this amount must be equal to the supply:

$$l^*y(w,r,p) = L(w,r,p). \tag{5.5.8}$$

Equation (5.5.8), which is really h equations, completes the model. It, together with (5.5.2) and the numeraire equation, is enough to determine all the variables.

There is more to (5.5.8) than meets the eye. The functions $y(w,r,p)$ and $L(w,r,p)$ have the supply of capital hidden in them. Let us suppose that the economy's supply of capital is, like the supplies of resources, a function of w, r and p: $K(w,r,p)$. The supplies and demands in the economy have always to satisfy the requirement that the total value of final demand is equal to the economy's total income:

$$py(w,r,p) = wL(w,r,p) + rK(w,r,p). \tag{5.5.9}$$

The meaning of this equation is discussed on p. 68 of Chapter 3. It connects the functions $y(w,r,p)$ and $L(w,r,p)$ with the function $K(w,r,p)$. The demands for products, then, and the supplies of resources are linked with the supply of capital. If K increases, either y must increase or L must fall. Probably the supply of capital will present itself most conspicuously in the demand for products. For instance, the accumulation of capital will appear in our equations in the guise of an increase in the total of demand. And if, to take another example, the supply of capital depends rather elastically on the rate of profit, then the demand for products will also depend rather elastically on the rate of profit. It is a mistake to think that the demand functions result simply from consumers deciding what to consume. That may be true of the *composition* of demand, but certainly not of the total.

In this book I have repeatedly stressed that the demand for resources comes from capitalists. It takes capital to finance the employment of resources. Equation (5.5.8) makes the demand for resources look as though it is derived simply from consumers' decisions. But that is an optical illusion. It works because once capitalists have decided to provide a certain amount of capital, capable of employing a certain quantity of resources, then in their capacity as consumers they will offer just the right amount of final demand to buy (together with the demand from the owners of resources) the product of that quantity of resources.

Comparative Statics

Our model is contained in the equations (5.5.2), (5.5.8) and the numeraire equation. But we can compress it further. In (5.5.8) the demands for products and the supplies of resources are written as functions of w, r and p. But once a numeraire is given r and p are actually determined by w through (5.5.2). So we may write y and L as functions of w only: $y(w)$ and $L(w)$. Equation (5.5.8) is then

$$l^* y(w) = L(w),$$

a system of L equations determining the L components of w. If we define the function

$$E(w) = l^* y(w) - L(w)$$

we can write the equation simply as

$$E(w) = 0. \qquad (5.5.10)$$

$E(w)$ stands for the **excess demand** for the resources, their demand less their supply. For $L(w)$ is the supply of resources and $l^* y(w)$ is, in a sense, the demand for resources; it is what is called a "derived demand" because it is derived from the demand for products. E is an h-dimensional column vector.

To do comparative statics we want to try out the effects of shifting the supply functions or the demand function. A way of doing that is to put in the functions a "shift parameter" σ as an extra argument. So we write them $y(w,\sigma)$ and $L(w,\sigma)$. Then we arrange the effect of σ on y and L to represent just the change we want to investigate. To represent a decrease in the supply of the first resource we make

$$\frac{\partial L_1}{\partial \sigma} < 0$$

and all the other partial derivatives nought:

$$\frac{\partial L_2}{\partial \sigma} = \frac{\partial L_3}{\partial \sigma} = \ldots \frac{\partial L_h}{\partial \sigma} = \frac{\partial y_1}{\partial \sigma} = \frac{\partial y_2}{\partial \sigma} = \ldots \frac{\partial y_n}{\partial \sigma} = 0.$$

To represent an increase in the demand for the first product we make:

$$\frac{\partial y_1}{\partial \sigma} > 0 \text{ and } \frac{\partial y_2}{\partial \sigma} = \frac{\partial y_3}{\partial \sigma} = \ldots \frac{\partial y_n}{\partial \sigma} = \frac{\partial L_1}{\partial \sigma} = \frac{\partial L_2}{\partial \sigma} = \ldots \frac{\partial L_h}{\partial \sigma} = 0. \quad (5.5.11)$$

And so on. We must be careful to make our shifts conform to the constraint (5.5.9), so that (differentiating (5.5.9)):

$$p \frac{\partial y}{\partial \sigma} = r \frac{\partial K}{\partial \sigma} + w \frac{\partial L}{\partial \sigma}.$$

Thus if, for instance, we want a shift to affect neither the supply of capital nor the supply of resources we must make

$$p \frac{\partial y}{\partial \sigma} = 0.$$

So in this case we cannot increase the demand for one product without decreasing the demand for another.

Now let us set our shift parameter to work. The excess demand E must of course now also be written as a function $E(w, \sigma)$ of σ, so equation (5.5.10) is

$$E(w, \sigma) = 0.$$

Differentiate it totally with respect to σ:

$$\frac{\partial E}{\partial w} \left(\frac{dw}{d\sigma} \right)' + \frac{\partial E}{\partial \sigma} = 0.$$

$$\therefore \quad \left(\frac{dw}{d\sigma} \right)' = - \left(\frac{\partial E}{\partial w} \right)^{-1} \frac{\partial E}{\partial \sigma} \qquad (5.5.12)$$

(assuming that $\partial E/\partial w$ is non-singular).

On the left of (5.5.12) is a vector showing the effect of the shift represented by σ on the prices w of resources. This is what we are interested in; once we know how w changes we can work out from (5.5.2) how p and r change. On the right multiplied by an inverse matrix that I shall talk about later, is a vector showing the initial effects of the shift on excess demand. This is what we control to represent the change we want to study.

What conclusions can we draw from (5.5.12)? First, the effects on w (and r and p) of a shift depend only on what the shift does to the *excess* demand for resources. Decreasing the supply of a resource has exactly the same effect as increasing the demand for it. Now increasing the demand for a *product* effectively increases the demand for a number of resources simultaneously. To be more precise it increases the demand for the product's *profile* of resources. Thus, for instance, suppose we increase the demand for the first product. Then (5.5.11) applies and the effect on excess demand is

$$\frac{\partial E}{\partial \sigma} = l^* \frac{\partial y}{\partial \sigma} = \frac{\partial L}{\partial \sigma} = \frac{\partial y_1}{\partial \sigma} l_1^*.$$

The symbol l_1^* stands for the first column of l^*, which is the first product's resource profile. The effect of this change, then, is exactly the same as the effect of decreasing the supply of resources in the proportions of the resource profile l_1^*. So this is the way the demand for products exerts its influence on prices: through the impact of their resource profiles.

A second conclusion from (5.5.12) is that it is very hard to find any general rules about the detailed effects of a change. It all depends on the matrix $(\partial E/\partial w)^{-1}$. We should really like to know something about the signs of its elements. For instance, it would be natural to expect its diagonal elements to be negative because that would mean that increasing the excess demand for a resource increases its price. But there is no guarantee that even this much is true, and it is very hard to find assumptions that will make it true; we saw on pp. 169–174 that even under drastic simplifying assumptions valuation effects could still cause an increase in a resource's price to result from an increase in its supply. There is no better reason to hope for rules about the off-diagonal elements of $(\partial E/\partial w)^{-1}$ either. The trouble is that what goes into making this matrix is immensely complicated: the supply of resources, the demand for products working indirectly through their resource profiles, the effect of the prices of resources on the prices of products, the supply of capital, and so on.

Third, we can draw a rather negative conclusion about the effect of the demand for a product on its own price. That effect works by two steps: the demand for a product affects the distribution of income (the prices of resources), which in turn determines the price of the product. In the first step the demand works its effect through the product's resource profile, which is given by technology alone, but precisely what its effect will be on the resources' prices depends also on the shape of their excess demand functions, on whether their supplies are elastic or inelastic and so on. In the second step the product's price is determined by equation (5.5.5). This equation is not affected at all by the excess demand functions; it contains only the prices of resources and the product's compounded requirements of resources. The latter depend on technology and the rate of profit; they may be similar to the resource profile if the rate of profit is small but they are not normally the same. Thus the influence of a product's demand on distribution and the reaction of distribution on the product's price pass by quite different channels. Therefore there is no reason to think that the connection between a product's demand and its price will be a simple one. And there is no reason to think that increasing a product's demand will increase its price.

Comparative Statics with a Constant Rate of Profit

Few definite results have emerged from all this. But in previous sections we have been able to gain some ground by making the rather special assumption that the rate of profit stays constant. And that will help us here too. So now in our comparative statics let us assume that when we look at changes in demand and supply they are always of a sort that leaves the rate of profit unaltered. There are two ways of justifying this assumption. We might say that there are reasons why the rate of profit should actually stay constant in the economy.

These are discussed on p. 170; the simplest one is that capitalists might adjust the supply of capital to have this effect — they might supply capital elastically at a particular rate of profit. The other justification is simply to say that this assumption allows us to make some progress; it is at least a way of discovering something about the economy's comparative statics. Changes in the rate of profit are a further complication that can be dealt with separately.

It happens to be convenient to change our numeraire. So far the numeraire has been a collection of products. But a resource can do the job equally well, and I am now going to take as numeraire the last resource, the h'th. That is to say

$$w_h = 1.$$

Equation (5.5.8) is, taking this numeraire into account,

$$l^* y(w_1, \ldots w_{h-1}, 1, r, p_1, \ldots p_n) = L(w_1, \ldots w_{h-1}, 1, r, p_1, \ldots p_n).$$

(I have simply written the vectors out in full.) It may be written

$$l^* y(w_-, 1, r, p) = L(w_-, 1, r, p) \tag{5.5.13}$$

if we use the symbol w_- to stand for the abbreviated vector

$$w_- = (w_1, w_2, \ldots w_{h-1}).$$

Equation (5.5.5) with this new numeraire is

$$p = (w_1, w_2, \ldots w_{h-1}, 1)\hat{l}(r)$$

or
$$p = w_- \hat{l}_-(r) + \hat{l}_h(r), \tag{5.5.14}$$

if we make $\hat{l}_-(r)$ stand for the matrix $\hat{l}(r)$ without its last row and $\hat{l}_h(r)$ for the vector that constitutes that last row.

Equations (5.5.13) and (5.5.14) between them contain $n + h$ equations. They contain $n + h$ unknowns too: r, the n components of p and the $(h-1)$ components of w_-. But now we are going to assume that supply and demand are always such as to make the rate of profit equal to some given level, say $\bar{r}$. So the solution of equations (5.5.13) and (5.5.14) must always make r equal to $\bar{r}$. That means that one of the equations contained in (5.5.13) is redundant. Given that r is equal to $\bar{r}$ the other $(h-1)$ together with (5.5.14) will fix values for p and w_-. The remaining equation will have to be — demand and supply must be such that it is — satisfied by the same values and $\bar{r}$; otherwise the system would not be in equilibrium with this rate of profit. We may take any of equations in (5.5.13) to be the redundant one, so let us for convenience make it the last. Without it (5.5.13) may be written

$$L^* y(w_-, 1, r, p) = L_-(w_-, 1, r, p)$$

where L_- is the vector L without its last component and L^* is the matrix l^* without its last row.

Now let us put a shift parameter into the functions, so that

$$L^*_y(w_-, 1, r, p, \sigma) = L_-(w_-, 1, r, p, \sigma),$$

and differentiate with respect to σ:

$$l^*_-\frac{\partial y}{\partial w_-}\left(\frac{dw_-}{d\sigma}\right)' + l^*_-\frac{\partial y}{\partial p}\left(\frac{dp}{d\sigma}\right)' + l^*_-\frac{\partial y}{\partial \sigma}$$

$$= \frac{\partial L_-}{\partial w_-}\left(\frac{dw_-}{d\sigma}\right)' + \frac{\partial L_-}{\partial p}\left(\frac{dp}{d\sigma}\right)' + \frac{\partial L_-}{\partial \sigma}.$$

(Remember that since r does not change $dr/d\sigma$ is nought.) Rearrange:

$$\left(l^*_-\frac{\partial y}{\partial p} - \frac{\partial L_-}{\partial p}\right)\left(\frac{dp}{d\sigma}\right)' + \left(l^*_-\frac{\partial y}{\partial w_-} - \frac{\partial L_-}{\partial w_-}\right)\left(\frac{dw_-}{d\sigma}\right)' = -\left(l^*_-\frac{\partial y}{\partial \sigma} - \frac{\partial L_-}{\partial \sigma}\right).$$

Rearrange again:

$$(l^*_-, I)\begin{pmatrix}\frac{\partial y}{\partial p} & \frac{\partial y}{\partial w_-}\\ -\frac{\partial L_-}{\partial p} & -\frac{\partial L_-}{\partial w_-}\end{pmatrix}\begin{pmatrix}\left(\frac{dp}{d\sigma}\right)'\\ \left(\frac{dw_-}{d\sigma}\right)'\end{pmatrix} = -\left(l^*_-\frac{\partial y}{\partial \sigma} - \frac{\partial L_-}{\partial \sigma}\right). \qquad (5.5.15)$$

Differentiating (5.5.14) gives

$$\frac{dp}{d\sigma} = \frac{dw_-}{d\sigma}\hat{l}_-$$

because $dr/d\sigma$ is nought. Therefore

$$\left(\frac{dp}{d\sigma}\right)' = \hat{l}'_-\left(\frac{dw_-}{d\sigma}\right)',$$

and (5.5.15) can be written

$$(l^*_-, I)\, J\begin{pmatrix}\hat{l}'_-\\ I\end{pmatrix}\left(\frac{dw_-}{d\sigma}\right)' = -\left(l^*_-\frac{\partial y}{\partial \sigma} - \frac{\partial L_-}{\partial \sigma}\right)$$

where J stands for the matrix

$$J = \begin{pmatrix}\frac{\partial y}{\partial p} & \frac{\partial y}{\partial w_-}\\ -\frac{\partial L_-}{\partial p} & -\frac{\partial L_-}{\partial w_-}\end{pmatrix}.$$

Finally, premultiply both sides of the equation by $dw_-/d\sigma$:

$$\left(\frac{dw_-}{d\sigma}\right)(l^*_-, I)\, J\begin{pmatrix}\hat{l}'_-\\ I\end{pmatrix}\left(\frac{dw_-}{d\sigma}\right)' = -\left(\frac{dw_-}{d\sigma}\right)\left(l^*_-\frac{\partial y}{\partial \sigma} - \frac{\partial L_-}{\partial \sigma}\right). \quad (5.5.16)$$

Now, suppose for a moment that we happened to know that the left side of (5.5.16) is negative. Then we should know that

$$\frac{dw}{d\sigma}\left(l_-^*\frac{\partial y}{\partial\sigma}-\frac{\partial L_-}{\partial\sigma}\right)>0. \qquad (5.5.17)$$

What would follow?

Well, let us use our parameter σ to represent an increase in the supply of the first resource. So we shall make

$$\frac{\partial L_1}{\partial\sigma}>0 \text{ and } \frac{\partial y_1}{\partial\sigma}=\frac{\partial y_2}{\partial\sigma}=\ldots\frac{\partial y_n}{\partial\sigma}=\frac{\partial L_2}{\partial\sigma}=\frac{\partial L_3}{\partial\sigma}=\ldots\frac{\partial L_{h-1}}{\partial\sigma}=0. \qquad (5.5.18)$$

When we set up a shift like this we need to make sure that it does not alter the rate of profit. But the way I have set up the equation means that we do not have to worry about that explicitly. The effect of the shift on L_h, $\partial L_h/\partial\sigma$, does not appear in (5.5.16). Consequently we can always assume that L_h is adjusted to keep the rate of profit constant without having to work out precisely what that adjustment needs to be; it makes no difference to the equation. But it is worth remembering that it is always this last resource, the numeraire, that is, as it were, taking up the slack whenever we shift a supply or a demand. Now we are increasing the supply of the first resource it is plain that the supply of the last will have to decrease in order to keep the rate of profit constant.

Fitting (5.5.18) into (5.5.17) tells us that

$$\frac{dw_1}{d\sigma}\frac{\partial L_1}{\partial\sigma}<0$$

and in fact that

$$\frac{dw_1}{d\sigma}<0.$$

An increase in the supply of the first resource decreases its price. More precisely: an increase in the supply of the first resource, balanced by a decrease in the supply of the last so as to leave the rate of profit unaltered, will reduce the price of the first resource in terms of the last as numeraire. Of course, we could have used any resource instead of the last as numeraire, and increased the supply of any resource instead of the first, so the conclusion is a general one. Here, then, we have the prices of resources behaving as one would expect.

But all this depends on the left of (5.5.16) being negative. Is there any reason to think it will be? Well, it will certainly be negative if two conditions are fulfilled. One is that the matrix J should be **negative quasi-definite**. The other is that L^* should be the same as $\hat{L}_-$. For by definition if J is negative quasi-definite then uJu' is negative for any row vector u, and if L^* is equal to $\hat{L}_-$ then the left of (5.5.16) has the form uJu' where

$$u=\frac{dw}{d\sigma}(l_-^*, I).$$

So these two conditions, if true, would lead to the result we want. I shall discuss each of them in turn.

Whether or not J is negative quasi-definite is to do with the behaviour of consumers and the owners of resources. It is obviously a technically abstruse condition, and it is beyond the scope of this book to go into it in detail. It is quite possible for it to be true but on the other hand it is quite a restrictive condition on people's behaviour and it might easily be false. To give you an idea of what is involved in it I can say that it will be true if all products and resources are **gross substitutes** for each other, if, that is to say, an increase in the price of one product or one resource leads people to buy more of all the other products and sell less of all the other resources. It may also be true even if the goods are not gross substitutes. I have in this book often made very restrictive assumptions about the demand for products and the supply of resources, in order to simplify the analysis. For instance, I have sometimes assumed that the composition of final demand is not affected by prices, and that the supply of a resource is only affected by its own price. To assume that J is negative quasi-definite is much less restrictive than that.

The condition that l^* should be the same as $\hat{l}$ I have talked about before (p. 158). Differences between the matrices, between the product's integrated requirements of resources and their compounded requirements, we have found to be a potent source of "perversities" in the behaviour of prices, in the direction of switches of technique, and so on. Here once again they can have the same effect. If we are to be sure that an increase in the supply of a resource will decrease its price, the integrated and compounded requirements need to be the same. Normally, of course, they will be different. But the smaller is the rate of profit the closer they will be, and the better is the chance that the prices of resources will behave in the expected way.

Let us now look at final demand for products and what its effects are. Let us assume in doing so that both the conditions I have mentioned are satisfied, so that (5.5.17) is true. Let us make the shift parameter increase the demand for the first product:

$$\frac{\partial y_1}{\partial \sigma} > 0 \text{ and } \frac{\partial y_2}{\partial_6} = \frac{\partial y_3}{\partial \sigma} = \ldots \frac{\partial y_n}{\partial \sigma} = \frac{\partial L_1}{\partial \sigma} = \frac{\partial L_2}{\partial \sigma} = \ldots \frac{\partial L_{h-1}}{\partial \sigma} = 0.$$

(Again it is implicit that the supply of the last resource adjusts to keep the rate of profit constant; in this case it will increase.) Then

$$\frac{dw}{d\sigma} = l_1^* - \frac{\partial y_1}{\partial \sigma} > 0.$$

(The symbol l_{1-}^* stands for the first column of L^*.) It is plain from this that the impact of the change on the prices of resources is through the product's resource profile l_{1-}^*, as I explained on p. 185. Its impact on the prices of products is, as usual, complicated by the difference between the integrated and compounded requirements of resources. But if it should happen that l_{1-}^* is proportional to $\hat{l}_{1-}$ then it would follow that

$$\frac{\mathrm{d}w}{\mathrm{d}\sigma} = l_1 - \frac{\partial y_1}{\partial \sigma} > 0.$$

But by (5.5.14)

$$\frac{\mathrm{d}w}{\mathrm{d}\sigma} = l_1 - = \frac{\mathrm{d}p_1}{\mathrm{d}\sigma}$$

so that

$$\frac{\mathrm{d}p_1}{\mathrm{d}\sigma} \frac{\partial y_1}{\partial \sigma} > 0.$$

Since $\partial y_1 / \partial \sigma$ is positive, so is $\mathrm{d}p_1 / \mathrm{d}\sigma$. Here, then, we have an increase in the demand for a product raising its price. But to reach this point of course, we have had to make a long chain of restrictive assumptions.

Conclusion

The result of all this comparative statics is that we have managed to find a number of conditions under which the effects of demands and supplies will be as one would expect: an increase in the supply of a resource will reduce its price and an increase in the demand for a product will increase its price. But the conditions are stringent: demands and supplies must change in such a way that the rate of profit is unaffected, the integrated requirements of resources must be the same as their compounded requirements, and the way demands and supplies are influenced by prices must satisfy a particular technical condition. To put the conclusion another way, natural expectations about the behaviour of prices can go wrong in three ways: the rate of profit may change, compounded and integrated requirements of resources may diverge, or the behaviour of supplies and demands may not conform to a particular technical requirement.

Section 5.6 Scarcity and Demand

Scarcity is often supposed to be the centre of economics. So one might imagine that earlier chapters of this book must have been seriously misleading because they ignored it. Especially one might imagine they must have underestimated the importance of consumers' demand (particularly in Section 3.6). It is common to think of economics as ultimately no more than the working of demand and supply; the demand from consumers acts on the limited supply of scarce resources. So in this section I shall ask what difference introducing scarcity makes to the working of the model, and particularly to the role of consumers' demand.

One thing is certainly true: the more scarce resources there are the more scope there is for demand to have detailed and specific effects on prices. The prices of products are completely determined by the prices of resources and the rate of profit, the economy's distributional variables. In a model with no scarce resources apart from labour, distribution can only change in one dimension; the rate of profit can rise or it can fall. So prices are very rigidly bound together. An increase in a product's demand can either raise the rate of profit (if the product is capital intensive) or lower it (if the product is labour intensive). If it does the former, prices will move one way; if it does the latter, prices will move the opposite way. Any change in demand can only have one or other effect. But each extra resource in the economy adds an extra dimension to the possible variations in the distributional variables. Hence it gives an extra freedom to the movement of relative prices. Products are characterized not just by their degrees of capital intensity but by their many-dimensional resource profiles. It is the products' resource profiles that determine how their demands act on distribution. If their profiles differ their demands will have different effects on the prices of resources and hence on the prices of products; the demand for a specific product will have a specific effect. And the more resources there are the better is the chance that products will have different resource profiles.

So demand has more specific effects. But that does not mean that a product's demand necessarily has a specific effect on its own price. Take a little example. Suppose that building buses uses a small amount of the rare metal Broomium, whose supply is inelastic. Then an increased demand for buses will raise the price of Broomium a lot, and that may slightly raise the price of buses. But the most dramatic effect will be on Broomium jewellery, which is made entirely of Broomium; its price will shoot up. A specific effect of the demand for buses, then, is on the price of this jewellery. On the other hand the demand for Broomium jewellery may have very little effect on its own price. Jewellery may absorb only a minute fraction of the total supply of Broomium, so that the demand for the jewellery may scarcely affect Broomium's price at all.

This example emphasizes one point I have made before (p. 185): the influence of final demand on distribution works through the resource profiles of the products, but it also depends on the resources' excess demand functions. The former are specific to particular products but the latter are not. Therefore there is no reason to expect that the effect on distribution of some product's demand will be reflected back precisely where it came from, to affect precisely that product's price. Furthermore, since the reflection back from distribution to prices works not through resource profiles but through the compounded requirements of resources, which may be quite different, it is likely to be diverted even further away from its original source.

Demand will have more *specific* effects in an economy with many resources, but there is no reason to think its influence will be *quantitatively* bigger. It depends on the economy's fertility. If its fertility is low then, as I explained in Section 3.6, most production will be aimed at supplying inputs to further production. Final demand will be only a small part of total demand, it will have little effect on the structure of production, on the distribution of income or on prices. This point is discussed thoroughly in Section 3.6. Adding scarce resources to the model does not affect the discussion except that it makes possible one type of exception. There may be a resource that is used in basic industries very little or not at all. It may be principally used in the final production of some consumer goods. In that case its price will be influenced directly and perhaps very much by the demand for these goods. If, also, the resource is a major constituent of these goods its price may strongly influence theirs. So in a case like this the demand for a product may influence its price directly and strongly.

Finally I want to mention another idea that is common in economics: the idea that the role of the prices of goods is to reflect their scarcity; that prices carry information to buyers and sellers about how scarce goods are; that goods in short supply, compared with the demand for them, will be expensive, plentiful goods cheap. No doubt this idea can be interpreted in various ways, but it is hard to see how it can be reconciled with the possibility that a resource may rise in price when its supply increases. We know that such a perverse movement of price is a possibility, and we have gone some way in analysing why. In the simple case where we were able to reach the most definite conclusions—the case where the rate of profit is constant—we found two possible causes. One is to do with how consumers (who are also the owners of resources) behave. The quantities of products people choose to buy and the quantities of resources they choose to sell will be functions of prices, and unless these functions conform to special conditions the prices of resources can move perversely. The second possible cause is a divergence between products' resource profiles l^* and their compounded requirements of resources $\hat{l}$. When l^* and $\hat{l}$ differ prices may move perversely. The difference between the two has nothing to do with the behaviour of consumers. It is built into the technology and the nature of capitalism. It occurs because profits are paid. The root of the trouble is that the prices of products do not reflect exactly the demands they make on the economy's scarce resources, but those demand compounded by profit. So there are at least two difficulties with the idea that prices reflect scarcity: one over the behaviour of consumers and this second, in a way more fundamental, difficulty over profit.

Questions on Chapter 5

---

1. Assume that land is free and plentiful. Suppose there are two techniques available for growing corn:

   α: 1/4 corn & 1 labour   →1 corn
   β: 1/8 corn   & 1 hard labour→1 corn.

   The supply of labour and hard labour is given as follows. There is a total labour force of 8 million. Each worker will do hard labour if the wage offered for it is at least one and a half times the wage offered for ordinary labour. Otherwise he or she will do ordinary labour.

   Find the wage rates at which the two techniques can be simultaneously in use. Show in a diagram the economy's gross and net production, and its distribution between workers and capitalists, for different levels of the supply of capital.

2. Suppose there are three qualities of land. Good land and medium land are owned by landlords and each is in a fixed supply of one million acres. Bad land is also owned by landlords but is very plentiful. Let the technology be:

   1/4 corn & 1 good land   & 1 labour →1 corn
   1/4 corn   & 1 medium land   & 3/2 labour →1 corn
   1/4 corn   & 1 bad land & 2 labour →1 corn.

   Assume that the supply of labour is infinitely elastic at a wage of 1/4.

   · Show how, as capital accumulates, at first only good land is cultivated, then also medium land, and finally bad land too. Will the rate of profit be different on the different sorts of land? How does the rate of profit change as capital accumulates? What is the rent on the three sorts of land when all are in cultivation? How much capital does the economy have before medium land is first cultivated? What is the rent on the three sorts of land then?

3. An economy employs this technology:

   1/4 corn & 1 labour & 1 corn land   →1 corn
   1/2 corn & 2 labour   & 1 pig land→1 pig.

   The supply of labour is infinitely elastic at a wage of 1/4. The supplies of corn land and pig land are both inelastic at 4 million acres and 5/4 million acres respectively. The supply of capital is inelastic at 15/4 million tons.

   Suppose that workers and capitalists consume corn and landlords consume pigs. Show that the economy is in equilibrium when the rent of corn land is 1/4 and the rent of pig land nought. Find the price of pigs relative to corn and the incomes of the three classes.

Now suppose that all classes consume pigs. Show that the economy is now in equilibrium when the rent of corn land is nought and the rent of pig land 5/3. Again find the price of pigs relative to corn and the incomes of the three classes.

Comment on the effects of this shift in demand.

4. A technology is given by an input–output matrix

$$A = \begin{pmatrix} 0 & 1/2 \\ 1 & 0 \end{pmatrix}$$

and a matrix of resource requirements

$$l = \begin{pmatrix} 1 & 2 \\ 2 & 4 \end{pmatrix}.$$

Work out the matrix of integrated resource requirements l^* and, as a function of the rate of profit, the matrix of compounded resource requirements $\hat{l}$. Show that the relative price of the products depends only on the rate of profit and not on the relative price of resources. What special feature of the technology makes this true?

6.

FURTHER DEVELOPMENTS

Section 6.1   Joint Production

Introduction

I have now developed our model as far as I can in this book with any degree of thoroughness. We have gained some insights into the workings of capitalist economies, but many additions still need to be made to the model if it is to come at all close to reality. This chapter describes some of them, and outlines the ways they can be fitted into the model. But it gives no more than outlines, and its arguments are not intended to be precise or complete.

An Example

The first addition to the model we shall look at takes account of production processes that have more than one product. An example is:

$\frac{1}{2}$ corn & 1 labour $\rightarrow$ 1 corn & 1 straw.

This is an instance of **joint production**.

Imagine an economy whose technology consists only of this technique. The value of a process's output is, as usual, the cost of production raised by the rate of profit. So

$$1 + p = (1 + r)(\tfrac{1}{2} + w) \tag{6.1.1}$$

where r is the rate of profit, w the wage in terms of corn and p the price of straw in terms of corn. There is here no determinate wage–profit equation. The relationship between wages and profits depends on p, and we shall obviously have to rely on the final demand for corn and straw to help fix p. So demand has a role we have not come across before in determining prices and the distribution of income.

There is a sense in which the real incomes of workers and capitalists must be inversely related: a worker's net production is half a unit of corn and one unit of straw, and this has to be divided between the worker and his or her employer. But the state of final demand can affect the value of net production in a way that obscures this real relationship. It can allow the rate of profit to rise even when the wage stays constant. Suppose, for instance, that workers consume only corn, and their wage remains constant in terms of corn. Capitalists consume both corn and straw, and suppose they suddenly decide to increase their demand for straw. The result will be an increase in straw's price, which will in turn inflate the rate of profit. Capitalists will have a nominally greater return on their capital. But they will receive in the end no more goods than they did originally, because workers will receive no fewer.

Now imagine that the economy also has this technique available:

$$\text{1/10 corn \& 5/4 labour} \rightarrow \text{1 straw.}$$

Given some wage, if the price of straw is high enough it will be profitable for capitalists to operate this technique as well as the other. Whether or not the price of straw is high enough will depend on the demand for it, so we have here a situation where demand can affect which techniques are used. The non-substitution theorem (p. 120) cannot be relied on when there is joint production.

Suppose this second technique does happen to be in use. Competition will ensure that it yields the same rate of profit as the other. So

$$p=(1+r)(1/10+(5/4)w. \tag{6.1.2}$$

This together with (6.1.1) gives a wage–profit equation

$$1 =(1+r)(2/5-(1/4)w),$$

and also the price of straw as a function of the wage:

$$p=(1/10+(5/4)w)/(2/5-(1/4)w).$$

We have obtained these more determinate results because we now have as many price equations — one for each technique — as there are products. And that is the situation we have always been in in previous chapters.

The wage–profit curve in this particular example slopes upwards. Figure 6.1.1 shows it. Once again it is of course impossible for the real incomes of both workers and capitalists to increase together. The curve slopes upwards simply because an increase in the wage inflates the price of straw so much (provided demand still keeps both techniques in operation) that there is room for the nominal rate of profit to increase too.

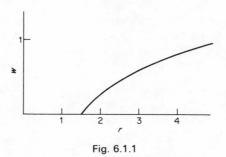

Fig. 6.1.1

The General Case

What I have been saying can be generalized. In any economy with joint production it is possible for fewer techniques to be employed than there are products, since one technique may produce several products. If this happens then final demand will have a direct influence on prices and the distribution of income. But if it should happen that the number of techniques in use is equal to the number of products then from the techniques in use one can determine a wage–profit curve (or if there are several resources a relationship between the rate of profit and the prices of resources). Also, once the distributional variables are fixed, so are the prices of products, by virtue of the technology alone. This is a state of affairs like the ones we are used to, but there are differences. One is that the wage–profit curve may slope upwards; we have seen an example. Another is that final demand can have a determining influence. *If* as many techniques are in operation as there are products then we do not need to refer to demand to determine the wage–profit curve or prices. But it may be the pattern of demand that determines how many techniques are employed in the first place.

Economies with Equal Numbers of Techniques and Products

It seems at the moment that it will be no more than good luck if the number of techniques in use happen to match the number of products. But we shall find in Section 6.2 that there is a good reason to pay special attention to what happens if they do. So I shall sketch an approach to analysing that particular case.

Let us look, then, at an economy that has n products and also n techniques for making them. Its technology may be set out like this:

$$a_{11} \text{ product } 1 \text{ \& } \ldots \text{ \& } a_{n1} \text{ product } n \text{ \& } l_{11} \text{ resource } 1 \text{ \& } \ldots$$
$$\text{\& } l_{h1} \text{ resource } h \rightarrow b_{11} \text{ product } 1 \text{ \& } \ldots \text{ \& } b_{n1} \text{ product } n$$

$$a_{1n} \text{ product } 1 \text{ \& } \ldots \text{ \& } a_{nn} \text{ product } n \text{ \& } l_{1n} \text{ resource } 1 \text{ \& } \ldots$$
$$\text{\& } l_{hn} \text{ resource } h \rightarrow b_{1n} \text{ product } 1 \text{ \& } \ldots \text{ \& } b_{nn} \text{ product } n.$$

The technology may be represented more briefly by collecting the coefficients into matrices. Let A be the $n \times n$ **input matrix** whose coefficients are the a's in the formula above; let B be the $n \times n$ **output matrix** whose coefficients are the b's; and let l be the $h \times n$ matrix of resource coefficients whose components are the l's.

Let x be the n-dimensional column vector of **activity levels**. That means that if, for instance, x_1 is one then the first technique is working at the scale set out in the formula above. But if x_1 is two then it is working at twice that scale, and so on. Then the economy's gross outputs will be the vector Bx. Its inputs of products will be Ax. So its net outputs will be

$$y = Bx - Ax = (B - A)x. \tag{6.1.3}$$

In our earlier models without joint production we knew that, provided the economy was productive, there was always a (non-negative) vector x of activity levels (equivalent in those models to gross productions) that would lead to any (non-negative) vector of net productions we might choose. Any pattern of net production was technically possible if enough resources were available. In mathematical terms we knew that

$$x = (I - A)^{-1} y$$

and that $(I - A)^{-1}$ had no negative components (p. 39). So to any given y without negative components there corresponded an x without negative components. But with joint production things are less simple. Even if $(B - A)$ is non-singular so that (6.1.3) leads to

$$x = (B - A)^{-1} y$$

there is no guarantee that $(B - A)^{-1}$ will not have negative components. So x may have negative components even if y does not. A negative component in x means giving some technique a negative activity level, which is obviously impossible. So some patterns of net production may simply not be possible; no pattern of activity levels will deliver them. It is easy to see why this might be: when activities produce goods jointly in fixed proportions it is not surprising if the economy cannot produce them in every conceivable combination.

If we assume, as I said we would, that each technique is in use, then each technique must be yielding the same rate of profit r. Let w be the vector of resource prices and p the vector of product prices. Then it is easy to see that

$$pB = (1+r)(pA + wl).$$

This equation can be manipulated in a familiar way:

$$pB - (1+r)pA = (1+r)wl.$$
$$\therefore\; p(B - (1+r)A) = (1+r)wl.$$
$$\therefore\; p = (1+r)wl(B - (1+r)A)^{-1}.$$

(Assume that $(B - (1+r)A)$ is non-singular.) We have here a formula for the prices of products in terms of the rate of profit and the prices of resources. Now let the vector z of products be the numeraire, so that pz is one. Then

$$pz = (1+r)wl(B - (1+r)A)^{-1}z.$$
$$\therefore\; 1 = (1+r)wl(B - (1+r)A)^{-1}z.$$

Here is the wage–profit equation or, if there are several resources, the equation that relates the prices of resources and the rate of profit.

In this sort of way the model can be developed as in earlier chapters. There will be many complications on the way. But rather than delving into them I want to turn to a case where there is a wider range of techniques available.

The Choice of Technique

Suppose now that the economy has n products but has available more than n techniques. We can pick out **systems of techniques** from the complete range. Each system must have exactly n techniques altogether and include for each of the n products a technique that produces it. We may also admit as systems collections of techniques that do not produce every product, provided they use as materials only the products they do produce, and provided they contain exactly as many techniques as they have products. The point of this concession is to allow, for instance, systems that make no use of some particular intermediate product or (as we shall be seeing) of some machine beyond a particular age. But we shall definitely not count as a system any collection of techniques that has fewer techniques than products.

Each system is a putative technology of the sort I have been describing. Each can be represented by matrices A, B and l. Each will lead to a definite relationship between the rate of profit and the prices of resources. Figure 6.1.2 shows the wage–profit curves for a number of systems within a technology that employs no resources besides labour. Now, unfortunately there is no guarantee that at a given wage capitalists will select the system whose curve is farthest to the right. Not every system, we have seen on p. 198, is necessarily able to produce every conceivable pattern of net production, and this particular system may not be suitable for supplying the final demand that happens to exist. Demand may force capitalists to adopt another system, or else no system at all: they may adopt some collection of techniques that includes fewer techniques than products.

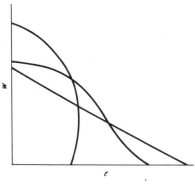

Fig. 6.1.2

As a general rule, then, a diagram like Fig. 6.1.2 will not tell us which techniques the economy will employ. Analysing the choice of technique will be a more complicated business. However, we shall find in Section 6.2 that in some significant circumstances capitalists will indeed select the system whose wage–profit curve lies furthest to the right. In those circumstances the diagram will serve its purpose.

Summary

The brief glimpse we have had of joint production suggests that it might force on us a radical revision of the conclusions we have reached earlier in this book. An economy where joint production was common might behave in ways quite different from those we are used to. In particular it seems that final demand might have a direct and important role. It also seems that our familiar methods may not be very successful at analysing such an economy.

The next section, however, examines the most practically important species of joint production, and its conclusions are much less pessimistic.

Section 6.2 Instruments of Production

Instruments as Joint Products

I have always assumed so far that inputs into the production process are all used up in a single period. But there are many important inputs, such things as machinery, tools and buildings, that do not fit this assumption. I call these the **instruments of production**, and I now want to take account of them.

The best way to fit instruments into our model is to treat an instrument as it remains at the end of a production process as an output of the process. Instruments enter a process as inputs and emerge as outputs one period older. Imagine, for example, that a farming technology employs horses. A horse has a useful life of three years and needs more attention as it gets older. The technology might be:

$$\left.\begin{array}{lll} \text{1/4 corn} & \text{\& 1 new horse} & \text{\& 1 labour} \to \text{1 corn} \\ & & \text{\& 1 one-year-old horse} \\ \text{1/4 corn} & \text{\& 1 one-year-old horse} & \text{\& 2 labour} \to \text{1 corn} \\ & & \text{\& 1 two-year-old horse} \\ \text{1/4 corn} & \text{\& 1 two-year-old horse} & \text{\& 4 labour} \to \text{1 corn} \\ \text{1/2 corn} & & \text{\& 1/2 labour} \to \text{1 new horse.} \end{array}\right\} \quad (6.2.1)$$

By expressing them this way processes that employ instruments of production can be brought under the heading of joint production.

So our analysis of joint production puts us in a position to analyse economies that use instruments. Indeed this is the principal reason for paying attention to joint production in the first place; the use of instruments is a much more significant feature of real economies than are other sorts of joint production. We have seen that joint production can lead to radical departures from the rules about economies' behaviour that we learnt in earlier chapters. For instance, there may be no such thing as a wage–profit curve. But the joint production associated with instruments is a very special sort, and economies that employ instruments will probably behave in altogether more familiar ways than do economies with joint production in general.

A Special Property of Instruments as Joint Products

There are two reasons for thinking this. One is that if we make a few assumptions we can be sure that the economy will always have in operation as many techniques as there are products. That, as we saw in Section 6.1, is enough to ensure that there is a wage–profit curve, or more generally a relationship between the rate of profit and the prices of resources. And it ensures that, once the distributional variables are fixed, the prices of products will be determined without any reference to final demand.

The first assumption we shall need is that the economy's only joint production is the production of used instruments; no materials, consumer goods or new instruments are produced jointly. That means that for every product apart from a used instrument there is a separate technique that produces it. If we can also be sure that for each type of used instrument there is a further technique in operation, we shall have as many techniques as there are products of any sort.

Let us next assume that there is no demand from consumers for used instruments. Then no used instrument will command a price (other than nought) unless it is employed in a technique that is actually in operation. If an instrument has no price we can ignore it and not count it as a product at all, as I ignored a three-year-old horse in (6.2.1). So for every used instrument that matters there is a technique in operation that employs it. There will therefore be as many techniques in operation as there are products, provided only that each used instrument adds to the count a new technique of its own rather than one that has already been counted.

This, however, is not automatically the case. Both the following two examples have fewer techniques than products.

$$
\left.
\begin{array}{l}
\text{1 steel \& 1 new machine \ \& 1 labour} \rightarrow \text{1 car \& 1 scrap machine} \\
\text{1 scrap machine \& 1 labour} \rightarrow \text{1 steel} \\
\text{1 labour} \rightarrow \text{1 new machine.}
\end{array}
\right\} (6.2.2)
$$

$$
\left.
\begin{array}{l}
\text{1 scrap machine \& 1 new machine \& 1 labour} \rightarrow \text{1 car \&} \\
\hspace{6cm} \text{1 scrap machine} \\
\text{1 labour} \rightarrow \text{1 new machine.}
\end{array}
\right\} (6.2.3)
$$

We shall have to make assumptions that exclude examples like these. One way of excluding technology (6.2.2) and others of the sort is to assume that instruments spend all their lives in one industry; used instruments are never taken from one industry to be employed in another. This assumption excludes recycling activities from the model, which is a pity. There are other ways of achieving the same end (we might, for instance, realistically assume that for every recycled product there is a technique that produces the same product directly from natural resources) but this is the simplest. We need another assumption to exclude cases like (6.2.3), but I shall not go into the question of which is the best to choose. No doubt such cases have little practical importance, but they do serve to show that assumptions need to be chosen with care if we are to be sure that a model containing instruments will have equal numbers of techniques and products.

Nevertheless, it seems reasonable to suppose that cases where there are fewer techniques in use than products will be exceptional.

Another Special Property of Instruments as Joint Products

We may generally presume, then, that the economy will always employ enough techniques to form a system as I defined it on p. 199. I explained on p. 198 that a system with joint production cannot necessarily produce goods in every possible combination that may be demanded. But a system whose only joint production is the production of used instruments is a special case, because it will normally be able to supply any pattern of final demand that may arise. This is the second reason why we may expect an economy that employs instruments to behave in more familiar ways than an economy with other sorts of joint production. I shall explain why, but the explanation will have to be very sketchy.

Let us suppose, then, that an economy is operating a system of techniques that has no joint production amongst new products, namely amongst consumer goods, materials and new instruments. And let us suppose that the system is productive in the sense of p. 39. Let us also make the assumption I mentioned above that an instrument spends all its life in one industry. Then the economy can be clearly divided into industries, each devoted to producing a single new product and nothing else. Each industry may employ several techniques, and many of the techniques may produce used instruments jointly with the industry's final product. But all these joint products are used up within the industry itself.

An industry will require as inputs the products (including new instruments) of other industries. To produce, net, a quantity of some new product, the product's own industry will have to operate, and also the industries that supply its inputs, and those that supply the inputs for its inputs, and so on. We can divide the economy up by *segments* as we did on p. 59. Each segment is a collection of industries in appropriate proportions so that they together produce, net, a single new product. Each segment may operate on any desired scale (provided enough resources are available) in order to produce any desired quantity of its own product. Its scale is independent of the scale of other segments. So the economy can produce, net, any pattern of new products that may be demanded.

That is not the end of the argument, however, because if the economy is growing there will be some final demand for used instruments as well as new goods. Although any combination of new goods can be produced, that is certainly not true of any combination of new and used goods. Nevertheless it is true that any combination of new and used goods that may actually be demanded in the course of economic growth can be produced, provided we continue to assume that consumers only demand new products. This is something I shall have to ask you to accept without an explanation.

Our conclusion, then, is that any system of techniques will generally be able to supply any pattern of final demand that may actually arise.

Obsolescence and the Choice of Technique

An economy that employs instruments inevitably has a number of systems of techniques to choose from. An instrument may be **retired** from use at different ages, and each age of retirement leads to a different system. Technology (6.2.1), for instance, contains within it these two systems:

$$\beta\begin{cases} \text{1/4 corn \& 1 new horse} & \& \quad \text{1 labour} \rightarrow \text{1 corn \& 1 one-year-old} \\ & \qquad\qquad\qquad\qquad\qquad\qquad \text{horse} \\ \text{1/4 corn \& 1 one-year-old horse} & \& \quad \text{2 labour} \rightarrow \text{1 corn} \\ \text{1/2 corn} & \& \quad \text{1/2 labour} \rightarrow \text{1 new horse} \end{cases}$$

$$\gamma\begin{cases} \text{1/4 corn \& 1 new horse} & \& \quad \text{1 labour} \rightarrow \text{1 corn} \\ \text{1/2 corn} & \& \quad \text{1/2 labour} \rightarrow \text{1 new horse} \end{cases}$$

and the whole of technology (6.2.1) is a third system α. In drawing up these systems I have simply not counted an instrument due for retirement as a product. In this I am following the instruction on p. 202 to ignore a used instrument whose price is nought. An instrument due for retirement has no further use and therefore no price.

Because of its connection with retirement, analysing the choice of technique is a particularly pressing matter in an economy that employs instruments. Fortunately we are in a position to deal with it. Whatever techniques the economy may adopt, we know that they will definitely form a system. And each system will have a wage–profit curve (or if there are several resources a relationship between the rate of profit and the prices of resources). Figure 6.2.1 shows the wage–profit curves of the systems α, β and γ in technology (6.2.1).

We found on p. 199 that in economies with joint production we cannot be sure that the system selected will be the one whose wage–profit curve lies furthest to the right in a diagram like Fig. 6.2.1. The reason is that this system might not be able to supply net production in the right proportions to satisfy final demand. But when the only joint production is of instruments we now know that every productive system is capable of producing any pattern of net production that may be demanded. Capitalists will therefore choose the system that the diagram shows to be most profitable. In our example system β will be chosen instead of α if the wage is above a certain level; a high wage causes horses to be retired early.

We may conclude, then, that once we know the wage (and the prices of other resources if there are any) we know what system will be selected. We know

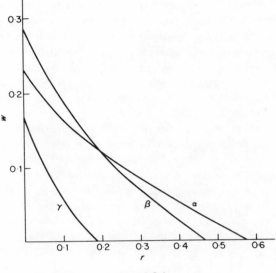

Fig. 6.2.1

what the rate of profit will be, and the prices of all the products. Final demand has no direct influence on these things. It is fair to say that the non-substitution theorem (p. 120) continues to apply.

Summary

Our brief look at instruments of production suggests that their existence does not radically alter the conclusions we drew in early chapters of this book. But of course this section has been only an introduction to their analysis.

Section 6.3 Increasing and Decreasing Returns to Scale; a Market in Capital

Technology

I have always assumed so far that any technique of production can be used unaltered on any scale. But in practice that is unlikely to be true. Many techniques, for one thing, will use indivisible inputs; a technique that requires machinery, for instance, can be run on a scale that needs one machine or two but not half a machine or one and a half. And many techniques will require workers to do specialized jobs and cooperate together in ways that are only possible when the labour force is large. On the other hand the difficulties of managing production on a large scale may create some inefficiency, so that the techniques available become progressively less productive as the scale increases. This section considers how our model can take account of possibilities like these.

An industry consists of a number of separate enterprises. The techniques available to an enterprise may depend on its own size, or they may also depend on the size of the whole industry. I shall primarily be discussing the former possibility, where the effects of scale are **internal** to the enterprise. The latter, **external**, effects I shall mention at the end of the section. For the moment I shall ignore them.

The most comprehensive way of representing a technology that does not have constant returns to scale is to list all the various possible techniques with a note attached to each saying what scale or scales it can be applied on. For example:

$$\left.\begin{array}{l} \alpha: \ 1/4 \text{ corn } \& \quad 1 \text{ labour } \rightarrow \ 1 \text{ corn}; \text{ any output} \\ \beta: \quad 1 \text{ corn } \& \quad 3 \text{ labour } \rightarrow \ 4 \text{ corn}; \text{ output in multiples of four units} \\ \gamma: \quad 3 \text{ corn } \& \ 20 \text{ labour } \rightarrow 20 \text{ corn}; \text{ output between 20 and 40 units.} \end{array}\right\}(6.3.1)$$

With this technology each of these is possible, for instance:

$$6\beta: \qquad 6 \text{ corn } \& \ 18 \text{ labour } \rightarrow 24 \text{ corn}$$
$$(6/5)\gamma: \ 18/5 \text{ corn } \& \ 24 \text{ labour } \rightarrow 24 \text{ corn}.$$

Of course a technology might have a continuous gradation of techniques rather than the sharp separation shown in (6.3.1). For instance, increasing the scale of production might progressively decrease the inputs needed per unit of output or, as a result of inefficiences, increase them. A production function may often be a convenient way of representing continuous technologies like this, as we found in Chapter 4. But everything I shall be saying applies as much to continuous technologies as to discrete ones.

Firms

A capitalist will have some amount of capital which, when it is invested in an industry, will determine the size of his or her enterprise. A farmer in our example might have enough capital to employ five workers. In that case three can be put on to technique β but the remaining two will have to use α, which is less productive and less profitable. It is plain that when an industry does not have constant returns to scale capitalists in the industry are likely to receive different rates of return on their capital, depending on how much capital they happen to have.

But this situation creates an obvious incentive for groups of capitalists in an industry to amalgamate their capitals, or perhaps divide them up, so as to set up enterprises of the right size to exploit the most profitable technique. They will create **firms**, which for the moment we shall treat as **cooperatives of capitalists**. Each firm will have a number of shareholders.

So let us assume that an industry's capital always organizes itself in this way. If the industry is to be competitive, as I shall want to assume it is, each firm will have to be small compared with the industry as a whole. So we shall have to assume that the scale required by the most profitable technique is comparatively small. A second consequence of this assumption is that the industry can expand or contract by the setting up of firms or by firms' closing down, and the lumpiness of the process will be slight enough to be ignored. Each individual firm will be able to stay always at the most profitable size and employ the most profitable technique. The industry will have, in effect, constant returns to scale even though the firms do not. It can change its scale without changing the technique in use, by changing the number of firms.

The Choice of Technique and Scale

Now we can analyse the firms' choice of technique in exactly the same way as before. From the collection of all the techniques in every industry we pick out systems of techniques in the usual way, simply ignoring the restrictions that limit the techniques to particular scales of output. Each system will define a wage–profit curve, or more generally a relationship between the rate of profit and the prices of resources. For any given wage, or given prices of resources, capitalists will adopt the system that delivers the greatest rate of profit. To do so they will have to organize each industry so that its firms are the right size for exploiting the most profitable technique. Figure 6.3.1, for instance, shows the wage–profit curves for technology (6.3.1). If the wage is less than 2/5 technique γ is the most profitable; if more than 2/5 β. If the wage moves through the switch point the industry will have to be reorganized; capitalists will have to combine their capitals in a new way. While technique γ is in use firms will need to produce an output between 20 and 40 units; while β is in use their output will need to be some multiple of four units.

All the analysis of previous chapters continues to apply without alteration to our new version of the model. The possible need for some reorganization at a switch point is the only significant new feature.

Management

The vision of firms as cooperatives of capitalists brings up the question of **management**. Implicitly I have always assumed that a capitalist manages his or her own enterprise. But now we have firms with several shareholders, and a

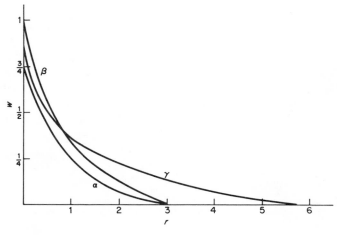

Fig. 6.3.1

single capitalist's capital may be divided between several firms, perhaps in several industries. To imagine that the shareholders cooperate in managing a firm is not very plausible. So let us assume that they employ managers. Managers will form a separate class in the society. We shall have to embody the need for management in the technology as an extra input. A typical technique might be:

3 corn & 20 labour & 1 management → 20 corn; output between 20 and 40 units.

Management is another scarce resource, analogous to labour. Our methods of analysis will continue to work perfectly well.

A Market in Capital; Entrepreneurs

There is a second rather unrealistic aspect to our vision of firms as cooperatives of capitalists. It suggests that capitalists of their own accord come together in groups of the right size. But it is more natural to suppose that a firm itself controls its size by *borrowing* capital in suitable amounts. Our model of capitalist society would represent modern capitalism more accurately if we incorporated into it a **market in capital**, where capital is borrowed and lent. Let us do so. The owners of capital, let us now suppose, do not apply it to production themselves but lend it to other people who do. The return they receive in exchange is **interest**. I shall assume that the market in capital is competitive, so that there is a uniform rate of interest.

Who borrows capital and applies it to production? We might take it to be the managers of firms, and there is no analytical difficulty in doing so. Managers would treat interest as a cost of production, and act so as to make the greatest possible income for themselves. But since the size of a firm determines the number of managers it has, it is a little awkward to assume that a firm's managers choose its size in order to maximize their incomes. That would be analogous to assuming that capitalists spontaneously form cooperatives of the most profitable size, which I have already condemned as unrealistic.

It is more traditional to suppose that each firm is controlled by a single **entrepreneur**. He or she borrows capital and uses it to buy materials, employ workers and so on, and also to employ managers if necessary. The entrepreneur's aim is to make the greatest income, and he or she selects the firm's size and the technique it uses to that end. Now that the return to capital is called interest we may call an entrepreneur's income "profit" (some people call it "pure profit"), but profit is now, of course, not to be thought of as a return to capital. Let us suppose that an entrepreneur may move freely from one industry to another, and set up a firm wherever he or she wishes. Consequently, competition amongst entrepreneurs will ensure that they receive the same profit in every industry.

The Choice of Technique and Scale

To fit entrepreneurs into our model we need to make their presence explicit in the technology. Here is an example:

$$
\left.
\begin{array}{l}
\alpha:\ 1/4\ \text{corn \& 1 labour \& 1 entrepreneur} \rightarrow 1 \quad \text{corn; output} \\
\qquad\qquad\qquad\qquad\qquad\qquad\qquad\qquad\qquad\qquad\qquad 1\ \text{unit} \\
\beta:\ 1/2\ \text{corn \& 2 labour \& 1 entrepreneur} \rightarrow 9/4\ \text{corn; output} \\
\qquad\qquad\qquad\qquad\qquad\qquad\qquad\qquad\qquad\qquad\qquad 9/4\ \text{units} \\
\gamma:\ 3/4\ \text{corn \& 3 labour \& 1 entrepreneur} \rightarrow 3 \quad \text{corn; output} \\
\qquad\qquad\qquad\qquad\qquad\qquad\qquad\qquad\qquad\qquad\qquad 3\ \text{units.}
\end{array}
\right\} \quad (6.3.2)
$$

Notice that each technique is available only at a single scale of output, because a firm must have one entrepreneur, no more and no less. The example shows a case where increasing a firm's scale of production initially increases its productivity (perhaps by division of labour) and then decreases it again (perhaps because a single entrepreneur cannot control a large firm very effectively).

As we did before we pick out of the technology systems of techniques, taking no notice of the limitations on scale. Each system will fix a relationship between the wage, the rate of interest, the entrepreneurs' profit, and the prices of any other resources there may be. Technique α in (6.3.2), for instance, gives us this relationship:

$$1 = (1+i)(\tfrac{1}{4} + w + \pi)$$

where i is the rate of interest and w and π are the wage and profit, both in terms of corn. To continue with the example, we may draw a wage–interest–profit surface for each technique. Figure 6.3.2 shows the surfaces for techniques β and γ; since α will obviously never be selected I have not included it in the diagram. Given a wage and a rate of interest, entrepreneurs will adopt the technique that gives them the greatest profit, and they will fix the scales of their firms accordingly. Obviously that means that the wage–interest–profit surface

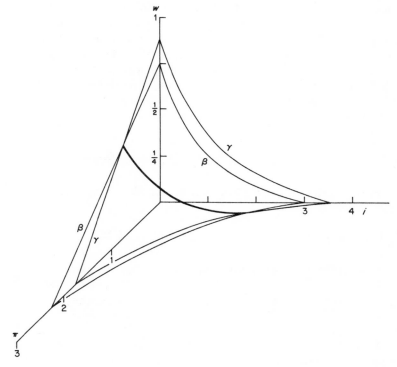

Fig. 6.3.2

for the economy as a whole is the outer envelope of the surfaces belonging to the individual techniques. And for any distribution of income the technique selected is the one that puts the economy on the outer envelope. This means that our analysis can proceed exactly as it has before, particularly in Chapter 5. In earlier versions of our model the choice of technique has always been in the hands of capitalists, who maximized the rate of return to capital given the prices of resources. Now it is in the hands of entrepreneurs, who maximize profit, given the prices of resources and the rate of return to capital. But that turns out to make no difference to the formal behaviour of the model; if profit were given and we maximized the rate of return to capital the result would be the same. We may simply treat entrepreneurs as a scarce resource and proceed as before. And none of our conclusions will be any different.

Figure 6.3.2, then, shows as a heavy line the locus of switch points where the scale of output from each firm will be switched between two units and three units. Increasing profit through the switch point causes a switch to production on a larger scale. (This is what one would naturally expect, but I do not offer it as an invariable rule.)

External Effects

It is possible for the techniques available to an enterprise to be affected by the scale of the entire industry it belongs to. This can happen, for example, if the industry depends on some scarce resource. If the resource belongs to someone who charges a rent for using it then the analysis of Chapter 5 covers the case. But if, like the stock of fish in the oceans, it belongs to nobody then Chapter 5 does not help. It is often best not to treat a resource of this sort explicitly as an input but instead say that it leads to decreasing returns to scale in the industry. The larger the industry the greater the pressure on the resource and consequently the bigger will be the amounts of other inputs needed per unit of output. If the fishing industry expands it will be more difficult to catch a ton of fish. Increasing the scale of an industry can, on the other hand, lead to increasing returns. A large industry, for instance, may spread amongst the population useful skills that individual enterprises will benefit from.

These are examples of **external effects**; the techniques available to an enterprise are affected by causes outside the enterprise itself. Let us assume for simplicity that there are not simultaneously any internal effects; we have already dealt with those. And let us assume that every enterprise is small compared with its industry. Then every enterprise in an industry will have the same techniques available to it, and no enterprise will, by expanding or contracting, have any noticeable influence over the techniques available.

The simplest way of incorporating external effects into our model is to make the "coefficients" of the technology (the requirements of inputs per unit of output) functions of the industries' outputs. In the model of Chapter 3, for instance, the input–output matrix A and the vector l of labour requirements will have to be written $A(x)$ and $l(x)$, where x is the vector of gross outputs. This formulation has the advantage that one industry's coefficients may be affected by another industry's output, as may plausibly happen if, for instance, both exploit the same resource.

Most of our equations will be the same as before. Prices, for example, will still be given by costs raised by the rate of profit:

$$p = (1 + r)(pA(x) + wl(x)).$$

Net and gross outputs will still be connected in the same way:

$$y = (I - A(x))x.$$

And so on. Our analysis, then, will not be totally altered. But there will be one obvious difference: the composition of production, which is partly determined by final demand, will have ubiquitous effects. We have generally been able to examine the relationships between prices and distributional variables without paying any attention to the pattern of demand or of production. But with external effects that will no longer be possible. In drawing up a wage–profit curve, for example, we shall have to take account of the different patterns of demand that workers and capitalists may have.

But I am not going to pursue the analysis, and that is all I have to say about external effects.

Summary

Giving up the assumption of constant returns to scale, when the effect was internal to the enterprises, forced us to add a market in capital to our model. But it made no difference to our methods of analysis or our conclusions. There are two reasons. One is that maximizing the profit of entrepreneurs, given a rate of return to capital determined in the capital market, has exactly the same effect as would maximizing the rate of return to capital, given a level of entrepreneurs' profit, and maximizing the rate of return to capital is what all our previous analysis has been based on. The other is that industries will still have constant returns to scale even if firms do not, provided firms are small compared with the industry and provided there are no external effects.

But if external effects do exist then new analysis is called for, and many of our conclusions will be threatened.

Section 6.4   Other Extensions

Differing Periods of Production

A process of production takes some definite length of time to complete. But by artificially treating part-finished goods as products the process may be broken down into a number of shorter steps. The process

$$1 \text{ cloth} \qquad \& \ 10 \text{ labour} \ \rightarrow 1 \text{ suit} \qquad\qquad (6.4.1)$$

may be broken down into

$$\left.\begin{array}{l} 1 \text{ cloth} \qquad\quad \& \ \ 5 \text{ labour} \ \rightarrow 1 \text{ half-made suit} \\ 1 \text{ half-made suit} \ \& \ \ 5 \text{ labour} \ \rightarrow 1 \text{ suit.} \end{array}\right\} \ (6.4.2)$$

If the original process takes ten weeks, each of the steps will take five. By dividing a process up more and more finely its steps may be made as short as need be.

Division into steps is a convenient way of fitting into our theory processes of production that take different lengths of time. The different processes simply need to be divided into steps of the same length. Each step can be treated as a technique in its own right, and we shall have a technology where every technique takes the same time to complete. This artificial technology will fit our theory perfectly. It is worth remembering that by dividing processes into steps we shall similarly divide profit. From a process that takes ten weeks a capitalist will expect roughly ten times the return on capital than from a step that takes one week, because capital invested in the latter will earn its profit ten times in ten weeks (actually rather more, because profit can be earned on profit).

Dividing up processes into steps is not a mere formality; it implies some definite changes in the model's assumptions. One is this: in treating each step as a separate technique we are implicitly assuming that all steps can be operated simultaneously; we do not have to wait till one batch of finished products has emerged before starting on the next. For most manufactuing industries that brings the model closer to reality. In many of these industries production is almost continuous; new batches are started down the line at short intervals. But there are also seasonal industries, especially agriculture, where production is confined to an annual cycle. If our model is to take proper account of seasonal industries then when we divide processes into steps we shall have to recognize that not every step is available at every time of year. This will demand some changes in the analysis.

A second implication of dividing up processes is in the timing of wage payments. Writing the process of suit-making as (6.4.1) implies, given the way the model is developed, that the wages are paid ten weeks before the suit is ready. But writing it as (6.4.2) implies that they are paid in two instalments, the second only five weeks before the suit is ready. To make a suit by (6.4.2) will actually require rather less capital than by (6.4.1), because some of the wages do not need to be financed for so long a period. This result of dividing up processes can be seen as an advantage rather than a disadvantage. In reality workers are generally paid at regular intervals of a week or a month, which are the same in every industry and often much shorter than the industry's period of production. They are not usually paid in a lump at the beginning of the process they work on. So dividing processes into weekly or monthly steps seems to bring us closer to reality. And this suggests something else. Workers are generally paid at the end of a week's or a month's work, and not at the beginning. So it seems that once we have split processes into short steps we shall move even closer to reality if we assume that workers are paid at the end of a step.

At first sight this move looks as if it will cause significant changes in many of the conclusions we have reached in this book. It means that wages do not need to be financed by capital, and the assumption that they do has played a large part in our analysis. But actually the change is not very great. It is obvious, on thinking about it, that by the time processes have been divided into short steps it cannot make much difference whether workers are paid at the beginning or the end of them. Capitalists, whose production processes generally take many weeks, are in practice going to need little more capital to cover wages if they are paid a week in advance than if they are paid a week in arrears. How this appears in the formal analysis is as follows. The more finely we divide a process into steps the more of its capital will formally be tied up in part-finished goods and the less in wage payments. When tailoring, for instance is looked at in (6.4.1) as a single process it needs capital only to buy cloth and pay wages. But when it is split up in (6.4.2) capital is also needed to finance half-made suits. Of course no more capital is needed than before; it is just that part of what previously appeared as capital to pay wages now appears as capital to buy or hold half-made suits. By the time a process is split into steps as short as a week, only a little of its capital will formally pay wages; and if we now assume that wages are paid a week in arrears, none at all. But the capital that finances part-finished goods is still really capital that pays wages viewed in another form. If the wage goes up, this part of capital will have to go up, because an increase in the wage will increase the price of part-finished goods relative to the final product. Wages are still effectively financed out of capital even if formally it does not appear so.

International Trade

International trade is really too big a subject to take up even sketchily in this book. But it is worth mentioning, I think, that in simple conditions it will fit into our model easily.

Assume that imported and exported goods are bought and sold in competitive world markets. That means that if an individual country buys or sells these goods abroad it will not influence their prices. Their prices are given to it, and let us suppose they are given in terms of some international currency called "foreign exchange".

We can treat foreign exchange formally as one of the country's products. Foreign exchange is "produced" by exporting and used as an input in importing. The activities of exporting and importing may be written as techniques. Exporting oil, for instance, might be

15 oil & shipping→1 foreign exchange,

and importing cars

2 foreign exchange & 4 shipping→1 cars.

In this way the costs of trading, such as shipping costs, can be taken into account. So can the profits of the trader, since these techniques will earn profits like any others. Since the activity of trading may take only a short time compared with genuine production, we shall have to rely on the method I have just described for accommodating processes of different lengths.

We have only to add all the exporting and importing activities to whatever techniques the economy possess for genuine production, and we shall have a technology for the economy that can be analysed in precisely the usual way. One of the things that will emerge from the model's working will be a price for the "product" foreign exchange, expressed in terms of whatever good happens to be numeraire. This price tells us how much of the numeraire will buy a unit of foreign exchange. It tells us, in effect, the country's exchange rate.

The technology, together with the exporting and importing techniques, will offer some choices of technique. Each good that the country might export provides a possible technique in the foreign exchange "industry". A conclusion we can draw at once is that generally only a single good will be exported. Unless the economy happens to be at one of the foreign exchange industry's switch points, which is not likely, only one technique—one exporting activity—will be in use within the industry. So far as importing is concerned, each importing activity amounts to an alternative technique to making the good domestically. Unless, again, the economy is at a switch point, it will choose one or the other; it will import the good or make it at home but not both.

Lack of Competition

To assume, as I have done, that the economy is entirely competitive is not very realistic. In practice the capitalists in an industry often have some control over their product's price, and capital does not flow freely between industries to equalize their rates of profit.

Consequently rates of profit may be different in different industries. This is something that can quite easily be put into our equations. Let us go back to the fundamental equation of Chapter 3, (3.3.2) on p. 46:

$$p = (1+r)(pA + wl).$$

This is really n separate equations, one for each industry:

$$p_1 = (1+r)(p_1 a_{11} + p_2 a_{21} + \ldots + p_n a_{n1} + wl_1)$$

and so on down to

$$p_n = (1+r)(p_1 a_{1n} + p_2 a_{2n} + \ldots + p_n a_{nn} + wl_n).$$

If, now, the different industries have different rates of profit, the equations will have to be written

$$p_1 = (1+r_1)(p_1 a_{11} + p_2 a_{21} + \ldots + p_n a_{n1} + wl_1)$$

and so down to

$$p_n = (1+r_n)(p_1 a_{1n} + p_2 a_{2n} + \ldots + p_n a_{nn} + wl_n)$$

where $r_1, r_2, \ldots r_n$ are the rates of profit in the different industries. Let us define a *matrix r* as

$$r = \begin{pmatrix} r_1 & 0 & \ldots & 0 \\ 0 & r_2 & \ldots & 0 \\ . & . & & . \\ . & . & & . \\ . & . & & . \\ 0 & 0 & \ldots & r_n \end{pmatrix}.$$

The equations may then be put back into vector form as

$$p = (pA + wl)(I + r). \tag{6.4.3}$$

(I is the identity matrix.) This equation can be manipulated in much the way I manipulated (3.3.2) in Chapter 3.

The equations of (6.4.3) contain $2n+1$ unknowns: the wage w, the n prices $p_1, \ldots p_n$ and the n rates of profit $r_1, \ldots r_n$. There are $n+1$ equations, counting an extra one for fixing the numeraire. Consequently, if n unknowns, such as all the rates of profit, were determined in some way independently of the equations all the other unknowns would follow. For one thing, then, the equations fix a relationship between the wage and the rates of profit. Figure 6.4.1 illustrates for an economy of just two industries.

The relationship is bound to be a negative one. That is to say, if the wage increases at least one rate of profit must decrease, and if one rate of profit increases either the wage or some other rate of profit must decrease. The

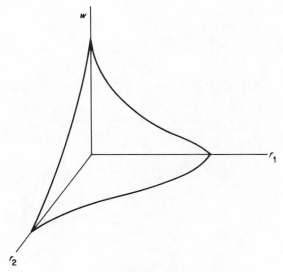

Fig. 6.4.1

arguments I presented on p. 50 of Chapter 3 are enough to establish this fact; I leave it to you to apply them to the new circumstances. They do allow one exception worth mentioning: the rate of profit in a non-basic industry may alter without altering the wage or any other rate of profit. It is obvious how this can happen: the price of a non-basic product may rise or fall without having any effect except to increase or decrease the industry's rate of profit.

So we have once more a familiar situation: the economy's distributional variables, representing the incomes of different people, are linked together negatively. One group's income can grow only at the expense of another's. Capitalists in one industry can improve their position only by damaging workers' or other capitalists'.

All this is no more than a framework for a theory of the economy's behaviour when competition fails, not a theory in itself. It sets limits on what can happen but does not tell us what will happen. The next step would be to decide what determines the individual rates of profit. It is easy to list some of the likely influences. An industry's rate of profit will depend on how effectively its capitalists can prevent new capital from entering the industry. It will depend on the nature of the demand for the industry's product; an inelastic demand is more easily exploited by pushing up the price. It will depend on how the industry's capitalists interact, on whether they cooperate or compete, and how. And so on. But putting these influences together to make a theory is something that will have to be left out of this book.

SOME SUGGESTED BOOKS
FOR FURTHER READING

Smith, A., *An Inquiry Into the Nature and Causes of the Wealth of Nations* (Clarendon Press 1976) (originally 1776; there are several other reprinted editions). The origin of many of the concepts used in this book, particularly of its concept of capital (see particularly Book II of Smith).

Ricardo, D., *The Principles of Political Economy and Taxation*, Volume I of *The Works and Correspondence of David Ricardo* edited by P. Sraffa (Cambridge University Press 1951) (first edition originally 1817; there are several other reprinted editions). A careful theoretical analysis of the distribution of income and its connection with prices. The origin of what is called the "Ricardian" method in economics, which this book by and large adopts.

Marx, K., *Capital*, Volume I (Penguin 1976) (originally 1876; there are several other reprinted editions). Develops some of Ricardo's ideas in a different direction from this book's. From a labour theory of value derives a theory of exploitation and follows up its implications.

Sraffa, P., *Production of Commodities by Means of Commodities* (Cambridge University Press 1960). The main source of much of the material in this book. Develops and modifies Ricardo's theory by working out its consequences in detail for an economy with many products.

Meek, R., *Studies in the Labour Theory of Value*, Second Edition (Lawrence and Wishart 1973). An account of the value theories of Smith, Ricardo and Marx, which sets them in their context. The new Preface to the Second Edition also discusses Sraffa's contribution.

Dobb, M., *Theories of Value and Distribution Since Adam Smith* (Cambridge University Press 1973). Another account of the theories of these four authors and others.

Morishima, M., *Marx's Economics* (Cambridge University Press 1973). A mathematical reinterpretation of Marx, using the sort of methods described in this book.

Bliss, C., *Capital Theory and the Distribution of Income* (North-Holland and American Elsevier 1975). A very thorough and authoritative treatment of many of the topics covered in this book, with a more advanced mathematical method and a different point of view.

Pasinetti, L., *Lectures on the Theory of Production* (Macmillan 1977). A textbook covering some of the same ground as this one. A more mathematical treatment, and particularly designed as an exposition of Sraffa and Marx.

Burmeister, E., *Capital Theory and Dynamics* (Cambridge University Press 1980). Another textbook, more confined to the theories of capital and growth.

Craven, J., *The Distribution of the Product* (George Allen and Unwin 1979). Another textbook, dealing particularly with different theories of distribution. Avoids difficult mathematics.

Harcourt, G., *Some Cambridge Controversies in the Theory of Capital* (Cambridge University Press 1972). An account of alternative theories of capital.

Brown, M., K. Sato and P. Zarembka (eds), *Essays in Modern Capital Theory* (North-Holland 1976). A collection of papers by various authors on topics in the theory of capital.

Leontief, W., *Input-Output Economics* (Oxford University Press 1966). A collection of essays by Leontief, which illustrate how some of the methods described in this book can be used to analyse the structure of real economies.

Kornai, J., *Mathematical Planning of Structural Decisions* (North-Holland 1967). Applications to a planned economy.

Hicks, J., *Capital and Time; A neo-Austrian Theory* (Clarendon Press 1973). Investigates something this book has only touched on sketchily: the "traverse" of economies between states of proportional growth. Treats capital in a novel way, which has some affinities with this book's treatment, and some differences.

Steedman, I. *Trade Amongst Growing Economies* (Cambridge University Press 1979). Applications to international trade.

Pasinetti, L. (ed.), *Essays in the Theory of Joint Production* (Macmillan 1980). A collection of essays by Pasinetti and others dealing with joint production and instruments of production.

Morishima, M., *Equilibrium, Stability and Growth* (Oxford University Press 1964). A technical monograph that extends some of the theory in this book. A source for some of Section 5.5.

APPENDIXES

Appendix A. Competitive Markets

This appendix is a brief outline of what a competitive market is, for readers who have not come across the notion before.

Think about the exchanges that take place in a capitalist economy of one good for another, say of bread for currency. (In our models it will generally be some good such as corn that plays the role of currency.) All the exchanges of bread for currency throughout the economy are called the bread **market**. When an exchange takes place, say of ten loaves for five units of currency, the rate of exchange, half a unit per loaf, is called the **price** of bread in terms of currency.

Suppose there are a large number of buyers and sellers of bread, none of whom buys or sells more than a small fraction of the total. Suppose they all act independently of each other, that they are all well informed about the prices other buyers and sellers are prepared to offer or accept, that they all act in their own best interest, and that there is nothing (such as legal constraints or transport costs) to stop any buyer from dealing with any seller. An obvious consequence is that, if this market is to be in equilibrium, there can only be one price in it; all exchanges of bread for currency will take place at the same price. Another is that no individual buyer or seller has any control over the equilibrium price. Each will have to accept whatever price is established in the market; everybody is a **price taker**. All that people can do is respond to the price passively by deciding how much to buy or sell. Of course their decisions will collectively help to determine what price emerges, but that process is beyond any individual's control.

What I have just described is a **competitive market**. *A competitive market is best defined as a market where there is only one price and everyone takes that price as given.*

Let us look at the quantity of bread sold during the course of some fixed period, say a year. Acting in response to a given price in the market the sellers of bread will have to decide how much they want to sell in a year. For different prices they may decide on different quantities. We can write the supply of bread as a function $S(p)$ of the price, p, of bread in terms of currency. Similarly there will be a demand function $D(p)$. Figure A1 shows typical graphs of these two functions; the graphs are known as a **supply curve** and a **demand curve**. By tradition these graphs are drawn with the independent variable, price, on the vertical axis.

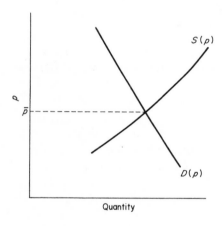

Fig. A1

If there is to be **equilibrium** in the market the year's demand will have to be equal to the year's supply. Otherwise there would be opportunities for some buyers and sellers to do better for themselves. So for equilibrium

$$S(p) = D(p).$$

The price $\bar{p}$ in Fig. A1 is the equilibrium price.

A steep demand curve or supply curve is said to be **inelastic**; a change in price has only a small effect on demand or supply. A vertical curve is **perfectly inelastic**. A demand or supply curve with a small slope is **elastic** and a horizontal one **perfectly elastic**. To be precise, the elasticity of demand is defined as

$$-\frac{p}{D}\frac{dD}{dp},$$

and of supply

$$\frac{p}{S}\frac{\mathrm{d}S}{\mathrm{d}p}.$$

The signs in these definitions are arranged so that a downward sloping demand curve has a positive elasticity and so does an upward sloping supply curve. The reason is that it is most normal for a demand curve to slope downwards and a supply curve upwards.

Appendix B. Matrix Algebra

This appendix outlines the matrix algebra that is used in the book from Chapter 3 onwards. Some more difficult concepts and methods, which are used only in Section 5.5, are described in Appendix C.

A **matrix** is a collection of numbers arranged in a rectangular pattern like this

$$\begin{pmatrix} -2 & 0.5 \\ 1.3 & -2.8 \\ 0 & 10 \end{pmatrix}.$$

The **dimensions** of this matrix are (3×2). When specifying a matrix's dimensions we always write the number of its rows first, then the number of its columns. An $m \times n$ matrix has m rows and n columns. A matrix with the same number of rows and columns is called **square**.

We often give a matrix a name consisting of a letter, so as to be able to refer to it easily. The matrix above we might call "B", so that

$$B = \begin{pmatrix} -2 & 0.5 \\ 1.3 & -2.8 \\ 0 & 10 \end{pmatrix}.$$

The numbers that make up a matrix are called its **components** or **elements**. To refer to an element we generally use a letter with two subscripts attached. The first subscript always specifies the element's row, the second its column. For instance, if we chose to use the letter "b" to refer to the elements of the matrix B above then

$$b_{11} = -2 \qquad b_{12} = 0.5$$
$$b_{21} = 1.3 \qquad b_{22} = -2.8$$
$$b_{31} = 0 \qquad b_{32} = 10.$$

A matrix with only one row, such as

$$(5, -3, -1\cdot3)$$

is called a **row vector**. This one is a three-dimensional row vector. A matrix with only one column, such as

$$\begin{pmatrix} 2 \\ 0 \end{pmatrix}$$

is called a **column vector**. This one is a two-dimensional column vector. To refer to the components of a vector we may use a letter with a single subscript. For instance, we might call the row vector above p and its components p_1, p_2 and p_3. Then

$$p = (p_1, p_2, p_3) = (5, -3, -1\cdot3),$$
$$\text{and } p_1 = 5, p_2 = -3 \text{ and } p_3 = -1\cdot3.$$

The **transpose** of a matrix is another matrix made out of the same elements, but with rows exchanged for columns and columns for rows. The transpose of a matrix B is written B'. So for instance if B is the (3×2) matrix above its transpose is

$$B' = \begin{pmatrix} -2 & 1\cdot3 & 0 \\ 0\cdot5 & -2\cdot8 & 10 \end{pmatrix}.$$

And

$$(5, -3, -1\cdot3)' = \begin{pmatrix} 5 \\ -3 \\ -1\cdot3 \end{pmatrix}.$$

An ordinary number is called a **scalar** to distinguish it from a matrix. Any matrix can be **multiplied by a scalar**; the product of a matrix B and a scalar r is written Br or rB. To multiply a matrix by a scalar simply multiply every component of the matrix by the scalar. The result is a matrix with the same size and shape as the original one. For instance

$$2\begin{pmatrix} -2 & 0\cdot5 \\ 1\cdot3 & -2\cdot8 \\ 0 & 10 \end{pmatrix} = \begin{pmatrix} -4 & 1 \\ 2\cdot6 & -5\cdot6 \\ 0 & 20 \end{pmatrix}$$

and $$(-1)(l_1, l_2, l_3) = (-l_1, -l_2, -l_3).$$

For any matrix B the product $(-1)B$ of B and the scalar (-1) is written $-B$. So $-B$ is the same as B except that every component is negated. For instance

$$-\begin{pmatrix} 1 \\ -2 \end{pmatrix} = \begin{pmatrix} -1 \\ 2 \end{pmatrix}.$$

Two matrices can be **added** together provided they have the same size and shape. The sum of the matrix B and the matrix C is written $B+C$ or $C+B$. To add matrices add together their corresponding components and write the sums as a new matrix the same size and shape as the originals. For instance

$$(1, -1)+(0.5, 1)=(1.5, 0)$$

and

$$\begin{pmatrix} a_{11} & a_{12} \\ a_{21} & a_{22} \end{pmatrix} + \begin{pmatrix} b_{11} & b_{12} \\ b_{21} & b_{22} \end{pmatrix} = \begin{pmatrix} a_{11}+b_{11} & a_{12}+b_{12} \\ a_{21}+b_{21} & a_{22}+b_{22} \end{pmatrix}$$

but

$$(2, 0)+\begin{pmatrix} 1 \\ 2 \end{pmatrix}$$

does not exist.

The sum $B+(-C)$ is written $B-C$. For instance

$$(a_1, a_2)-(1, 1)=(a_1-1, a_2-1).$$

A matrix that consists only of noughts is given the name "0" and called a **null matrix**. The symbol "0" can therefore refer to many different matrices, such as

$$(0, 0), \begin{pmatrix} 0 \\ 0 \\ 0 \end{pmatrix} \text{ and } \begin{pmatrix} 0 & 0 \\ 0 & 0 \end{pmatrix},$$

but the context usually makes it clear precisely which it refers to. For any matrix B

$$B+0=B$$
$$\text{and } B-0=B$$
$$\text{and } B-B=0.$$

The context here shows that in each case "0" refers to a matrix with the same dimensions as B.

If a matrix B has the same number of columns as a matrix C has rows, the two can be **multiplied** to form a product BC. (The order of the matrices in this expression is important; BC is not the same as CB.) The rule for multiplying matrices is complicated; to explain it I shall start with the simple special case of multiplying vectors.

If b is a row vector and c a column vector then the product bc exists provided b and c have the same dimension. For then b has the same number of columns (i.e. components) as c has rows (i.e. components). To calculate bc start by multiplying the first component of b by the first component of c, then the second of b by the second of c and so on. Then add up all these separate products and the result is the product bc. So bc is a scalar. For instance:

$$(p_1, p_2, p_3) \begin{pmatrix} x_1 \\ x_2 \\ x_3 \end{pmatrix} = p_1 x_1 + p_2 x_2 + p_3 x_3$$

and
$$(1, -1) \begin{pmatrix} 10 \\ 12 \end{pmatrix} = 10 - 12 = -2.$$

But
$$(1, 2, 3)(5, 3)$$

does not exist.

Now to multiplying matrices in general. We want to find BC, where B has as many columns as C has rows. Suppose B's dimensions are $(m \times n)$ and C's $(n \times k)$. Think of each row of B as a row vector and each column of C as a column vector. These vectors all have the same dimension: n. We shall in turn multiply every row of B by every column of C in the way I have just described. The products we shall arrange in a matrix. In the first row and first column of this matrix we shall put the product of B's first row and C's first column. In its second row and first column we shall put the product of B's second row and C's first column. In its fifth row and third column we shall put the product of B's fifth row and C's third column. And so on. This matrix, when it is finished, is the product BC we wanted. It will have the same number of rows as B and the same number of columns as C. Its dimensions will be $(m \times k)$ in fact.

Here are some examples of matrix multiplication:

$$\begin{pmatrix} a_{11} & a_{12} \\ a_{21} & a_{22} \end{pmatrix} \begin{pmatrix} x_1 \\ x_2 \end{pmatrix} = \begin{pmatrix} a_{11}x_1 + a_{12}x_2 \\ a_{21}x_1 + a_{22}x_2 \end{pmatrix},$$

$$(1, 2, 3) \begin{pmatrix} 0 & -1 \\ 1 & 0 \\ 0 & -1 \end{pmatrix} = (2, -4),$$

$$\begin{pmatrix} 1 & 2 & 3 \\ -1 & -1 & -1 \end{pmatrix} \begin{pmatrix} 0 & -1 \\ 1 & 0 \\ 0 & -1 \end{pmatrix} = \begin{pmatrix} 2 & -4 \\ -1 & 2 \end{pmatrix},$$

$$\begin{pmatrix} 0 & -1 \\ 1 & 0 \\ 0 & -1 \end{pmatrix} \begin{pmatrix} 1 & 2 & 3 \\ -1 & -1 & -1 \end{pmatrix} = \begin{pmatrix} 1 & 1 & 1 \\ 1 & 2 & 3 \\ 1 & 1 & 1 \end{pmatrix}.$$

But
$$\begin{pmatrix} x_1 \\ x_2 \end{pmatrix} \begin{pmatrix} a_{11} & a_{12} \\ a_{21} & a_{22} \end{pmatrix}$$

does not exist. Two of these examples show that BC need not be the same as CB even if both exist.

A square matrix such as

$$\begin{pmatrix} 1 & 0 & 0 \\ 0 & 1 & 0 \\ 0 & 0 & 1 \end{pmatrix}$$

with ones on the diagonal that runs down from left to right and noughts elsewhere is called an **identity matrix**. It is generally given the name "I". "I" can stand for an identity matrix of any size; the size is normally made clear by the context. All identity matrices are square. It is easy to check that for any matrix B

$$BI = B$$
$$\text{and } IB = B.$$

Notice that, unless B is square, I in these two equations will stand for identity matrices of different sizes.

For most square matrices B we can define another matrix that we call its **inverse** and write B^{-1}. The defining property of B^{-1} is that both

$$BB^{-1} = I$$
$$\text{and } B^{-1}B = I.$$

For instance the inverse of

$$B = \begin{pmatrix} 2 & 5 \\ 1 & 3 \end{pmatrix}$$

$$\text{is } B^{-1} = \begin{pmatrix} 3 & -5 \\ -1 & 2 \end{pmatrix}$$

because

$$BB^{-1} = \begin{pmatrix} 2 & 5 \\ 1 & 3 \end{pmatrix} \begin{pmatrix} 3 & -5 \\ -1 & 2 \end{pmatrix} = \begin{pmatrix} 1 & 0 \\ 0 & 1 \end{pmatrix} = I$$

$$\text{and } \quad B^{-1}B = \begin{pmatrix} 3 & -5 \\ -1 & 2 \end{pmatrix} \begin{pmatrix} 2 & 5 \\ 1 & 3 \end{pmatrix} = \begin{pmatrix} 1 & 0 \\ 0 & 1 \end{pmatrix} = I.$$

A matrix that is not square does not have an inverse. There are also some square matrices that do not have an inverse. That is to say, it is impossible to find for them a matrix having the property that defines their inverse. A square matrix that has no inverse is called **singular**.

I shall not describe the standard methods for finding whether a square matrix has an inverse and for finding its inverse if it has one. They would take up too much space. But I shall mention an alternative in a moment.

One use of matrices is to represent **systems of simultaneous linear equations**. The system

$$2x_1 + 3x_2 - 5x_3 = -3$$
$$x_1 - 2x_2 + x_3 = 5,$$

for instance, can be written

$$\begin{pmatrix} 2 & 3 & -5 \\ 1 & -2 & 1 \end{pmatrix} \begin{pmatrix} x_1 \\ x_2 \\ x_3 \end{pmatrix} = \begin{pmatrix} -3 \\ 5 \end{pmatrix}.$$

So instead of two equations we have a single vector equation saying that the vector on the left is equal to the vector on the right. In general the equation

$$Bx = c,$$

where B is a matrix and x and c are column vectors, represents a system of equations.

The example above is a system that cannot be solved for the unknowns x_1, x_2 and x_3 because there are fewer equations than unknowns. But if B should happen to be a square matrix the system represented by $Bx = c$ has the same number of unknowns and equations, so that as a general rule it can be solved. Suppose, for instance, that

$$B = \begin{pmatrix} 2 & 5 \\ 1 & 3 \end{pmatrix}, \ x = \begin{pmatrix} x_1 \\ x_2 \end{pmatrix} \text{ and } c = \begin{pmatrix} 3 \\ -1 \end{pmatrix}$$

then the equation $Bx = c$ represents the system

$$2x_1 + 5x_2 = 3$$
$$x_1 + 3x_2 = -1.$$

These equations can be solved in the ordinary way to give the solution

$$x_1 = 14$$
$$x_2 = -5.$$

But we can use matrix algebra to find the solution another way. The equations are, in vector form

$$Bx = c.$$

If B has an inverse B^{-1} we can multiply both sides of this equation by B^{-1}:

$$B^{-1}Bx = B^{-1}c.$$
$$\therefore \qquad Ix = B^{-1}c.$$
$$\therefore \qquad x = B^{-1}c.$$

It happens that for our particular example we know that B does have an inverse, and we know what it is, because I used it as an example of an inverse matrix just above. B^{-1} is

$$\begin{pmatrix} 3 & -5 \\ -1 & 2 \end{pmatrix}.$$

Therefore $x = B^{-1}c$

is

$$\begin{pmatrix} x_1 \\ x_2 \end{pmatrix} = \begin{pmatrix} 3 & -5 \\ -1 & 2 \end{pmatrix} \begin{pmatrix} 3 \\ -1 \end{pmatrix},$$

or

$$\begin{pmatrix} x_1 \\ x_2 \end{pmatrix} = \begin{pmatrix} 14 \\ -5 \end{pmatrix}.$$

And this is the same solution as we found by ordinary methods earlier.

So matrix algebra gives us a way of expressing the solution of a system of equations. The equations $Bx = c$, where B is square and non-singular, have the solution $x = B^{-1}c$. If B happens to be singular the equations have no solution. Furthermore, if we can calculate B^{-1} this is actually a method for solving the equations.

Conversely, solving equations in the ordinary way can save us from having to calculate a matrix's inverse; we can simply go back and solve the equations that originally gave rise to the inverse. Let us take an example. Chapter 3 explains that if x is the vector of an economy's gross outputs, y is the vector of its net output and A is its input–output matrix, then

$$x = (I - A)^{-1}y.$$

So if we are given y and A, by calculating the inverse of $(I - A)$ we can calculate x. But this equation may alternatively be written without the inverse as

$$(I - A)x = y.$$

If, for example

$$A = \begin{pmatrix} a_{11} & a_{12} \\ a_{21} & a_{22} \end{pmatrix}, \quad x = \begin{pmatrix} x_1 \\ x_2 \end{pmatrix} \text{ and } y = \begin{pmatrix} y_1 \\ y_2 \end{pmatrix},$$

then the equation is

$$\begin{pmatrix} 1 - a_{11} & -a_{12} \\ -a_{21} & 1 - a_{22} \end{pmatrix} \begin{pmatrix} x_1 \\ x_2 \end{pmatrix} = \begin{pmatrix} y_1 \\ y_2 \end{pmatrix}$$

or, as a system of separate equations

$$(1 - a_{11})x_1 - a_{12}x_2 = y_1$$
$$-a_{21}x_1 + (1 - a_{22})x_2 = y_2.$$

If we are given y and A (i.e. y_1, y_2, a_{11}, a_{12}, a_{21}, and a_{22}) we can solve the equations for x_1 and x_2 in the ordinary way. Without calculating the inverse $(I - A)^{-1}$, then, we can achieve the same end.

Appendix C. More Matrix Algebra

This appendix outlines some more matrix algebra, chiefly definitions, that is used in Section 5.5.

A fact about transposes: if B and C are matrices

$$(BC)' = C'B';$$

transposition reverses the order of multiplication. This fact is easily checked by multiplying out the matrices term by term.

A piece of notation: we can stack matrices up to make bigger matrices. For instance, if

$$B = \begin{pmatrix} b_{11} & b_{12} \\ b_{21} & b_{22} \end{pmatrix}$$

and

$$C = (c_1 \quad c_2)$$

then the matrix

$$\begin{pmatrix} b_{11} & b_{12} \\ b_{21} & b_{22} \\ c_1 & c_2 \end{pmatrix}$$

we write

$$\begin{pmatrix} B \\ C \end{pmatrix}.$$

And if

$$p = (p_1, p_2, p_3)$$

and

$$w = (w_1, w_2)$$

then

$$(p, w) = (p_1, p_2, p_3, w_1, w_2).$$

Of course matrices can only be stacked if they have the right dimensions to fit together.

A definition: an $n \times n$ matrix B is **negative quasi-definite** if and only if qBq' is negative for every n-dimensional row vector q other than nought.

Some notation for **differentiating** vectors and matrices: suppose B is a matrix that is a function $B(r)$ of a scalar r. That is to say, the elements of B are functions of r. Let

$$B(r) = \begin{pmatrix} b_{11}(r) & b_{12}(r) & \cdots & b_{1n}(r) \\ b_{21}(r) & b_{22}(r) & \cdots & b_{2n}(r) \\ & \vdots & & \\ b_{m1}(r) & b_{m2}(r) & \cdots & b_{mn}(r) \end{pmatrix}$$

Then by the notation dB/dr we mean

$$
\frac{dB}{dr} = \begin{pmatrix} \dfrac{db_{11}}{dr} & \dfrac{db_{12}}{dr} & \cdots\cdots & \dfrac{db_{1n}}{dr} \\[2ex] \dfrac{db_{21}}{dr} & \dfrac{db_{22}}{dr} & \cdots\cdots & \dfrac{db_{2n}}{dr} \\[2ex] \vdots \\[2ex] \dfrac{db_{m1}}{dr} & \dfrac{db_{m2}}{dr} & \cdots\cdots & \dfrac{db_{mn}}{dr} \end{pmatrix}.
$$

Suppose x is an m-dimensional *column* vector that is a function of an n-dimensional *row* vector p, so that

$$
x(p) = \begin{pmatrix} x_1(p_1, p_2, \ldots p_n) \\ x_2(p_1, p_2, \ldots p_n) \\ \vdots \\ x_m(p_1, p_2, \ldots p_n) \end{pmatrix}.
$$

By the notation $\partial x/\partial p$ we mean the $(m \times n)$ matrix

$$
\frac{\partial x}{\partial p} = \begin{pmatrix} \dfrac{\partial x_1}{\partial p_1} & \dfrac{\partial x_1}{\partial p_2} & \cdots\cdots & \dfrac{\partial x_1}{\partial p_n} \\[2ex] \dfrac{\partial x_2}{\partial p_1} & \dfrac{\partial x_2}{\partial p_2} & \cdots\cdots & \dfrac{\partial x_2}{\partial p_n} \\[2ex] \vdots \\[2ex] \dfrac{\partial x_m}{\partial p_1} & \dfrac{\partial x_m}{\partial p_2} & \cdots\cdots & \dfrac{\partial x_m}{\partial p_n} \end{pmatrix}.
$$

This notation allows us to write down a version of the **chain rule** for vectors. Suppose x is a column vector that is a function of a row vector p that is in turn a function of a scalar σ. Then

$$
\frac{d}{d\sigma} x(p(\sigma)) = \frac{\partial x}{\partial p} \left(\frac{dp}{d\sigma} \right).
$$

This formula can be checked by doing the differentiation component by component, as follows:

$$\frac{d}{d\sigma}x(p(\sigma)) = \frac{d}{d\sigma}\begin{pmatrix} x_1(p_1(\sigma), \ldots p_n(\sigma)) \\ \cdot \\ \cdot \\ \cdot \\ \cdot \\ x_m(p_1(\sigma), \ldots p_n(\sigma)) \end{pmatrix}$$

$$= \begin{pmatrix} \dfrac{d}{d\sigma}x_1(p_1(\sigma), \ldots p_n(\sigma)) \\ \cdot \\ \cdot \\ \cdot \\ \cdot \\ \dfrac{d}{d\sigma}x_m(p_1(\sigma), \ldots p_n(\sigma)) \end{pmatrix}$$

$$= \begin{pmatrix} \dfrac{\partial x_1}{\partial p_1}\dfrac{dp_1}{d\sigma} + \ldots \dfrac{\partial x_1}{\partial p_n}\dfrac{dp_n}{d\sigma} \\ \cdot \\ \cdot \\ \dfrac{\partial x_m}{\partial p_1}\dfrac{dp_1}{d\sigma} + \ldots \dfrac{\partial x_m}{\partial p_n}\dfrac{dp_n}{d\sigma} \end{pmatrix}$$

$$= \begin{pmatrix} \dfrac{\partial x_1}{\partial p_1} \cdots \dfrac{\partial x_1}{\partial p_n} \\ \cdot \\ \cdot \\ \cdot \\ \dfrac{\partial x_m}{\partial p_1} \cdots \dfrac{\partial x_m}{\partial p_n} \end{pmatrix}\begin{pmatrix} \dfrac{dp_1}{d\sigma} \\ \cdot \\ \cdot \\ \cdot \\ \dfrac{dp_n}{d\sigma} \end{pmatrix}$$

$$= \frac{\partial x}{\partial p}\left(\frac{dp}{d\sigma}\right)'.$$

INDEX

Demand and supply
  negative quasi-definite matrix,
    188–189
Demand for products
  aggregate, 23–25, 61–62, 68, 182
  composition of, 60–62, 120, 161
  final, 60–61, 67, 203–204
  functions, 67–68, 182
  influence on distribution of income, 61,
    62–63, 84–88, 123, 172–173, 197,
    204–205, 212
  influence on prices, 53, 64–66, 84–88,
    120, 173–174, 185, 189–192, 197,
    204–205, 212
  influence on economy's structure,
    60–62, 84–88, 123
  influence on techniques in use, 120,
    123, 196–197, 204–205, 212
Dated labour, *see* integrated requirement
    of labour as a dated series
Distribution of income, *see also* demand
    for products, influence on distri-
    bution of income, *and* prices of
    products and distribution of income,
    and resources, scarce, influence of
    supply on distribution of income,
    and wage–profit curve and equation,
    and wage–profit–rent surface and
    equation, 8, 15–16, 51
  and aggregate capital/labour ratio,
    20–21, 69–72, 106–110, 120–127, 167

Efficient production, 93
Entrepreneurs, 2, 209
Equilibrium, *see also* comparative statics,
    2, 72, 79
  long run and short run, 44–45
  stability of, 2–3
Euler's Theorem, 131

Factor–price frontier, *see* wage–interest–
    profit surface, *and* wage–profit curve
    and equation, *and* wage–profit–rent
    surface and equation
Free entry and exit, 44, 207
Fertility, 9, 16, 25, 36–37, 39, 52–53,
    85–86, 100, 192
Firms, 206–209

Gross production, *see also* net produc-

tion, relationship with gross pro-
    duction, 7, 34
Gross substitution, 189
Growth, 7–8, 21–23, 60, 72–79, 87–88,
    127, 149–151
  maximum, 37, 87
  proportional, 22, 28, 72–74, 82, 170

Indivisibilities, 206
Inflation, 2
Input matrix, 198
Input–output matrix, 32
Instruments of production, 7, 201–205
Integrated requirement, *see also* prices of
    products and integrated require-
    ments
  of capital, 17–18, 26, 43–44, 54–56,
    153, 157
  of labour, 9–10, 26, 39–40, 54–55, 157
  of labour as a dated series, 10, 40–41,
    57–58
  of land, 10, 147, 153, 157
  of resources, 180, 189
Interest, 208
Isoquants, 92–93, 97, 101–104

Joint production, 195–205

Labour, 6–7, 12–13
  demand for, 18–19, 27, 59–60
  distribution amongst industries, 60,
    62–66
  supply of, 18, 21–22, 59, 149, 152,
    159–162
Labour embodied, *see* integrated require-
    ment of labour
Labour market, *see also* labour, demand
    for, *and* labour, supply of, 17, 18–20,
    24–25, 26, 59, 105, 149, 159
Land, 5, 6, 12–13, 31, 147
  supply of, 152, 160–162
Land/labour ratio, 151, 159, 161,
    172–173, 175
  compounded, 158, 173–174, 176–177
  integrated, 151, 153, 158, 173–174,
    176–177
Land market, 149, 159
Landowners, 13, 147–148

Machinery, *see* instruments of produc-
    tion